DIRECTIONS 88

CORPORATE SPONSORS

AGFA GAVAERT CANADA LTD.
PROFESSIONAL FILM AND EQUIPMENT
SUPPLIER TO THE GRAPHICS INDUSTRY

AZTEC LTD., A KODAK COMPANY
MANUFACTURERS OF THE
REVOLUTIONARY AZTEC 3000-S
AND ACCESSORIES

BERT BELL & ASSOCIATES LTD.

BLUMER LEVON LTD.

**BRADBURY TAMBLYN &
BOORNE LTD.**
CELEBRATING TEN YEARS OF
QUALITY PRINTING

CANON CANADA INC.

**THE COMPOSING ROOM AT
COOPER & BEATTY**

EMPRESS GRAPHICS INC.

EUREKA FILMS LTD.

THE IMAGE BANK CANADA
STOCK ILLUSTRATION & PHOTOGRAPHY

**KIMBERLEY CLARK
CORPORATION
TECHNICAL PAPER**
MANUFACTURERS OF
HIGH-QUALITY DURABLE AND SPECIALTY
PRINTING PAPERS

KING WEST COMMUNICATIONS

KODAK CANADA INC.

**THE PARTNERS' FILM COMPANY
LIMITED**

**PROVINCIAL PAPERS
A DIVISION OF
ABITIBI-PRICE INC.**

STUDIO CENTRE
PROFESSIONAL PHOTOGRAPHIC/VIDEO
SALES, RENTALS AND FACILITIES

TECHNI PROCESS LIMITED

THE ART DIRECTORS CLUB
OF TORONTO
PRESIDENT
HEATHER COOPER

BOARD OF DIRECTORS
HEATHER COOPER, CHAIRPERSON
STUART ASH
BERT BELL
THEO DIMSON
LOUIS FISHAUF
GEORGES HAROUTIUN
TERRY ILES
DIETER KAUFMANN
KEN RODMELL

EXECUTIVE COMMITTEE
HEATHER COOPER, PRESIDENT
WALTER AUGUSTOWITSCH
CHRISTINE DOWNS
TERESA FERNANDES
ARNOLD KELLY
LISA MILLER
JIM WIDEMAN
JERRY WIESE
BARBARA WOOLLEY
VERN ZIMMERMAN

ADMINISTRATIVE STAFF
HEATHER LEISHMAN
ANDA VOPNI
LINDA VOPNI

A very special thanks to Linda Vopni and Heather Leishman.
Without their expertise and labours the judging weekend, the
show and this book would have been virtually impossible.

CREDITS

A publication of Applied Arts Inc.
20 Holly Street, Suite 208
Toronto, Ontario, Canada. M4S 3B1
Telephone (416) 488-1163

ART DIRECTOR
GEORGES HAROUTIUN

DESIGN CONSULTANT
LOUIS FISHAUF

EDITOR
PETER GIFFEN

DESIGNERS
BONITA BOCANEGRA-COLLINS
VALERIE RIOUX

CONTRIBUTING PHOTOGRAPHERS
BERT BELL
VINCENT NOGUCHI

ADVERTISING SALES MANAGER
WILLIAM COTRIC

CONTROLLER/OFFICE MANAGER
RITA HAROUTIUN

**DISTRIBUTION/
CIRCULATION MANAGER**
FRANCES MILLS

PRODUCTION
M.A.G. GRAPHICS

TYPESETTING
TECHNI PROCESS LIMITED

COLOUR SEPARATIONS
EMPRESS GRAPHICS INC.

PRINTING
BRADBURY TAMBLYN & BOORNE LTD.

PAPER
JENSON GLOSS 100 LB.
MANUFACTURED BY PROVINCIAL PAPERS,
A DIVISION OF ABITIBI-PRICE INC.

DISTRIBUTED BY

**CANADA
FIREFLY BOOKS LIMITED**
3520 PHARMACY AVENUE
UNIT 1C, SCARBOROUGH,
ONTARIO, CANADA. M1W 2T8

**WORLDWIDE
ROCKPORT PUBLISHERS**
5 SMITH STREET
ROCKPORT, MASS.
U.S.A. 01966

Applied Arts has tried its best to ensure that all the credits in
this publication are correct. However, if a mistake has been
made, we extend our apologies.

**PUBLISHED BY APPLIED ARTS INC.
PRESIDENT**
GEORGES HAROUTIUN

COPYRIGHT 1988
APPLIED ARTS INC.

ISBN 0-921940-00-9
ISSN 0480-8769

JUDGES

ADVERTISING PRINT

MICHAEL McLAUGHLIN
Vice-President, Creative Director,
MacLaren Advertising

Having worked for some of Canada's top agencies—Ogilvy & Mather, Vickers & Benson and Carder Gray—the Toronto adman has received numerous awards for his work, including the Gold Lion at Cannes and seven Gold Marketing Awards.

JARL OLSEN
Copywriter, Fallon McElligott

At the Minneapolis agency, Olsen has worked on such accounts as Hush Puppies Shoes and ITT Life. He says his many awards do not include a New York Art Directors' cube, because "they just give them to art directors, who are notorious for not sharing."

DANIELLE RENFER
Vice-President, Senior Art Director,
McKinney & Silver

Before joining the Raleigh, North Carolina agency, Renfer taught art at Vance Academy. Work for such clients as Piedmont Airlines, Fannie Mae and Norwegian Cruise Line has won her spots in many award shows.

ADVERTISING BROADCAST

BRUCE CAMPBELL
Senior Vice-President, Creative Director,
Hal Riney & Partners

In addition to Gallo, Anheuser-Busch, Sterling Automobiles and other account responsibilities at the San Francisco agency, Bruce has worked on Chrysler, Ralston-Purina and the Tuesday Team (the committee to reelect President Reagan).

RICH SILVERSTEIN
Creative Director and Principal, Goodby,
Berlin & Silverstein

One of the first art directors at *Rolling Stone*, Silverstein's "unequivocal passion for the quality of advertising" helped him create successful campaigns at various big-name firms before starting his own San Francisco agency.

MARTIN SHEWCHUK
Vice-President, Creative,
Leo Burnett Advertising

Shewchuk's work on such accounts as Kellogg Salada and Pepsi has won the Toronto adman numerous awards at home and abroad. He was named the top art director at the 1987 Canadian Festival of Television Advertising.

EDITORIAL

ANN KWONG
Art Director, New York Woman

Born in Hong Kong, Kwong has been with *New York Woman* since its launch in 1986. She was previously art director at *Elle* and *Restaurant Hotel Design*.

HELENE SILVERMAN
Art Director, Metropolis Magazine

The New York designer has previously worked at *Mademoiselle*, the *Seattle Times* and the *Rocket*. Her freelance clients include Abbeville Press, EMI-Manhattan Records and Condé Nast.

MATTHEW DRACE
Art Director, San Francisco Focus

Since his arrival, Drace has redesigned and redirected the look of the city magazine: designing covers with a poster-like treatment, using white backgrounds and "leaving the blondes in bathing suits behind."

LUCY BARTHOLOMAY
Art Director, The Boston Globe Magazine

Formerly art director of *The Real Paper* and *The Boston Monthly*, Bartholomay has won numerous awards from the New York Art Directors Club, the Society of Publication Designers and the Society of Newspaper Designers.

GRAPHIC DESIGN

SCOTT TAYLOR
Partner, Taylor & Browning
Design Associates

In his 15 years of graphic communications work for leading Canadian and American businesses, the Toronto designer has won dozens of awards for the annual reports, identity programs, brochures and promotional materials that he has produced.

JAY LOUCKS
President, Loucks Atelier

Active in the Houston design community for over 20 years, Loucks is the winner of many awards, and his work has been featured in exhibitions and magazines, including *Graphis, Communication Arts* and *Print*.

KATHERINE McCOY
Cochairman of the Department of Design,
Cranbrook Academy of Art

The Michigan designer is also a partner at McCoy & McCoy Associates. Her work has been exhibited and published internationally, and clients have included Chrysler, MIT Press, Formica Corp. and NV Philips.

ALYSSA ANN ADKINS
Designer, Carbone Smolan Associates

Involved in concept development, design and project management, the New York designer has done work for such companies as the New York Stock Exchange, Merrill Lynch and the Louis Dreyfus Property Group.

The Art
of persuasion
is a gift.

Use it wisely

HEATHER COOPER, PRESIDENT

KEN RODMELL

Superb art director, witty copywriter, fine teacher and so-so golfer BY JIM DONOAHUE

TORONTO LIFE FASHION WINTER ISSUE: PUBLISHED OCTOBER 1, 1987/ TORONTO LIFE FASHION, 59 FRONT ST E. 364-3333

1. Poster designed for the 10th anniversary of *Toronto Life Fashion* magazine. Illustrated by Jeff Jackson.

2. Poster for Kertész exhibition and book launch. Rodmell also designed the book.

3. Invitation for a 1959 exhibition organized by Cooper & Beatty.

4. Symbol for Toronto Arts Awards.

5. Promotional poster for *Toronto Life*. All magazine covers art directed by Rodmell.

1.

2.

A few weeks ago Theo Dimson called to tell me that my good friend Ken Rodmell had been chosen as this year's winner of the Les Usherwood Award. I couldn't have been happier. Ken had been told of the award and asked to put together a show of his work for this evening's presentation. I called to congratulate him, and in typical Rodmell style, he immediately suggested 10 people he felt were more deserving of the award than he. I strongly disagreed with him. There's no doubt in my mind that Ken deserves the award, but considering the contribution he has made, I'm not sure one is enough.

For the past 16 years, Ken has been with *Toronto Life* magazine. For the first seven he was the art director. He has also art directed *Toronto Life Fashion, Canadian Business* and *Quill & Quire*. He designs ads, writes copy and the occasional article, and even takes a picture or two. Every magazine he works on, he affects, not only its visual style but its editorial direction as well.

Over the years he's handed out hundreds of assignments to illustrators, photographers and designers. Through his encouragement, his

stimulation and his insight, a lot of great stuff has shown up in *Toronto Life*, and with his help many brilliant careers have been launched on those pages. I doubt that *Toronto Life* would be the fine magazine that it is today if Ken had not been around to help guide it. Aside from the staggering number of magazines Ken has worked on, there have been a fair number of books he's done with much harder covers. One of my favorites is the André Kertész book, a photo collection of the famous Hungarian photographer. Ken's superb eye and his careful typography make it a joy to behold. Ken tells me that Mr. Kertész was pleased. As a book designer, Ken has always approached the written word with a great deal of respect. And when he turns his hand to writing, he does it with substance and style. The one-liners in his copy have been breaking me up for years.

Every fall for the last 17 years, he has found time to teach a couple of classes at the Ontario College of Art. I know he has always felt that it is important to give something back, and he certainly does that. Ask any student who's had the good fortune to be in one of his classes. Perhaps,

the visual craft of William Golden

3.

4.

TORONTO ARTS 1986 AWARDS

Toronto Life covers the things that make Toronto great. That's why over 340,000 people read each issue!

5.

because Ken is such a student of life, he has become a great teacher.

Ken and I first met at OCA more than 30 years ago. We both came from Hamilton, and most Fridays during the school year, he'd jump on a bus and go back to the steel town to play trombone in a band. He still plays his trombone, though he doesn't take any more out-of-town gigs.

After graduating from the college, Ken went to work for Allan Fleming as his assistant at Cooper & Beatty. At that time, Allan taught a Wednesday afternoon class at OCA, a class we had both looked forward to a great deal as students. I went to Montreal, and a year and a half later, returned to join Allan and Ken at Cooper & Beatty. We had a terrific time. Ken and I found out the difference between Bembo, Bodoni and Broadway, and among the three of us, we won our share of awards. At this point, Ken decided it was time to study the subtle differences between single-malt whiskies and find out if it was true that Guinness really was good for you, so he took off for England with a couple of friends. There are rumors that he worked a little while he was there, but they appear unfounded. The best part, I suspect, was meeting Jane, his

wife of 25 years. I think she was well worth the trip. Back in Toronto, he took a job as art director of the *Imperial Oil Review*, then followed that with the *Canadian Magazine*, both of which he art directed beautifully. Then came *Toronto Life*, and the rest, as they say, is history.

There are a couple more things about Ken Rodmell that I'd like to share with you. He's a golfer, a serious student of the game. I haven't played with many people who hit longer drives into the woods. He has a great little sailboat that he loves, and handles it beautifully. He does water colors, and shows no one. Jurgen Gothe would approve of his record collection, as would Mozart. He and Jane have raised bright boys. One of them also hits a golf ball a long way, usually on the fairway. He is, by now, as you might have guessed, a connoisseur of single-malt whisky.

If all of this sounds like Ken Rodmell, Renaissance man, it may be so. I can't think of too many people with more wit, wisdom, awareness and sensitivity than Ken.

And I can't think of anyone more deserving of the Les Usherwood Award. I'm sure Les would approve.

ADVERTISING POSTER, SINGLE

6

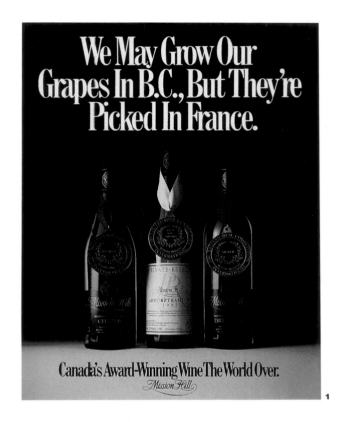

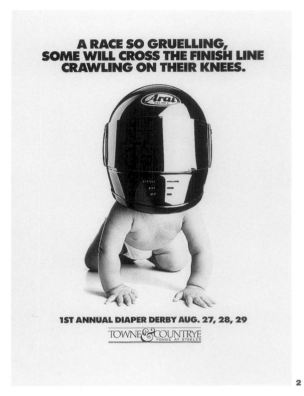

"The world of advertising and design is not short of awards. Every year there seems to be more.

"Some created as publicity stunts. Some, frankly, to make money.

"But only one in Britain is dedicated solely to encourage excellence.

"Design and Art Direction.

"This is its twenty-fifth show.

"Like all those before, the juries who judged the best work were hugely talented, vastly argumentative and typically hard-hearted.

"From 27,000 entries they selected only 377.

"They rejected work that had won gold awards in other festivals.

"And of 249 possible silver pencils they awarded only 25.

"But if their standards weren't so high, this show wouldn't be so good."

3

1	2	3
TITLE 3 BOTTLES	**TITLE** GRUELLING	**TITLE** D&AD '87 POSTER
ART DIRECTOR VINCE TASSONE	**ART DIRECTOR** PETER HOLMES	**ART DIRECTOR** ED CLEARY
AGENCY NATHAN FRASER ROSS ROY	**PHOTOGRAPHER** BRUCE HORN	**CLIENT** COOPER & BEATTY, LIMITED
CLIENT MISSION HILL	**PRODUCTION HOUSE** COOPER & BEATTY, LIMITED	**WRITER** TONY BRIGNULL
CREATIVE DIRECTOR ROBERT MONK	**AGENCY** FRANKLIN DALLAS	
	CLIENT TOWNE & COUNTRYE	
	WRITER PETER HOLMES	
	CREATIVE DIRECTOR PETER HOLMES	

ON MAY 22, SEE NINE MEN RACE AROUND MOSPORT ON ONE MOTORCYCLE.

That's because every motorcycle in the Q-107/RC30 Shootout during the Budweiser Victoria Day Sprints will be a Honda RC30 – 750 cc's of awesome motorcycle technology and power. Riders will compete for a $5,000 winner-take-all purse.

If you buy your Victoria Day Sprints ticket at a participating Honda dealer, you'll receive validation to park your motorcycle at the Honda Park preferred parking area near the grandstand. Entry is by the Porsche Gate.

Otherwise, just pick up your ticket at Mosport. And watch 'em shoot it out May 22.

HONDA

1

WHITE SALE.

The only daily non-stop to Washington begins May 1st. It's a capital idea.

And we're celebrating our return to Ottawa with a great return fare.

Beginning May 1st, you can fly from Ottawa to Baltimore/Washington for the low fare of only $211 return.

BALTIMORE/WASHINGTON
$211 Return

EASTERN
WE'VE GOT YOUR TICKET

And our flight leaves later and arrives earlier than any other airline. You depart at 7:00 a.m. and land at 8:14 a.m.

Non-stop.

So just call your travel agent, or Eastern Airlines toll-free at 1-800-361-3020.

It's the one seat in Ottawa you don't have to be elected to.

2

Fly Wardair Business Class to Britain and gain a few pounds.

£495.00* return

(That's $1,148 Canadian).

Wardair's daily scheduled non-stop flights to London are priced up to 50% less than the competition when you book 14 days in advance.* Or book up to day of departure and save almost 50%. Either way, that means you'll save your company a few pounds when you go to Britain.

But with Wardair's exceptional in-flight service, aboard one of our wide-bodie I aircraft, you might also be tempted to put on a few pounds during the flight. What with imported wine,

premium liquor, a two-course meal, full dessert trolley and after-dinner drinks, you could easily find yourself a few pounds heavier when you arrive.

So the next time business takes you to Britain, consider Wardair. Pound for pound it is the best Business Class to Britain.

Ask your travel agent to reserve your flight on Wardair. And find out about our new London Daylight, with the convenience of same day arrival to London.

Wardair Canada
We're in Business.

TORONTO

3

1

TITLE
ON MAY 22

ART DIRECTOR
SCOTT DUBE

WRITER
RAY ROUSSELL

AGENCY
AMBROSE CARR

CLIENT
HONDA

CREATIVE DIRECTORS
CARR/JOHANNSSON

2

TITLE
WHITE SALE

ART DIRECTOR
JAMIE WAY

WRITER
TERRY O'REILLY

PHOTOGRAPHER
IMAGE BANK

DESIGNER
LOWE, CANADA

CLIENT
EASTERN AIRLINES

CREATIVE DIRECTOR
TREVOR GOODGOLL

3

TITLE
GAIN A FEW POUNDS

ART DIRECTOR
DAVE KELSO

WRITER
BRAD RIDDOCH

AGENCY
J WALTER THOMPSON

CLIENT
WARDAIR CANADA LTD.

Be Bop A Lula.

Be Bop A Lula. She's my baby. Be Bop a Lula. Yeah. That's really her name. I think it's great. Kinda like Kareem Abdul-Jabbar. She changed it. Used to be Heather Wilson. So listen – have you seen her? She's the gal in the red blue jeans. Oh there she is – drinking the Molson Canadian. Hey Be Bop! Be Bop A Lula!

Molson Canadian.
Taste that'll stop you cold.

MOLSON CANADIAN Lager

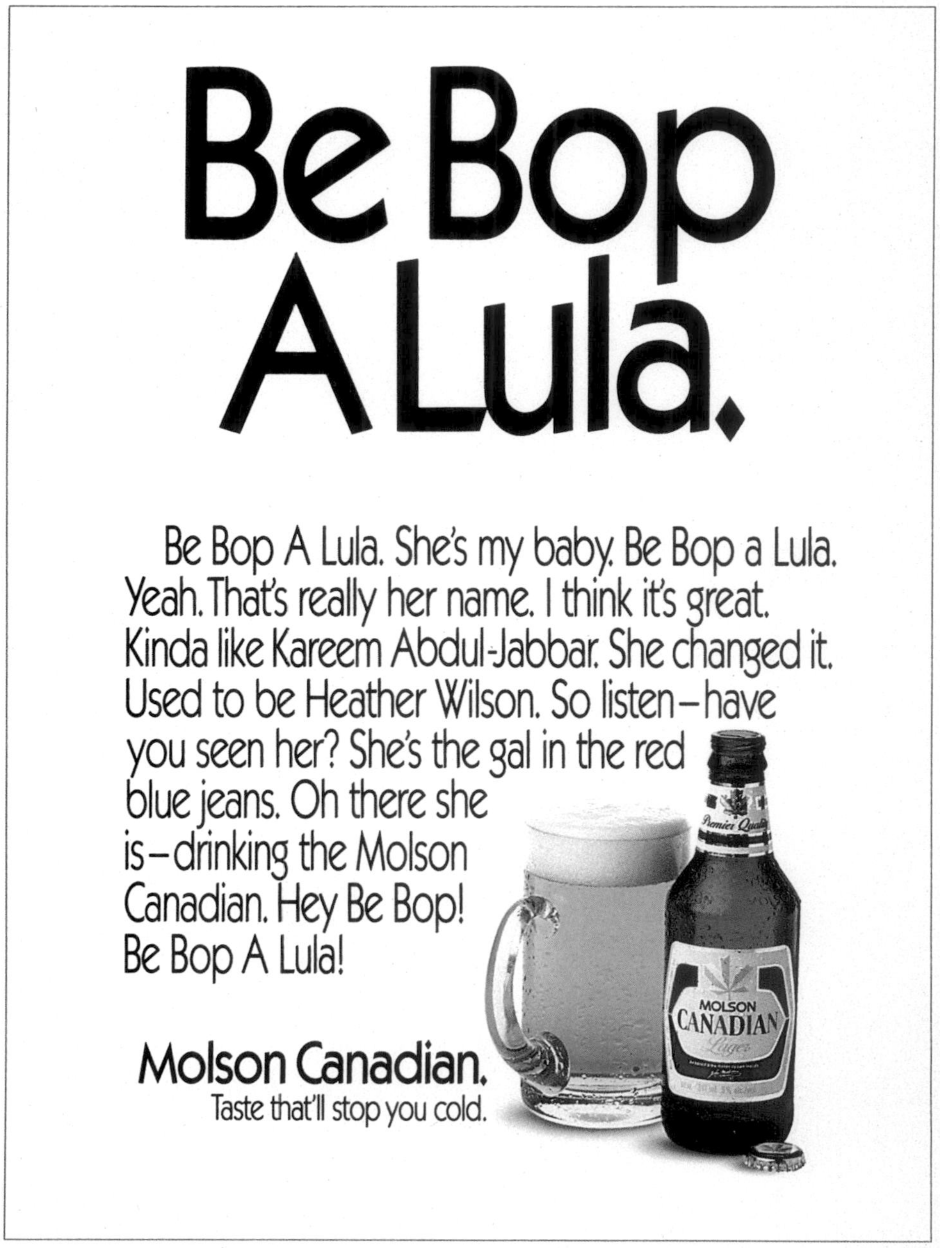

1

1

TITLE
BE BOP A LULA
ART DIRECTOR
MICHAEL McLAUGHLIN
WRITER
STEPHEN CREET
PHOTOGRAPHER
BERT BELL
AGENCY
MacLAREN ADVERTISING
CLIENT
MOLSON BREWERIES OF CANADA
CREATIVE DIRECTORS
STEPHEN CREET/MICHAEL McLAUGHLIN

Da Doo Ron Ron.

I met him on a Monday. And my heart stood still. Da doo ron ron. Da doo. Just kinda stopped. Like I was on pause or something. I wasn't scared or nothing. Actually it was really neat. Anyways this guy's name is Bill and he's a lot of fun and his favourite beer's Molson Canadian too. But that's weird about my heart huh?

Molson Canadian
Taste that'll stop you cold.

1

Doo Wah Diddy.

There she was. Just walking down the street. Singing doo wah diddy diddy dum diddy doo. Which ain't exactly normal. But what the heck. She looked good. In fact she looked really fine. So I caught up with her and asked her if she wanted to go for a Molson Canadian. Now we're together nearly every single day. Singing doo wah diddy diddy dum diddy doo.

Molson Canadian
Taste that'll stop you cold.

2

3

1	**2**	**3**
TITLE	**TITLE**	**TITLE**
DA DOO RON RON	DOO WAH DIDDY	COMFORT
ART DIRECTOR	**ART DIRECTOR**	**ART DIRECTOR**
MICHAEL McLAUGHLIN	MICHAEL McLAUGHLIN	GEOFFREY ROCHE
WRITER	**WRITER**	**WRITER**
STEPHEN CREET	STEPHEN CREET	TERRY BELL
PHOTOGRAPHER	**PHOTOGRAPHER**	**PHOTOGRAPHER**
BERT BELL	BERT BELL	CAILOR RESNICK
AGENCY	**AGENCY**	**AGENCY**
MacLAREN ADVERTISING	McLAREN ADVERTISING	SCALI, McCABE, SLOVES (CANADA) LTD.
CLIENT	**CLIENT**	**CLIENT**
MOLSON BREWERIES OF CANADA	MOLSON BREWERIES OF CANADA	VOLVO CANADA LIMITED
CREATIVE DIRECTORS	**CREATIVE DIRECTORS**	
MICHAEL McLAUGHLIN/STEPHEN CREET	MICHAEL McLAUGHLIN/STEPHEN CREET	

VOLVO

AN IMPORTANT NOTICE TO VOLVO OWNERS.

There is absolutely nothing wrong with your car. In fact, it is one of the nicer cars that anyone could hope to own. But pardon our immodesty. There is a car which is easily its equal and possibly its better. It's the Saab 9000. But we don't expect you to take our word for it, which is why we'd like to give you a Saab 9000 Turbo or 9000 S to test drive. Not for an hour or two, mind you. For 72 hours. This extraordinary measure is necessary, we believe, because the way you prize your car it may take us that long to win you over. Of course, we don't rule out love at first sight. See your Saab dealer for more details.

THE ABOVE LOGO IS THE REGISTERED TRADEMARK OF VOLVO CANADA LTD.

AN IMPORTANT NOTICE TO MERCEDES BENZ OWNERS.

There is absolutely nothing wrong with your car. In fact, it is one of the nicer cars that anyone could hope to own. But pardon our immodesty. There is a car which is easily its equal and possibly its better. It's the Saab 9000. But we don't expect you to take our word for it, which is why we'd like to give you a Saab 9000 Turbo or 9000 S to test drive. Not for an hour or two, mind you. For 72 hours. This extraordinary measure is necessary, we believe, because the way you prize your car it may take us that long to win you over. Of course, we don't rule out love at first sight. See your Saab dealer for more details.

THE ABOVE LOGO IS THE REGISTERED TRADEMARK OF MERCEDES-BENZ CANADA INC.

AN IMPORTANT NOTICE TO AUDI OWNERS.

There is absolutely nothing wrong with your car. In fact, it is one of the nicer cars that anyone could hope to own. But pardon our immodesty. There is a car which is easily its equal and possibly its better. It's the Saab 9000. But we don't expect you to take our word for it, which is why we'd like to give you a Saab 9000 Turbo or 9000 S to test drive. Not for an hour or two, mind you. For 72 hours. This extraordinary measure is necessary, we believe, because the way you prize your car it may take us that long to win you over. Of course, we don't rule out love at first sight. See your Saab dealer for more details.

THE ABOVE LOGO IS THE REGISTERED TRADEMARK OF VOLKSWAGEN CANADA INC.

1

TITLE
AN IMPORTANT NOTICE TO MERCEDES OWNERS
AN IMPORTANT NOTICE TO VOLVO OWNERS
AN IMPORTANT NOTICE TO AUDI OWNERS

ART DIRECTOR
MICHAEL EDWARDS

WRITER
BRUCE MacDONALD

AGENCY
MILLER MYERS BRUCE DALLA COSTA

CLIENT
SAAB

CREATIVE DIRECTORS
MARTIN MYERS/DENNIS BRUCE

NEWSPAPER AD, CAMPAIGN

Be Bop A Lula.

Be Bop A Lula. She's my baby. Be Bop a Lula. Yeah. That's really her name. I think it's great. Kinda like Kareem Abdul-Jabbar. She changed it. Used to be Heather Wilson. So listen – have you seen her? She's the gal in the red blue jeans. Oh there she is – drinking the Molson Canadian. Hey Be Bop! Be Bop A Lula!

Molson Canadian.
Taste that'll stop you cold.

Da Doo Ron Ron.

I met him on a Monday. And my heart stood still. Da doo ron ron. Da doo. Just kinda stopped. Like I was on pause or something. I wasn't scared or nothing. Actually it was really neat. Anyways this guy's name is Bill and he's a lot of fun and his favourite beer's Molson Canadian too. But that's weird about my heart huh?

Molson Canadian
Taste that'll stop you cold.

1

Doo Wah Diddy.

There she was. Just walking down the street. Singing doo wah diddy diddy dum diddy doo. Which ain't exactly normal. But what the heck. She looked good. In fact she looked really fine. So I caught up with her and asked her if she wanted to go for a Molson Canadian. Now we're together nearly every single day. Singing doo wah diddy diddy dum diddy doo.

Molson Canadian
Taste that'll stop you cold.

1
TITLE
DOO WAH DIDDY/BE BOP A LULA/DA DOO RON RON
ART DIRECTOR
MICHAEL McLAUGHLIN
WRITER
STEPHEN CREET
PHOTOGRAPHER
BERT BELL
AGENCY
MacLAREN ADVERTISING
CLIENT
MOLSON BREWERIES OF CANADA
CREATIVE DIRECTORS
MICHAEL McLAUGHLIN/STEPHEN CREET

- D I R E C T I O N S | 8 8 -

CONSUMER MAGAZINE AD, SINGLE

TO SEE WHAT OTHER VIDEO SYSTEMS DO TO A PICTURE THAT SUPER VHS WON'T, SQUINT YOUR EYES AND READ THIS AD.

Fuzzy pictures. Blurry words. This is what you're seeing right now as you attempt what the above headline suggests.

However, if you were to open your eyes wide, these words and pictures would be incomparably clearer. Sharper.

In essence, this is what Super VHS is all about. A picture that's that much clearer and sharper than any other video picture.

A picture that's 60% clearer, sharper.

Until now the standard video picture resolution has been a meager 240 lines.

Super VHS hasn't merely transcended this standard. It has obliterated it with more than 400 lines of picture resolution.

A picture that's 60% clearer and sharper. A picture that gives the term 'an eye opening experience' new meaning.

The Super VHS System.

JVC offers a completely integrated video component system in Super VHS.

At the heart of the system is the HR-S7000 VCR.

To produce the unprecedented 400 line resolution of the Super VHS picture, the HR-S7000 records the video signal at a much higher frequency, over a much broader frequency band.

In other systems these signals are input as a combined signal which causes cross-colour disturbance and moiré patterns.

With the signals separated, the Super VHS picture has colour reproduction true to life. With a marked reduction in picture disturbance.

Add to this all the other recent refinements in VHS technology including High Quality (HQ) system circuitry, Stereo Hi-Fi sound and MTS (Multichannel Television Sound).

And you may well call playing the HR-S7000, playing with a loaded deck.

The ultimate television picture.

Although the Super VHS picture can be enjoyed on a conventional television, JVC has introduced three high resolution Super VHS television monitors each with separated contrast and colour terminals for direct interfacing with the HR-S7000 VCR.

These Super VHS television monitors include the 28" AV-2637S, the sleekly designed 28" 560-line resolution AV-2687S and the giant 37" 560-line resolution AV-3587S (which, quite frankly, is such a major achievement in big screen TV. It deserves an ad of its own).

The first professional quality camcorders that are actually professional quality.

The Super VHS system has been extended into two professional quality camcorders.

The GR-S1000H features the remarkable picture resolution of Super VHS with a super-high resolution CCD pickup.

The GF-S1000H also features the same improved picture quality, as well as 6 hour/8 hour recording time on a full sized cassette, extraordinary CCD image resolution, professional editing features and Stereo Hi-Fi sound capability.

To take full advantage of the Super VHS format, a range of Super VHS cassette tapes and accessories are available. Super VHS tapes have a greater particle density which makes them the highest grade VHS tape available, even for normal recording with a conventional VCR.

Super VHS doesn't outdate VHS, it's an extension of VHS.

Even though Super VHS is a radical improvement in picture quality, it isn't anymore complicated to use than standard VHS equipment. The basic features are virtually identical.

And each component is compatible with conventional VHS components and all of your VHS recordings.

You can see the Super VHS picture only at an authorized JVC dealer. But to see how good it is in the meantime, read this ad again. Without squinting your eyes.

SUPER VHS. FROM THE PEOPLE WHO BROUGHT YOU VHS IN THE FIRST PLACE. JVC

MOST GREAT ITALIANS WILL BE AT FESTITALIA.
And we'd like you to join them from September 7th until October 1st.

Qualità è il nostro primo pensiero.

Michelin Sport EP-X tires are superb in corners.

1
TITLE SQUINT YOUR EYES
ART DIRECTOR PETER HOLMES
WRITER PETER HOLMES
PHOTOGRAPHER BRUCE HORN
PRODUCTION HOUSE COMPOSING ROOM
AGENCY FRANKLIN DALLAS
CLIENT JVC CANADA INC.
CREATIVE DIRECTOR PETER HOLMES

2
TITLE MONA
ART DIRECTORS JOHN FINN/DOMENIC SALLESE
WRITERS MICHAEL O'REILLY/TOM GOUDIE
PHOTOGRAPHER TDF STUDIOS
AGENCY YOUNG & RUBICAM LTD.
CLIENT FORD MOTOR COMPANY
PRODUCTION MARJ TAYLOR
CREATIVE DIRECTORS MICHAEL GARRETT/TERRY ILES

3
TITLE MICHELIN SPORT EP-X TIRES ARE SUPERB IN CORNERS
ART DIRECTOR STEVE THURSBY
WRITER ALLAN KAZMER
PHOTOGRAPHER TERRY COLLIER
AGENCY DDB NEEDHAM WORLDWIDE ADVERTISING LTD.
CLIENT MICHELIN TIRE CORP.
CREATIVE DIRECTOR ALLAN KAZMER

CONSUMER MAGAZINE AD, SINGLE

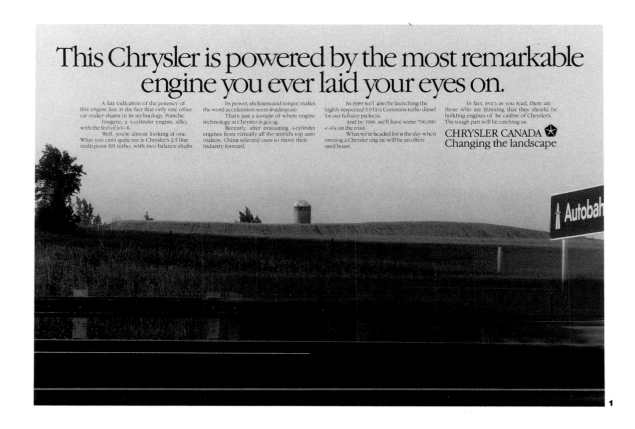

This Chrysler is powered by the most remarkable engine you ever laid your eyes on.

A fair indication of the potency of this engine lies in the fact that only one other car maker shares in its technology. Porsche.

Imagine, a 4-cylinder engine, silky, with the feel of a V-8.

Well, you're almost looking at one. What you can't quite see is Chrysler's 2.5 litre multi-point EFI turbo, with two balance shafts.

Its power, slickness and torque makes the word acceleration seem inadequate.

That's just a sample of where engine technology at Chrysler is going.

Recently, after evaluating 4-cylinder engines from virtually all the world's top auto makers, China selected ours to move their industry forward.

In 1989 we'll also be launching the highly respected 5.9 litre Cummins turbo diesel for our full size pickups.

And by 1996 we'll have some 700,000 4-6's on the road.

What we're headed for is the day when owning a Chrysler engine will be an often-used boast.

In fact, even as you read, there are those who are thinking that they should be building engines of the calibre of Chrysler's. The tough part will be catching us.

CHRYSLER CANADA ✦
Changing the landscape

1

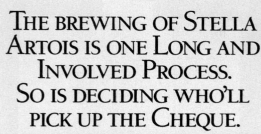

THE BREWING OF STELLA ARTOIS IS ONE LONG AND INVOLVED PROCESS. SO IS DECIDING WHO'LL PICK UP THE CHEQUE.

What's a small slip of paper between friends? Not much. Unless it's a cheque for Stella Artois. It is after all, a very expensive beer.

We scour all Europe for the finest raw ingredients. We employ the most fragrant hops (with flagrant disregard for the cost).

And we demand only the highest grade of barley (with similar scant respect for the expense incurred).

Then we leave our beer to mature for literally weeks on end. Knowing full well that many other beers are sent packing in less than half the time.

Despite all this apparent folly, Stella Artois is enjoyed around the world. It's proof that while all the money in the world can't buy friendships, it can buy one superb beer.

BREWED AS IF MONEY WERE NO OBJECT (BUT THEN, IT'S YOUR MONEY)

2

A tall tale from your true ale. Since we're talking ducks, me and old Dundee were out last fall. It was a beautiful day, but we weren't having our usual luck. In fact, we hadn't seen a bird all day. Suddenly, one flies right over us. Well, I line it up. And darned if my gun don't jam. Just then old Dundee takes off after him, he's holding my duck call in his mouth. Next thing I know, I hear Dundee blowing that duck call. The duck looks down for just a split second, all confused. And he flies right into a tree. Now, you know, my tale may be tall but my ale is true. If you don't believe me, just go and ask my old Dundee. Okay. **Oland Export. Your ale is true.**

3

1	2	3
TITLE	**TITLE**	**TITLE**
AUTOBAHN	PICK UP THE CHEQUE	TALE
ART DIRECTORS	**ART DIRECTOR**	**ART DIRECTOR**
BERNARD ROMANO/BORIS DAMAST	JEFF KATZ	LEIF NIELSEN
WRITER	**WRITER**	**WRITER**
BORIS DAMAST	T.J. HARRISON	STEVE CONOVER
PHOTOGRAPHER	**PHOTOGRAPHER**	**PHOTOGRAPHER**
GEORGE SIMHONI	BERT BELL	TIM SAUNDERS
DESIGNER	**AGENCY**	**AGENCY**
JEFF LAYTON	LOWE CANADA	YOUNG & RUBICAM LTD.
AGENCY	**CLIENT**	**CLIENT**
BAKER LOVICK ADVERTISING	CARLING O'KEEFE BREWERIES	OLAND BREWERIES
CLIENT	**TYPE**	**TYPE**
CHRYSLER CANADA LTD.	THE COMPOSING ROOM	WORDS OVER NORTH AMERICA
TYPE		**CREATIVE DIRECTOR**
THE COMPOSING ROOM		RICK DAVIS
CREATIVE DIRECTOR		
BORIS DAMAST		

14

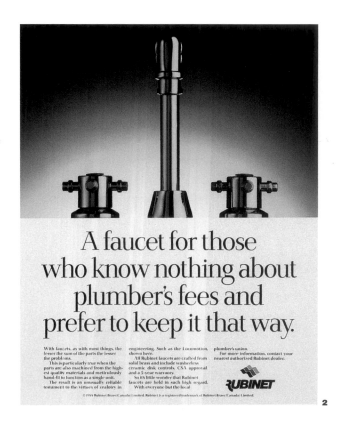

1

We've stretched the truth about MagicWagon.

The truth about Chrysler MagicWagon is better design from top to bottom.

To begin with, it's easier to step into because it's built lower to the ground. Like children.

And once inside, you'll notice that the floor is truly flat.

There's no drive-shaft-hump to bump into.

MagicWagon also gives you the smoother ride and car-like handling of front wheel drive. Features that have earned it the highest rating in customer satisfaction, and higher sales than Ford, GM, Toyota and VW minivans combined.[1]

And now we've stretched the truth 14.5".

The result? A Grand MagicWagon that carries passenger comfort and cargo room to even greater lengths.

And like the original, it also carries the longest powertrain warranty: 7 years or 115,000 km.

Which means the truth about MagicWagon is that it now comes in two versions. See them both at your Dodge or Plymouth dealer.

CHRYSLER CANADA ✶
Changing the landscape

14.5"

Grand version of Dodge Caravan and Plymouth Voyager offers extra cargo space, optional 8-passenger seating, 4 or 6 cyl. EFI engines available.

A faucet for those who know nothing about plumber's fees and prefer to keep it that way.

With faucets, as with most things, the lesser the sum of the parts the lesser the problems.

This is particularly true when the parts are also machined from the highest quality materials and meticulously hand-fit to function as a single unit.

The result is an unusually reliable testament to the virtues of zealotry in engineering. Such as the Locomotion, shown here.

All Rubinet faucets are crafted from solid brass and include washerless ceramic disk controls, CSA approval and a 5-year warranty.

So it's little wonder that Rubinet faucets are held in such high regard. With everyone but the local

plumber's union.

For more information, contact your nearest authorized Rubinet dealer.

RUBINET

© 1988 Rubinet Brass (Canada) Limited. Rubinet is a registered trademark of Rubinet Brass (Canada) Limited.

2

1

TITLE
STRETCHED THE TRUTH

ART DIRECTOR
JEFF LAYTON

WRITER
PHIL NICHOLAS

PHOTOGRAPHER
GEORGE SIMHONI

DESIGNER
JEFF LAYTON

AGENCY
BAKER LOVICK ADVERTISING

CLIENT
CHRYSLER CANADA LTD.

TYPE
THE COMPOSING ROOM

CREATIVE DIRECTOR
BORIS DAMAST

2

TITLE
PLUMBER'S FEES

ART DIRECTOR
PETER HOLMES

WRITERS
PETER HOLMES/JAY STANLEY

PHOTOGRAPHER
PAT LACROIX

PRODUCTION HOUSE
COMPOSING ROOM

AGENCY
FRANKLIN DALLAS

CLIENT
RUBINET BRASS (CANADA) LTD.

CREATIVE DIRECTOR
PETER HOLMES

Not if your feet are killing you. And poor unfortunate soles like Imelda's ought to know. So before you blow a small fortune on footwear, run out of closet space, or both, do a little sole searching of your own. At one of Feet First's total footcare centres. *Where To Begin* What seems to be the problem may

painstakingly adjusted to your exact needs. We can also do the same for your children in our special Kids Korner. And here's more good news. These corrective inserts can be slipped into all kinds of footwear (and the orthotic fees are often covered by extended healthcare plans). But Feet First total

Happiness isn't 3,000 pairs of shoes.

not necessarily the problem. That's why every Feet First consultation begins with a complete biomechanical video analysis. Translated into plain English, we videotape your walk and run on a special treadmill. Then we see how your feet bear up in terms of weight distribution, stability, shock absorption, and alignment. It's very much like having the wheels, steering and suspension checked out on your car. And the estimate's free. If all is as it should be, we can fit you up perfectly from our wide selection of name-brand sports, dress and leisure shoes. However, if your feet need extra help, we're there to help. *We're Very Supportive.* It's seldom too soon or too late to address foot problems. And that's where our professional support staff really come in to their own. Using a styrofoam imprint of your foot, they create a precise replica of your sole. This leads to the ingenious Feet First Orthotic—a scientifically designed shoe insert that's custom-molded and

footcare doesn't stop there. *Getting It Together* What's bad for the sole is often bad for the body—especially the knees, legs and back. Our EnerGym features the latest in biomechanical equipment including the Dynatrack, a computerized machine which monitors muscle strength and movement. Used in conjunction with individualized fitness programs designed by our expert staff, Dynatrack may help you regain and maintain 100% capacity of your foot, knee and leg muscles. It's yet another way in which Feet First can help you get back on track. Not to mention our full range of unique footcare products, including pads and specially formulated creams. *This Way To Paradise.* Running away from foot discomfort isn't going to get you anywhere. So why not make an appointment for your free biomechanical video analysis, today? And we'll get your feet off to a brand-new start. Yours too, Imelda.

The world's sole authorities.

We've moved.

To the top. To the top of the Financial Post's list of real estate leaders. And we're proud of our accomplishment. But let's give credit where it's due: To our Brokers and Sales Associates.

We've always said the reason RE/MAX is above the crowd is because our people are. And they've just proved it.

So if you're buying or selling real estate,

get Canada's top producers working for you. The cream of the crop. They're at RE/MAX. Now Canada's leading real estate organization.

An international network of independent member brokers.

They laughed when I sat down to refinish it.

But then they didn't know about Minwax. Minwax uncomplicates even the most daunting refinishing project by providing a fully integrated line of products for preparing, colouring, protecting and maintaining interior wood surfaces. Minwax always makes it easy to choose the

right products for results you can be proud of. Find out the steps and products you'll need by sending for a complimentary copy of the 32 page Minwax Tips booklet. It's the best start you could have on a beautiful finish.

Write to: Minwax, Div. of Sterling Drug, Ltd., 400 Yonge Street South, Aurora, Ontario L4G 3H6

MINWAX

1

TITLE
HAPPINESS

ART DIRECTOR
ERIC JUREWICH

WRITER
DAVID COMPTON

ILLUSTRATOR
TITUS VILLANEUVA

DESIGNER
ERIC JUREWICH

AGENCY
LASER KULEBA SHYLLIT

CLIENT
FEET FIRST

2

TITLE
WE'VE MOVED

ART DIRECTOR
GERALD SCHOENHOFF

WRITER
TOM WEISNER

PHOTOGRAPHER
JEAN DESJARDINS

AGENCY
LASER KULEBA SHYLLIT

CLIENT
RE/MAX

3

TITLE
THEY LAUGHED

ART DIRECTOR
DENNIS FORBES

WRITERS
VICKI GRANT/DENNIS FORBES

PHOTOGRAPHER
BILL McLEOD

CLIENT
MINWAX, DIV. OF STERLING DRUG

CREATIVE DIRECTOR
MICHAEL PAUL

Since childhood, all our chief designer wanted was to design Ferraris and Maseratis. He got his wish.

Perfection, by its very nature, is something few designers have the insight to understand, let alone the ardour and the genius to achieve.

Fortunately for us however, our chief designer is one of these few.

And as a consequence of his fascination with detail and penchant for precision, he courts perfection with startling, prodigious results.

The Eliseo designs shown here are instances of this engineering virtuosity.

As with all Rubinet faucets, these feature washerless, ceramic disk cartridges and quarter turn controls, all housed in solid brass constructions with epoxy-based finishes.

And although they come with a 5-year warranty and CSA approval, no faucet leaves our hands until it's been fanatically examined for even the smallest of imperfections.

All of which lends credence to the fact that not all of the world's penultimate examples of engineering are made to be parked in the garage.

For more information, contact your nearest authorized Rubinet dealer.

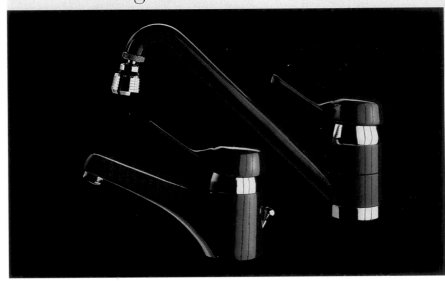

1

A faucet for those who know nothing about plumber's fees and prefer to keep it that way.

With faucets, as with most things, the lesser the sum of the parts the lesser the problems.

This is particularly true when the parts are also machined from the highest quality materials and meticulously hand-fit to function as a single unit.

The result is an unusually reliable testament to the virtues of zealotry in engineering. Such as the Locomotion, shown here.

All Rubinet faucets are crafted from solid brass and include washerless ceramic disk controls, CSA approval and a 5-year warranty.

So it's little wonder that Rubinet faucets are held in such high regard. With everyone but the local plumber's union.

For more information, contact your nearest authorized Rubinet dealer.

By adding quarter turn controls, we've turned faucet design completely around.

As those with even a cursory knowledge of engineering will attest to, the slightest twist in an archetypal design is often enough to start a revolution.

So it's understandable that our quarter turn controls have caused such a stir because, unlike faucets with conventional full turn controls, Rubinet faucets deliver the usual degrees of water flow, but within the unusual range of a mere quarter turn.

And due to their precisely machined parts and ceramic disk cartridges, they turn with a quiet, giddying smoothness.

Rubinet faucets also possess a panoply of other distinctive features including solid brass construction, a 5-year full warranty and an almost unscratchable epoxy-based finish.

Consequently, a Rubinet faucet like the Quadrice design shown here, is such an unmitigated pleasure to use, you may actually find yourself searching for opportunities to dirty your hands.

For more information, contact your nearest authorized Rubinet dealer.

1

TITLE
PLUMBER'S FEES/QUARTER TURN
FERRARIS AND MASERATIS

ART DIRECTOR
PETER HOLMES

WRITERS
PETER HOLMES/JAY SANKEY

PHOTOGRAPHER
PAT LACROIX

PRODUCTION HOUSE
COMPOSING ROOM

AGENCY
FRANKLIN DALLAS

CLIENT
RUBINET BRASS (CANADA) LTD.

CREATIVE DIRECTOR
PETER HOLMES

CONSUMER MAGAZINE AD, SINGLE

Not if your feet are killing you. And poor unfortunate soles like 'melda's ought to know. So before you blow a small fortune on footwear, run out of closet space, or both, do a little sole searching of your own. At one of Feet First's total footcare centres. *Where To Begin* What seems to be the problem may

painstakingly adjusted to your exact needs. We can also do the same for your children in our special Kids Korner. And here's more good news. These corrective inserts can be slipped into all kinds of footwear (and the orthotic fees are often covered by extended healthcare plans). But Feet First total

Happiness isn't 3,000 pairs of shoes.

not necessarily be the problem. That's why every Feet First consultation begins with a complete biomechanical video analysis. Translated into plain English, we videotape your walk and run on a special treadmill. Then we see how your feet bear up in terms of weight distribution, stability, shock absorption, and alignment. It's very much like having the wheels, steering and suspension checked out on your car. And the estimate's free. If all is as it should be, we can fit you up perfectly from our wide selection of name-brand sports, dress and leisure shoes. However, if your feet need extra help, we're there to help. *We're Very Supportive.* It's seldom too soon or too late to address foot problems. And that's where our professional support staff really come in to their own. Using a styrofoam imprint of your foot, they create a precise replica of your sole. This leads to the ingenious Feet First Orthotic—a scientifically designed shoe insert that's custom-molded and

footcare doesn't stop there. *Getting It Together* What's bad for the sole is often bad for the body—especially the knees, legs and back. Our Ener-Gym features the latest in biomechanical equipment including the Dynatrack, a computerized machine which monitors muscle strength and movement. Used in conjunction with individualized fitness programs designed by our expert staff, Dynatrack may help you regain and maintain 100% capacity of your foot, knee and leg muscles. It's yet another way in which Feet First can help you get back on track. Not to mention our full range of unique footcare products, including pads and specially formulated creams. *This Way To Paradise.* Running away from foot discomfort isn't going to get you anywhere. So why not make an appointment for your free biomechanical video analysis, today? And we'll get your feet off to a brand-new start. Yours too, 'melda.

The world's sole authorities. [F] FEET FIRST

FEET FIRST is a member of the Tridont Health Care Inc. group of companies.

TORONTO-CENTRAL
2404 Yonge Street
Phone: 481-FEET (3338)

TORONTO-DOWNTOWN
First Canadian Place
Maritime Level
Phone: 368-FEET (3338)

OSHAWA
Island Shopping Centre
380 King Street West
Phone: 434-FEET (3338)

OTTAWA
Bayshore Shopping Centre
100 Bayshore Drive, Nepean
Phone: 820-TOES (8637)

1

We've moved.

To the top. To the top of the Financial Post's list of real estate leaders. And we're proud of our accomplishment. But let's give credit where it's due: To our Brokers and Sales Associates.

We've always said the reason RE/MAX is above the crowd is because our people are. And they've just proved it.

So if you're buying or selling real estate,

get Canada's top producers working for you. The cream of the crop. They're at RE/MAX. *Now Canada's leading real estate organization.*

RE/MAX

An international network of independent member brokers.

2

They laughed when I sat down to refinish it.

But then they didn't know about Minwax. Minwax uncomplicates even the most daunting refinishing project by providing a fully integrated line of products for preparing, colouring, protecting and maintaining interior wood surfaces. Minwax always makes it easy to choose the

right products for results you can be proud of. Find out the steps and products you'll need by sending for a complimentary copy of the 32 page Minwax Tips booklet. It's the best start you could have on a beautiful finish.

Write to: Minwax, Div. of Sterling Drug Ltd., 400 Yonge Street South, Aurora, Ontario L4G 3H6

MINWAX

3

1

TITLE
HAPPINESS

ART DIRECTOR
ERIC JUREWICH

WRITER
DAVID COMPTON

ILLUSTRATOR
TITUS VILLANEUVA

DESIGNER
ERIC JUREWICH

AGENCY
LASER KULEBA SHYLLIT

CLIENT
FEET FIRST

2

TITLE
WE'VE MOVED

ART DIRECTOR
GERALD SCHOENHOFF

WRITER
TOM WEISNER

PHOTOGRAPHER
JEAN DESJARDINS

AGENCY
LASER KULEBA SHYLLIT

CLIENT
RE/MAX

3

TITLE
THEY LAUGHED

ART DIRECTOR
DENNIS FORBES

WRITERS
VICKI GRANT/DENNIS FORBES

PHOTOGRAPHER
BILL McLEOD

CLIENT
MINWAX, DIV. OF STERLING DRUG

CREATIVE DIRECTOR
MICHAEL PAUL

CONSUMER MAGAZINE AD, CAMPAIGN

16

Over time, the penetrating force of a single drop of rain will pierce metal like a bullet.

Rain is only the accomplice. The real killer is ferric oxide. The deadly combination of water, air and metal we call rust.

Triggered by a tiny scratch or chip, rust bores relentlessly through the body of your car, turning steel into red dust.

The only way to stop it is to make sure it never starts. Chrysler does it by protecting fenders, doors and hoods with a shield of pre-coated and double-galvanized steel. Then dipping the entire body in a 7-step anti-corrosion bath.

And for extra protection against stone chips, all lower bodysides are treated with a tough urethane shell. Only then are the paints applied and clear-coated.

This is why every Chrysler-built product carries the longest anti-corrosion warranty in the industry: 7 years or 160,000 km.

Because over time, the penetrating force of a single drop of rain will pierce metal like a bullet.

CHRYSLER CANADA ✦
Changing the landscape.

1

This Chrysler is powered by the most remarkable engine you ever laid your eyes on.

A fair indication of the potency of this engine lies in the fact that only one other car maker shares in its technology. Porsche.

Imagine, a 4-cylinder engine, silky, with the feel of a v-8.

Well, you're almost looking at one. What you can't quite see is Chrysler's 2.5 litre multi-point EFI turbo, with two balance shafts.

Its power, slickness and torque makes the word acceleration seem inadequate.

That's just a sample of where engine technology at Chrysler is going.

Recently, after evaluating 4-cylinder engines from virtually all the world's top auto makers, China selected ours to move their industry forward.

In 1989 we'll also be launching the highly respected 5.9 litre Cummins turbo diesel for our full-size pickups.

And by 1990 we'll have some 700,000 V-6's on the road.

What we're headed for is the day when owning a Chrysler engine will be an often-used boast.

In fact, even as you read, there are those who are thinking that they should be building engines of the calibre of Chrysler's. The tough part will be catching us.

CHRYSLER CANADA ✦
Changing the landscape

1

TITLE
DROP OF RAIN/AUTOBAHN/WARRANTY

ART DIRECTORS
BERNARD ROMANO/BORIS DAMAST

WRITER
BORIS DAMAST/PHIL NICHOLAS

PHOTOGRAPHER
GEORGE SIMHONI

DESIGNER
JEFF LAYTON

AGENCY
BAKER LOVICK ADVERTISING

CLIENT
CHRYSLER CANADA LTD.

CREATIVE DIRECTOR
BORIS DAMAST

ILLUSTRATOR
TERRY SHOFFNER

CONSUMER MAGAZINE AD, CAMPAIGN

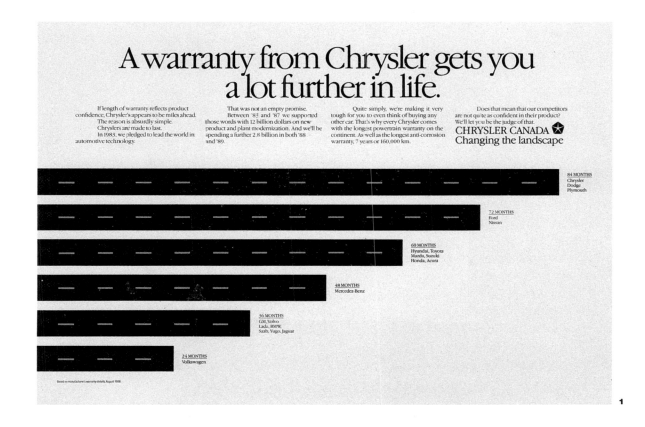

A warranty from Chrysler gets you a lot further in life.

If length of warranty reflects product confidence, Chrysler's appears to be miles ahead. The reason is absurdly simple. Chryslers are made to last. In 1983, we pledged to lead the world in automotive technology.

That was not an empty promise. Between '83 and '87 we supported those words with 12 billion dollars on new product and plant modernization. And we'll be spending a further 2.8 billion in both '88 and '89.

Quite simply, we're making it very tough for you to even think of buying any other car. That's why every Chrysler comes with the longest powertrain warranty on the continent. As well as the longest anti-corrosion warranty, 7 years or 160,000 km.

Does that mean that our competitors are not quite as confident in their product? We'll let you be the judge of that.

CHRYSLER CANADA ✶
Changing the landscape

	84 MONTHS Chrysler Dodge Plymouth
	72 MONTHS Ford Nissan
	60 MONTHS Hyundai, Toyota Mazda, Suzuki Honda, Acura
	48 MONTHS Mercedes-Benz
	36 MONTHS GM, Volvo Lada, BMW, Saab, Yugo, Jaguar
	24 MONTHS Volkswagen

Based on manufacturer's warranty details, August 1988.

1

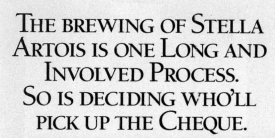

THE BREWING OF STELLA ARTOIS IS ONE LONG AND INVOLVED PROCESS. SO IS DECIDING WHO'LL PICK UP THE CHEQUE.

What's a small slip of paper between friends? Not much. Unless it's a cheque for Stella Artois. It is after all a very expensive beer. We scour all Europe for the finest raw ingredients. We employ the most fragrant hops (with flagrant disregard for the cost). And we demand only

the highest grade of barley (with similar scant respect for the expense incurred). Then we leave our beer to mature for literally weeks on end. Knowing full well that many other beers are sent packing in less than half the time.

Despite all this apparent folly, Stella Artois is enjoyed around the world. It's proof that while all the money in the world can't buy friendships, it can buy one superb beer.

BREWED AS IF MONEY WERE NO OBJECT (BUT THEN, IT'S YOUR MONEY)

AT STELLA ARTOIS, WE ACCEPT ONLY CERTIFIED CZECHS.

Czechoslovakian hops to be exact. They're certifiably the best money can buy. So we send our people armed with unshakeable discretion (and expense accounts) to gather the most fragrant of the lot. Even if it means paying through the nose. But that's not the only cheque that needs to be covered.

There are the bills we rack up when purchasing the finest barley. And yeast so superior, it even makes our prices rise. Finally there are extra wages to be paid (at union rates) to ensure our beer is brewed for a full seven weeks. So who pays for all this?

You do. Incidentally, please remember to carry sufficient funds when ordering Stella. We don't accept cheques. Certified or otherwise.

BREWED AS IF MONEY WERE NO OBJECT (BUT THEN, IT'S YOUR MONEY)

2

2

TITLE
CERTIFIED CZECHS/PICK UP THE CHEQUE

ART DIRECTOR
JEFF KATZ

WRITER
T.J. HARRISON

PHOTOGRAPHER
BERT BELL

AGENCY
LOWE CANADA

CLIENT
CARLING O'KEEFE BREWERIES

CREATIVE DIRECTOR
TREVOR GOODGOLL

CONSUMER MAGAZINE AD, CAMPAIGN

Since childhood, all our chief designer wanted was to design Ferraris and Maseratis. He got his wish.

Perfection, by its very nature, is something few designers have the insight to understand, let alone the ardour and the genius to achieve.

Fortunately for us however, our chief designer is one of these few.

And as a consequence of his fascination with detail and penchant for precision, he courts perfection with startling, prodigious results.

The Eliseo designs shown here are instances of this engineering virtuosity.

As with all Rubinet faucets, these feature washerless, ceramic disk cartridges and quarter turn controls, all housed in solid brass constructions with epoxy-based finishes.

And although they come with a 5-year warranty and CSA approval, no faucet leaves our hands until it's been fanatically examined for even the smallest of imperfections.

All of which lends credence to the fact that not all of the world's penultimate examples of engineering are made to be parked in the garage.

For more information, contact your nearest authorized Rubinet dealer.

© 1988 Rubinet Brass (Canada) Limited. Rubinet is a registered trademark of Rubinet Brass (Canada) Limited.

1

A faucet for those who know nothing about plumber's fees and prefer to keep it that way.

With faucets, as with most things, the lesser the sum of the parts the lesser the problems.

This is particularly true when the parts are also machined from the highest quality materials and meticulously hand-fit to function as a single unit.

The result is an unusually reliable testament to the virtues of zealotry in engineering. Such as the Locomotion, shown here.

All Rubinet faucets are crafted from solid brass and include washerless ceramic disk controls, CSA approval and a 5-year warranty.

So it's little wonder that Rubinet faucets are held in such high regard. With everyone but the local plumber's union.

For more information, contact your nearest authorized Rubinet dealer.

© 1988 Rubinet Brass (Canada) Limited. Rubinet is a registered trademark of Rubinet Brass (Canada) Limited.

By adding quarter turn controls, we've turned faucet design completely around.

As those with even a cursory knowledge of engineering will attest to, the slightest twist in an archetypal design is often enough to start a revolution.

So it's understandable that our quarter turn controls have caused such a stir because, unlike faucets with conventional full turn controls, Rubinet faucets deliver the usual degrees of water flow, but within the unusual range of a mere quarter turn.

And due to their precisely machined parts and ceramic disk cartridges, they turn with a quiet, giddying smoothness.

Rubinet faucets also possess a panoply of other distinctive features including solid brass construction, a 5-year full warranty and an almost unscratchable epoxy-based finish.

Consequently, a Rubinet faucet like the Quadrice design shown here, is such an unmitigated pleasure to use, you may actually find yourself searching for opportunities to dirty your hands.

For more information, contact your nearest authorized Rubinet dealer.

© 1988 Rubinet Brass (Canada) Limited. Rubinet is a registered trademark of Rubinet Brass (Canada) Limited.

1

TITLE
PLUMBER'S FEES/QUARTER TURN
FERRARIS AND MASERATIS

ART DIRECTOR
PETER HOLMES

WRITERS
PETER HOLMES/JAY SANKEY

PHOTOGRAPHER
PAT LACROIX

PRODUCTION HOUSE
COMPOSING ROOM

AGENCY
FRANKLIN DALLAS

CLIENT
RUBINET BRASS (CANADA) LTD.

CREATIVE DIRECTOR
PETER HOLMES

CONSUMER MAGAZINE AD, CAMPAIGN

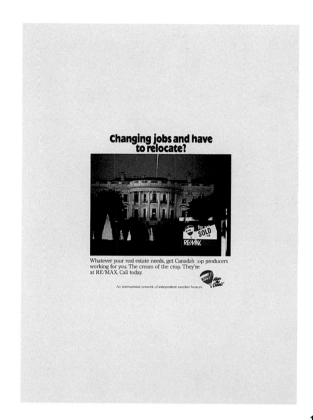

1

1

TITLE
WHITE HOUSE/TAJ MAHAL/ACROPOLIS

ART DIRECTOR
JOE SHYLLIT

WRITER
JERRY KULEBA

PHOTOGRAPHER
STOCK (DAN GARSON)

AGENCY
LASER KULEBA SHYLLIT

CLIENT
RE/MAX

TRADE AD, SINGLE

20

You'd never have to put up with

1

GOLD AWARD

delays like this if you had the world's fastest graphic workstation.

At Hewlett-Packard, we design on the premise that a workstation should work with you. Not after you.

That's why, whether performing relatively simple 2-D manipulations or highly sophisticated 3-D solid modeling, all our HP 9000 graphic workstations

function in real time. They never leave you staring at a blank screen.

That gives us a substantial performance edge over the leading competition.

And it gives you a real advantage in productivity. With no disadvantage in quality or range.

That's because Hewlett-Packard workstations offer not just the most realistic modeling but a complete set of solutions for the engineer, architect, or software developer as well.

And all these features are available at a price much lower than you'd expect.

Or the competition could deliver.

The Hewlett-Packard workstations. The only graphic workstations that can really keep up with you.

 HEWLETT PACKARD

1
TITLE
DELAYS
ART DIRECTOR
DENNIS FORBES
WRITER
VICKI GRANT
AGENCY
SMW ADVERTISING
CLIENT
HEWLETT PACKARD
CREATIVE DIRECTOR
MICHAEL PAUL

TRADE AD, SINGLE

People who think all oils are the same should have their heads examined.

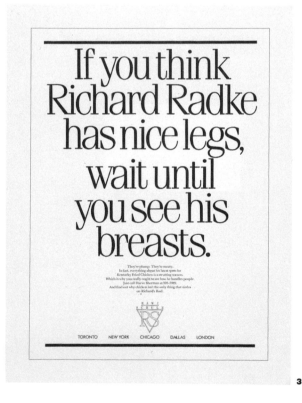

1

TITLE
HEADS EXAMINED

ART DIRECTOR
MARIO RICCI

PHOTOGRAPHER
MICHAEL KOHN

AGENCY
PALMER BONNER BCP

CLIENT
VALVOLINE

CREATIVE DIRECTOR
BRUCE McCALLUM

2

TITLE
COMPARE THE PRICE TAGS

ART DIRECTOR
DENNIS FORBES

PHOTOGRAPHER
DAVE SLOAN

CLIENT
HEWLETT PACKARD

CREATIVE DIRECTOR
MICHAEL PAUL

3

TITLE
CHICKEN

ART DIRECTOR
GEOFFREY ROCHE

AGENCY
CHIAT DAY

CLIENT
RAWI SCHULZ

CREATIVE DIRECTORS
RICHARD HADDEN/GEOFFREY ROCHE

ADVERTISING ILLUSTRATION

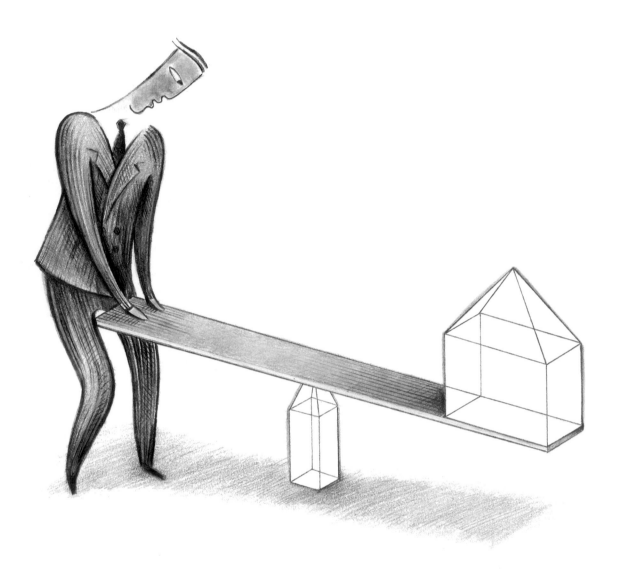

ART DIRECTOR
ROBERT BURNS

ILLUSTRATOR
FRANK VIVA

GOLD AWARD

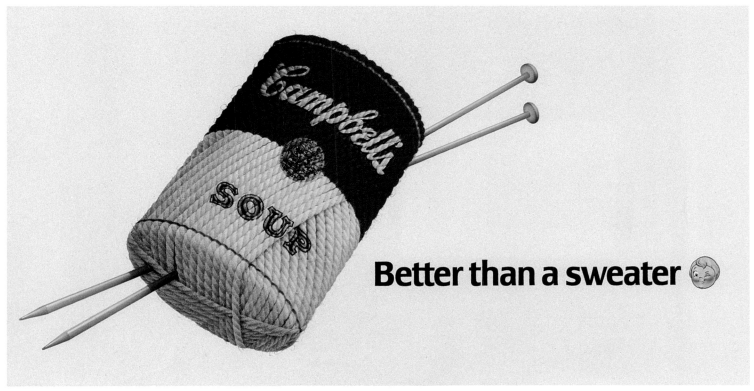

Better than a sweater

1

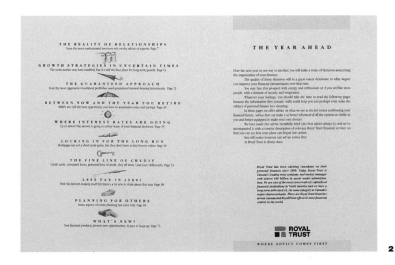

2

1

TITLE
BETTER THAN A SWEATER

ART DIRECTOR
JIM BROWN

WRITER
BRAD MYERS

ILLUSTRATOR
ROGER HILL

AGENCY
OGILVY & MATHER

CLIENT
CAMPBELL SOUP CO. LTD.

CREATIVE DIRECTOR
KEITH RAVENSCROFT

2

TITLE
THE YEAR AHEAD

ART DIRECTOR
ROBERT BURNS

ILLUSTRATOR
FRANK VIVA

DESIGNER
GREGORY HALLAS

CLIENT
ROYAL TRUST

CREATIVE DIRECTOR
ROBERT BURNS

ADVERTISING PHOTOGRAPHY

24

1

2

1

TITLE
HEATHER COOPER

ART DIRECTOR
GEOFFREY ROCHE

PHOTOGRAPHER
BERT BELL

CLIENT
APPLIED ARTS

WRITER
JACK NEARY

EDITOR
GEORGES HAROUTIUN

2

TITLE
MESSAGE IN A BOTTLE

ART DIRECTOR
CARL JONES

PHOTOGRAPHER
TIM SAUNDERS

AGENCY
VICKERS & BENSON

WRITER
PAUL JOYCE

ART DIRECTOR
CARL JONES
PHOTOGRAPHER
TIM SAUNDERS

26

Eliminate overhead.

Pulsar NX.

NISSAN
Built for the Human Race.

1

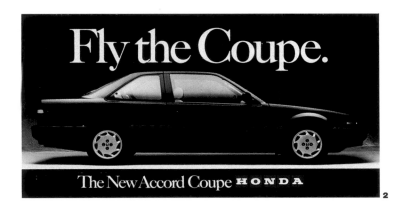

Fly the Coupe.

The New Accord Coupe HONDA

2

Take one a day for the cold.

Once a Campbell's kid, Always a Campbell's kid

3

1	2	3
TITLE OVERHEAD	**TITLE** FLY THE COUPE	**TITLE** ONE A DAY
ART DIRECTOR GEOFFREY ROCHE	**ART DIRECTOR** JOHN LLOYD	**ART DIRECTOR** JIM BROWN
PHOTOGRAPHER SMITH & NELSON	**AGENCY** SCHUR PEPPLER	**WRITER** BRAD MYERS
AGENCY CHIAT/DAY	**CLIENT** HONDA CANADA INC.	**ILLUSTRATOR** ROGER HILL
CLIENT NISSAN	**CREATIVE DIRECTOR** DAN PEPPLER	**AGENCY** OGILVY & MATHER
CREATIVE DIRECTORS GEOFFREY ROCHE/RICHARD HADDEN		**CLIENT** CAMPBELL SOUP CO. LTD.
		CREATIVE DIRECTOR KEITH RAVENSCROFT

ART DIRECTOR
JIM BROWN

ILLUSTRATOR
ROGER HILL

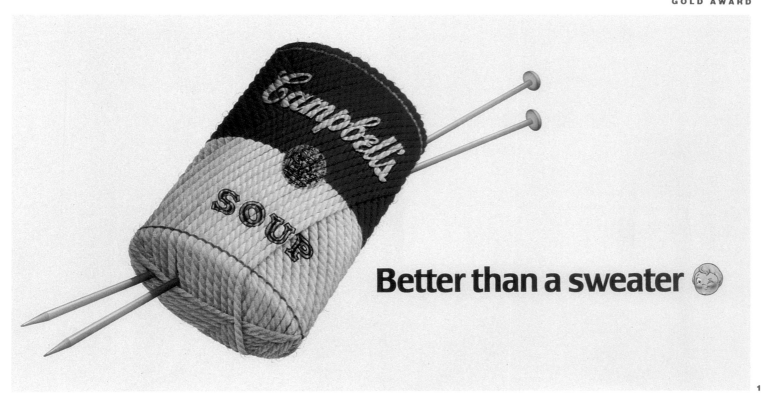

Better than a sweater

1

If you let Crunchie melt in your mouth, it'll last all the way to the end of the line.

A delicious honeycomb centre covered with the taste of Cadbury's chocolate.

However, if you crunch a Crunchie quickly, you can finish it before the next stop.

2

You can crunch a Crunchie in as little time as it takes to read this.

On the other hand, you could let Crunchie's honeycomb centre, covered with the great taste of Cadbury's chocolate, melt ever so slowly in your mouth. You could eat it so slowly, in fact, that you could make Crunchie last as long as it takes to read this. I mean, that's if you wanted to. Who says you have to take the name of the bar literally anyway? Certainly not us. While we do understand how much fun it is to crunch a Crunchie, it can be just as tough not to slowly savour Crunchie's honeycomb centre, as long as you can.

But, as Kierkegaard wrote, an individual's choice of one mode

3

1

TITLE
BETTER THAN A SWEATER

ART DIRECTOR
JIM BROWN

WRITER
BRAD MYERS

ILLUSTRATOR
ROGER HILL

AGENCY
OGILVY & MATHER

CLIENT
CAMPBELL SOUP CO. LTD.

CREATIVE DIRECTOR
KEITH RAVENSCROFT

2

TITLE
END OF THE LINE

ART DIRECTOR
RANDY DIPLOCK

PHOTOGRAPHER
GEORGE SIMHONI

AGENCY
SCALI, McCABE, SLOVES (CANADA) LTD.

CLIENT
WILLIAM NEILSON LTD.

CREATIVE DIRECTOR
GARY PROUK

3

TITLE
KIERKEGAARD

ART DIRECTOR
RANDY DIPLOCK

PHOTOGRAPHER
GEORGE SIMHONI

AGENCY
SCALI, McCABE, SLOVES (CANADA) LTD.

CLIENT
WILLIAM NEILSON LTD.

CREATIVE DIRECTOR
GARY E. PROUK

OUTDOOR POSTER/BILLBOARD OR TRANSIT, CAMPAIGN

1

If you let Crunchie melt in your mouth, it'll last all the way to the end of the line.

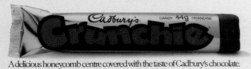

A delicious honeycomb centre covered with the taste of Cadbury's chocolate.

However, if you crunch a Crunchie quickly, you can finish it before the next stop.

2

You can crunch a Crunchie in as little time as it takes to read this.

On the other hand, you could let Crunchie's honeycomb centre, covered with the great taste of Cadbury's chocolate, melt ever so slowly in your mouth. You could eat it so slowly, in fact, that you could make Crunchie last as long as it takes to read this. I mean, that's if you wanted to. Who says you have to take the name of the bar literally anyway? Certainly not us. While we do understand how much fun it is to crunch a Crunchie, it can be just as tough not to slowly savour Crunchie's honeycomb centre, as long as you can.

But, as Kierkegaard wrote, an individual's choice of one mode

1

TITLE
RITZ/OREO

ART DIRECTOR
BARRY CHEMEL

ILLUSTRATOR
DESMOND MONTAGUE

AGENCY
McCANN-ERICKSON ADVERTISING

CLIENT
CHRISTIE BROWN & CO.

WRITER
KURT HAGAN

CREATIVE DIRECTOR
WAYNE HILINSKI

2

TITLE
KIERKEGAARD/END OF THE LINE

ART DIRECTOR
RANDY DIPLOCK

PHOTOGRAPHER
GEORGE SIMHONI

AGENCY
SCALI, McCABE, SLOVES (CANADA) LTD.

CLIENT
WILLIAM NEILSON LTD.

WRITER
RANDY DIPLOCK

CREATIVE DIRECTOR
GARY E. PROUK

TYPE
TYPSETTRA LTD.

30

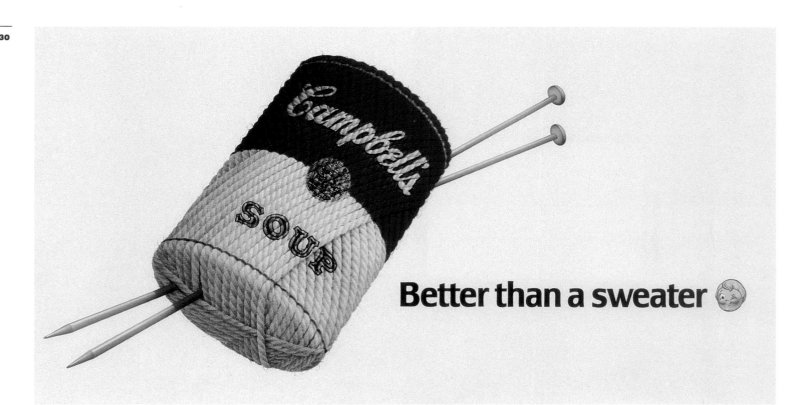

Better than a sweater

GOLD AWARD

1

GOLD AWARD

Take one a day for the cold.

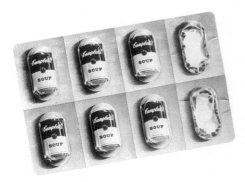

1

TITLE
BETTER THAN A SWEATER/ONE A DAY

ART DIRECTOR
JIM BROWN

ILLUSTRATOR
ROGER HILL

AGENCY
OGILVY & MATHER

CLIENT
CAMPBELL SOUP CO., LTD.

WRITER
BRAD MYERS

CREATIVE DIRECTOR
KEITH RAVENSCROFT

If your skin is as smooth as this card, call 691-7086.

Beachcomber Hairstyling and Grooming.

1

If the ends of your finger-tips look like the ends of this card, call 691-7086.

Beachcomber Hairstyling and Grooming.

1

TITLE
SMOOTH/FINGERTIPS

ART DIRECTOR
RICHARD CLEWES

DESIGNER
RICHARD CLEWES

CLIENT
BEACHCOMBER

WRITER
RICHARD CLEWES

THE "A" LIST

Lori Abrams • David Adams • Charles Adorjan • Harry Agensky • Leonard Aguanno • Howard Albert • Roy Albon • David Allan • Jim Allen • Howard Alstad • Larry Anas • Bob Anderson • Shigeshi Aoki • Glen Arnold • Stuart Ash • Bev Atkinson • Roland Aubert • Lawrence Ayliffe • Nadia Bailey • Ulrike Balke • Inacio Barata • Mario Basile • Doug Beatty • Lindsay Beaudry • Bert Bell • Terry Bell • Jay Belmore • Nina Berkson • Richard Billinghurst • Yolanda Biron • Kevin Bird • Baiba Black • Stephen Boake • Marilyn Bouma-Pyper • Bill Boyko • Ken Boyd • Donna Braggins • Keith Branscombe • Philip Brazeau • Katherine Brown • Jim Brown • Max Brown • Paul Browning • Ann Brown-Onyette • Dennis Bruce • Duncan Bruce • Neil Bruce • Robert Burns • Paul Cade • Silvio Calcagno • Gail Campbell • Jim Carpenter • Susan Casey • Steve Catlin • Renzo Cattoni • Barry Chemel • Wanda Chirnside • Michael Chortyk • Ozzie Ciliberti • David Clark • Keith Clarriage • Ed Cleary • Richard Clewes • Peter Coates • Cate Cochran • Jim Cochrane • Dean Coldham • Jai Cole • Kathryn Cole • Heather Cooper • John Cormier • Salvatore Corrado • Stephen Creet • Chris Crofton • Dianne Croteau • Michael Crunkhorn • John Cruickshank • Mark Cryns • Boris Damast • Stanley Davidson • Robert Davidson • Rick Davis • Jack Dawkins • Skip Dean • Kasper deLine • Rod Della Vedova • Micheal Dempsey • Jean Luc Denat • Rudi Desiato • Theo Dimson • Luba Diduch • Patti DiSciascio • Peter Dixon • Yuri Dojc • Jim Donoahue • Christine Downs • Vivian Ducas • Claude Dumoulin • Carmen Dunjko • Philip Dunk • Bill Durnan • Diane Eastman • John Edmonds • Jane Edwards • Michael Edwards • Bruce English • Peter Enneson • Roslyn Eskind • Ken Etheridge • Robin Fennell • Teresa Fernandes • Michael Fiala • Martin Finesilver • Jayne Finn • Maggie Finnegan • Louis Fishauf • Tim Forbes • Michael Fog • Ted Forrest • Patrick Fong • Lynn Franklin • Pam Freir • David Frieberg • Kevin Fullarton • Aviva Furman • Lyn Gaby • Lionel Gadoury • B.J. Galbraith • Paul Gallaugher • Paul Ganyon • Alan Gee • Gerald George • Bob Glynn • Dennis Goddard • Nester Golets • Robbie Goulden • Martine Gourbault • Heidi Graf • Allen Graham • Jack Graham • Anita Granger • John Grant • Michael Gregg • Remzi Hacioglu • Kofi Hadjor • Susan Halle • Graham Hallett • Robin Hamilton • Georges Haroutiun • Julia Harris • James Harrison • Norman Hathaway • Greg Herriott • Catherine Haughton • Carmen Hickson • Christine Higdon • Wayne Hilinski • Keith Hillmer • Peter Holmes • Allan Holman • Marlene Hore • David How • Karen Howe • Thomas Howlett • Robert Hyland • Terry Iles • James Ireland • Janice Ivory • Ken Jackson • Richard Jacobson • Paul Jarsky • Elaine Jewell • Ursula Kaiser • Dennis Kane • Allan Kazmer • Dieter Kaufmann • Arnold Kelly • Tony Kerr • Syd Kessler • Dela Kilian • David Kinoshita • Tanya Koehnke • Michael Kohn • Diane Kolev • Wendy Korentager • Larry Kuzoff • Bill Kyles • J.P. LaCroix • Pat LaCroix • Wes Laing • Derek Lamarque • Peter Land • Peter Lanyon • Ted Larson • Ed Lea • Daniel LeBlanc • Dan LeBrun • Chris Lee • Timothy Lee • Tiffany Leger • Krysia Leszczynski • Elvin Letchford • Nancy Leung • Holly Levine • Michael Levy • Robert M. Lewis • Vera Litynski • Gerry L'Orange • Benard Low • Joe Lum • Brad MacIver • Alex Macleod • Vera Maidan • Richard Male • Marcy Maloney • Michael Malloy • Jay Mandarino • Steve Manley • Malcolm Marcus • Judy Margolis • Bill Martin • Kim Martin • Jose Martucci • Carolyn Martyn • Nadia Maryniak • Maria Mastromarco • Emilio Mazzonna • Donald McLean • Geoffrey McFarlane • Michael McLaughlin • Paul McClimond • Stephen McLachlan • Dennis McManus • Nicole Mentis • Linda Menyes • Lisa Miller • Bryan Mills • Sue Milne • Michele Miodonski • Jenny Molloy • Russell Monk • Barry Montgomery • Brian Moore • Patricia Morley • Timothey Morley • Bryan Morris • Chris Morris • Janice Morris • Julia Moss • Marian Mustard • Shawn Murenbeeld • Steve Mykolyn • Julie Nasmith • Ed Nanni • Rodney Nash • Phil Nicholas • Dermot O'Brien • Suzanne O'Callaghan • Karen Okada • Peter Oliver • Terrence O'Malley • Mary Opper • John Ormsby • Terry O'Reilly • Liz Pardal • Rick Padulo • Derrick Pao • Mario Parisell • Sandra Parsons • Roxanne Pearce • Gregory Peek • William Perry • George Phair • Kathleen R. Picton • Ingrid Piil • Fernanda Pisani • Barry Platt • Kerry Plumley • Laura Pollard • Len Preskow • Gord Pronk • Gary Prouk • Michael Rafelson • Tim Raleigh • Raj Rama • Robert Ramsay • Keith Ravenscroft • Mario Remillard • Paul Renaud • Sue Reynolds • Brian Richards • Lisa Richards • Bruce Richardson • Debra Richman • Peter Robbers • Doug Robinson • Beverley Rockett • Mannuel Rodenkirchen • Ken Rodmell • Ross Rogers • Rudi Rodrigues • Jim Ronson • Gabrielle Rosen • Philip Rostron • Hal Roth • Michael Rouleau • Marsha Rovan • Therese Schechter • Martin Shewchuck • Rene Schoepflin • Chris Solari • Anna Spencer • Michel St. Jean • Marika Steel • Russell Steventon • Leslie Styles • John Speakman • Marc Stewart • Rod Stothers • Evelyn Stoynoff • Gary Stuber • Nina Stultz • Philip Sung • Stephen Sussman • James Sweetland • Michael Szucs • Andre Talbot • Viv Tate • Scott Taylor • Tiit Telmet • Del Terrelonge • Frank Teskey • Mark Tharme • Robert Thompson • Ebbe Thomsen • Steve Thursby • Derek Timmerman • Chris Tivey • Les Trevor • Jonas Tse • Bev Tudhope • Kent Turcotte • Judy Turner-Blain • Robin Uchida • Klaus Uhlig • John Uiberall • Ron Uliani • Philip Unger • Elsie Usherwood • Ron Vandenberg • Alex Vassallo • Richard Verdiccio • John Vennare • Michael Viau • Mike Visser • Jon Vopni • H.E. Wallis • Earl Walker • Paul Walker • George Walton • Eddie Wawrychuk • Martha Weaver • Melanie Weston • Robert White • Michael Wilde • Elizabeth Williams • Tiziana Williams • Pamela Wimbush • Cork Winter • Curtis Wolowich • Don Wong • David Woodside • Barbara Woolley • Carol Young • Eric Young • Richard Zemnicks • Rose Zgodzinski

ART DIRECTORS CLUB OF TORONTO MEMBERS 1988

TO PUT YOUR NAME ON THE "A" LIST, CALL THE A.D.C.T. AT 416 483 1400

CREATIVE

B

CELEBRATING
10 YEARS
OF EXCELLENCE

**Bradbury Tamblyn
& Boorne Ltd.**

25 POLLARD STREET
RICHMOND HILL, ONTARIO
CANADA L4B 1A8
TELEPHONE (416) 731 6052
TORONTO LINE (416) 226 2001
FAX (416) 731 4549
ATLANTA, GA (404) 233 6326

At BTB, a balanced blend

of modern technology and

experienced craftsmanship

ensures that the excellence

of your work is reflected in

the quality of

our printing

A PART OF YOUR

CREATIVE PROCESS

CONCEPT/DESIGN · REACTOR ART & DESIGN

CONSUMER COMMERCIAL, SINGLE

GOLD AWARD

LARGE FRAME	SMALL FRAME	AUDIO
CU Passport; Hong Kong being stamped on it.	CU girl on plane intercom.	VO INTERCOM: Please enjoy your stay in Hong Kong.
Hero's hand picking up leather garment bag. Cathay Pacific tag is prominent in frame.	CU girls in flight.	MVO: When it's important
Hero hefts bag onto his shoulder.	CU plane taking off.	
¾ overhead shot of hero walking through throng of people in airport.	CU food on tray.	that your needs as a business person
Hero walking purposefully toward camera (as in print shot).	CU girl turning, smiling.	be reconciled with your wants as a traveller…
As Hero passes by camera frame freezes and blows out to white. SUPER LOGO: Cathay Pacific. Arrive in better shape.		Cathay Pacific… Arrive in better shape.

TITLE
SERVICE
ART DIRECTOR
MALCOLM MARCUS
WRITER
JANET KESTIN/BASIL MINA
CREATIVE DIRECTOR
TONY HOUGHTON
PRODUCER
JILL WADE
DIRECTOR
JIM SONZERO
PRODUCTION HOUSE
PARTNERS FILM CO.
MUSIC/SOUND
CONNIE VAN BEEK—CHICAGO
AGENCY
LEO BURNETT COMPANY LTD.
CLIENT
CATHAY PACIFIC

SILVER AWARD

VIDEO	AUDIO		
Open on Hogan at a typical backyard barbecue.		Hogan speaks to dog.	(TO DOG): If I was you I'd make me self scarce.
Hogan speaks to camera. A man cooks in background.	HOGAN: G'day. My mates invited me over for a fine Canadian tradition —a Barby.	Hogan looks to camera. PRODUCT SHOT: Can, Hot Dog. SUPER: The Golden Throat Charmer. Brewed in Canada.	ANNCR (VO): Foster's. The Golden Throat Charmer.
Hogan speaks to cook.	(TO COOK): What's cookin' mate?		
Cook turns to speak and throws a scrap to a dog.	COOK: Steak.		
Hogan speaks again to camera as he takes a can of Foster's from a cooler.	HOGAN: Ace. Just like in Oz, when you're hungry enough to eat a Wallaby, and you'd like something while you're waitin', Foster's, the Golden Throat Charmer.		
Hogan pours himself a can of Foster's.			
Cook turns to speak to Hogan and gestures to barbecue.	COOK: You know if you're that hungry I can throw on a dog for ya!		
Hogan looks at dog. Dog looks at Hogan. Hogan speaks to man.	HOGAN: No thanks mate.		

TITLE
HOT DOG
ART DIRECTOR
DAVE KELSO
WRITER
BRAD RIDDOCH
CREATIVE DIRECTOR
BRAD RIDDOCH
PRODUCER
PAT WHITE
DIRECTOR
DAVID ASHWELL
PRODUCTION HOUSE
DAVID ASHWELL FILM CO.
AGENCY
J. WALTER THOMPSON
CLIENT
CARLING O'KEEFE
BREWERIES OF CANADA

CONSUMER COMMERCIAL, SINGLE

SILVER AWARD

	VIDEO	AUDIO

TITLE
EXPEDITION

ART DIRECTOR
CHUCK BEISCH

WRITER
PHILLIPPA EWING

CREATIVE DIRECTOR
CHUCK BEISCH

PRODUCER
DEE ANDERSON

PRODUCTION HOUSE
PARTNERS FILM CO.

AGENCY
THE LONG GROUP

CLIENT
LOBLAWS
SUPERMARKETS LTD.

VIDEO

Open on a room similar to a 1940's classroom. There are men standing around wearing Polar exploration gear. The leader is seated at a desk working intently. Behind him is a blackboard on which is a map of the Polar route.

An applicant enters wearing snow shoes. He is fully dressed in furry Polar Exploration gear.

Cut to CU of leader speaking to the applicant. The leader barks out his demands.

Applicant displays them.

Leader peers forward. Applicant holds up two large mittened hands.

Leaders ticks items off his list.

Applicant responds.

AUDIO

LEADER: Here to sign up for the Polar Expedition?

APPLICANT: Yes.

LEADER: Show us your snow shoes.

LEADER: Snow shoes.

LEADER: Mittens?

LEADER: Two.

LEADER: Any objections to living with dogs?

APPLICANT: No.

Very dictatorially, the leader commands the other men.

Men begin to chant.

A large fish slaps down on the desk. The applicant looks horrified.

The leader looks surprised.

Applicant looks as if what he's saying is quite logical.

Leader looks up and shouts.

Men take up new chant.

Attached to applicant's coat front is a pouch resembling a bed roll. He pulls strings and unrolls it to reveal it as a marvelous carrier and display for cheeses. About 15 or 20 can be seen. Applicant points to different ones.

LEADER: Let's see if he eats the raw fish.

MEN: Yum, yum, yum, yum.

APPLICANT: Er...no thank you.

LEADER: Well, if you won't eat raw fish, how do you expect to conquer the Pole?

APPLICANT: I thought I'd take cheese.

LEADER: Cheese?

MEN: Cheese, cheese, cheese.

APPLICANT: There's brie for the soft going, goat's cheese for the hilly sections. Trappist Monk, Stilton...

Men are chanting and moving in unison. We hear the chanting under.

Applicant continues and we see the cheeses again.

Leader questions him indignantly.

Applicant produces two Loblaws bags of cheese. We can see the logo.

Men chant and move.

Leader interrupts them.

Applicant continues.

Leader contemplates first the raw fish. Then the cheeses.

Cut to Monty Python type animation. Flag is raised with "Loblaws does it again" and logo.

MEN: (under) Cheese, cheese, cheese.

APPLICANT: ...limburger so they can find us. I've got 150 different cheeses here.

LEADER: Where would you get 150 different cheeses?

APPLICANT: Just around the corner.

MEN: Cheese, cheese, cheese.

LEADER: Will you shut up.

APPLICANT: ...you don't have to go all around the world to get the world's oldest cheeses.

LEADER: Nice cold raw fish...or 150 different kinds of cheese. Well, no accounting for taste.

APPLICANT VO: Loblaws does it again.

SILVER AWARD

LARGE FRAME	SMALL FRAME	AUDIO

TITLE
RELIABILITY

ART DIRECTOR
MALCOLM MARCUS

WRITER
JANET KESTIN/BASIL MINA

CREATIVE DIRECTOR
TONY HOUGHTON

PRODUCER
JILL WADE

DIRECTOR
JIM SONZERO

PRODUCTION HOUSE
PARTNERS FILM CO.

MUSIC/SOUND
CONNIE VAN BEEK
—CHICAGO

AGENCY
LEO BURNETT COMPANY LTD.

CLIENT
CATHAY PACIFIC

LARGE FRAME

Open on airport door sliding open as traveller walks through. Written: Hong Kong International Airport in English and Chinese. It moves out of frame.

Hero turns and recognizes Chinese business associate who has come to meet him in a chauffeur-driven Rolls.

Hero shakes hands with Chinese businessman.

SMALL FRAME

Flight engineer walking around plane doing final external flight check.

ECU Rolls-Royce engine.

Cut to airport video screen showing time of CX-801 departure. Changes to read "Departed."

AUDIO

AIRPORT SOUNDS

MVO: When it's essential that you get

where you're going precisely

Hero casually tosses the bags into the trunk.

ECU Cathay Pacific baggage tag as hero's bag goes into trunk.

Hero and associate are seated in car talking. We see them through the window.

Car pulls away. Frame freezes and blows out to white.
SUPER LOGO: Arrive in better shape. Cathay Pacific.

Plane is in motion. Wheels turn to camera.

Cut to plane taking off.

when you have to be there...

Cathay Pacific... Arrive in better shape.

CONSUMER COMMERCIAL, SINGLE

VIDEO	AUDIO
Opens on man with television on his head. He reaches up and turns it on. SUPER: McDonald's (logo).	MUSIC: Fast-paced electro-beat with lots of weird and wild sounds scored to picture.
	SINGERS: What's new. What's new. (ELECTRO)
Man is separated into three on the screen: his legs, torso and head. Then, in a series of quick cuts, his legs, body etc. is switched with characters such as 'Fred Flintstone' and with young target group boy and girl. SUPER ON SMURFETTE: Smurf™ © 1988 PEYO	What's new at McDonald's?
	Canada's Wonderland Cups
	Free with every medium soft drink.
	Flintstones, Jetsons, and…Smurfs…
SUPER ON CUPS: At participating McDonald's while supplies last.	a new one each week.
	Oh yeah! McDonald's also has…

Cut to head of man with television. Footage comes on screen.
SUPER: Applies to regular passport only. No purchase necessary for coupon.

Final scene is the cups coming into frame. And then McDonald's logo.
SUPER: Free with every medium soft drink.

Discount coupons for four dollars off…
Canada's Wonderland Passports…

Good time, great taste,
At McDonald's.

TITLE
ELECTRO SWITCH

ART DIRECTOR
TOM FENNEY

WRITER
RON THOMSON

CREATIVE DIRECTOR
PAUL JOYCE

PRODUCER
FRANCA PIACENTE

DIRECTOR
STEVE CHASE

PRODUCTION HOUSE
CHAMPAIGN

MUSIC/SOUND
RICK SHURMAN

AGENCY
VICKERS & BENSON
ADVERTISING

CLIENT
McDONALD'S RESTAURANTS
OF CANADA LIMITED

AUDIO

MUSIC TRACK
THROUGHOUT

TITLE
ALL THAT SNOW

ART DIRECTOR
TREVOR McCONNELL

WRITER
BRUCE WALKER

PRODUCER
GEORGE ARCHER

PRODUCTION HOUSE
PARTNERS FILM CO.

MUSIC/SOUND
DAVID FLEURY MUSIC

AGENCY
MULTICOM

CLIENT
TRAVEL ALBERTA

CONSUMER COMMERCIAL, SINGLE

VIDEO   **AUDIO**

TITLE
COPS

ART DIRECTOR
MARTIN SHEWCHUK

WRITER
JODY OVEREND

CREATIVE DIRECTOR
TONY HOUGHTON

PRODUCER
AGGIE BROOK

PRODUCTION HOUSE
BRATKOWSKI PRODUCTION

MUSIC/SOUND
AIR COMPANY

AGENCY
LEO BURNETT
COMPANY LTD.

CLIENT
PEPSI-COLA CANADA LTD.

VIDEO	AUDIO		
Open on Scott and buddy driving down highway. Two girls, driving in a car beside his, are flirting.	VOCALS: Are you up? Are you in? Are you ready to begin?	Scott and lady cop flirt.	COP: What are you looking at?
Scott hears siren and pulls over. Girls drive away.	Are you ready for the show?	Scott does one handed opening of 7UP and takes a drink. Lady cop and Scott are still flirting as she writes out his ticket.	VOCALS: Are you up for it? Are you up for it? Are you up for it?
	SFX: SIREN	Male cop rips ticket off her pad as lady cop looks on nervously. He gives ticket to Scott and the two cops walk off.	MUSIC TRACK
Scott gets out and leans against car. Two cops approach. Buddy is laughing and drinking 7UP.	Come on baby, he let's go Alright. MUSIC TRACK		COP: Have a nice day MUSIC TRACK
Big male cop stops by Scott.	COP: You're a real smart guy huh? Come down here with your fancy car…	Cut to Scott as he reads her phone number on the back of the ticket. Scott smiles. Cut away to two cops walking back to their cruiser.	VOCALS: Are you up for it? Are you up for it?
Lady cop gets license plate. She takes off her hat and lets her blond hair down as Scott watches.	VOCALS: You really want to go for it	Cut to Scott and buddy in car. Scott puts on his sunglasses. SUPER: Are you up for it? And 7UP logo.	BUDDY: See the way she looked at me? SCOTT: Yeah
Lady cop walks over to action. Buddy looking on longingly.	Rock and Roll Roll with it Having some fun with it Are you up for it?		VOCALS: 7UP 7UP.

AUDIO

TITLE
IMAGES

ART DIRECTOR
PAUL HAINS

WRITERS
BRUCE McCALLUM
/PAUL HAINS

CREATIVE DIRECTOR
BRUCE McCALLUM

PRODUCER
KAY BROWN

PRODUCTION HOUSE
PARTNERS FILM CO.

MUSIC/SOUND
CONNIE VAN BEEK

AGENCY
PALMER BONNER BCP

CLIENT
CARLING O'KEEFE
BREWERIES OF CANADA LTD.

MUSIC TRACK
THROUGHOUT

CONSUMER COMMERCIAL, SINGLE

AUDIO

WOMAN: At first he'd be an hour late for dinner. Then two. Then one night, he just didn't come home.

SFX: (Whistle traffic noises, bike gears).

WOMAN: I was devastated. But the truth was, she was giving him what he really hungered for.

SFX: (Birds chirping).

GRANDMA: This will be our little secret.

WOMAN: Now I give him nothing but Purina Meow Mix. Did you know, it's the only food with the tastes of Tuna, Liver and Chicken? It's what he always asked for. I guess I just wasn't listening.

ANNCR: Purina Meow Mix. If you don't feed it to your cat, who will?

SFX: (Barbershop door chime rings, traffic noises).

BARBER: This'll be our little secret.

TITLE
EXPOSÉ 1

ART DIRECTOR
JOHN SPEAKMAN

WRITER
TERRY BELL

CREATIVE DIRECTOR
GARY PROUK

PRODUCER
MARLA DIGIACOMA

DIRECTOR
CHRISTOPHER SANDERSON

PRODUCTION HOUSE
MISTRAL FILM PRODUCTIONS

MUSIC/SOUND
STRESS INC.— MARK STAFFORD

AGENCY
SCALI, McCABE, SLOVES (CANADA) LTD

CLIENT
RALSTON PURINA INC.

VIDEO | **AUDIO**

Open on a super that reads: it's commercial time.

SUPER: But wait, before you go to the bathroom.

SUPER: Take this. A pack rolls up into frame.
SUPER: Continuous cleaning Sani-Flush.

SUPER: Drop it in the tank. Pack, as if in water falls through frame behind type.

SUPER: Every flush releases chlorine cleaning power.

SUPER: That kills toilet bowl germs.

SFX: We hear melodic classic music.

SUPER: So your toilet stays clean for up to 4 months.

We see all the type fall through the screen.
Four month pack comes to rest.
SUPER: Continuous cleaning Sani-Flush 4 month.
SUPER: O.K. You can go now!

SFX: Ker-chung! We hear a toilet flush.

MVO: Continuous cleaning Sani-Flush, it's like a brush every time you flush.

TITLE
KER CHUNG

ART DIRECTOR
MALCOLM MARCUS

WRITER
BASIL MINA

CREATIVE DIRECTOR
TONY HOUGHTON

PRODUCER
BRENDA SURMINSKI

PRODUCTION HOUSE
STUDIO 422

AGENCY
LEO BURNETT COMPANY LTD.

CLIENT
BOYLE MIDWAY

42

VIDEO **AUDIO**

TITLE RODEO	winged statue—Mont Royal Park, Montreal	(music begins)
ART DIRECTOR JOHN McINTYRE	cruise ship at Canada Harbour Place—Vancouver	
CREATIVE DIRECTORS JOHN McINTYRE/ ARNOLD WICHT	sacred buffalo skull—Head Smashed In Buffalo Jump, Alberta	
PRODUCERS BOB KIRK/ CANDACE CONACHER	Delta Police Band—Vancouver	
DIRECTOR STEPHEN YEATES	diddly boppers—Edmonton	
PRODUCTION HOUSE THE DIRECTORS FILM CO. LTD.	jammer bus—Waterdon National Park	
MUSIC/SOUND CRAWFORD-GOLDSMITH	polo—Gormley, Ontario	
AGENCY CAMP ASSOCIATES ADVTG. LTD.	waterfall—Takkakaw Falls, Yoho National Park, B.C.	
CLIENT TOURISM CANADA	little girl going down steps—Vancouver	
	Vistadome train in tunnel—Field, B.C.	
	people on beach—Wendake Beach, Ont.	

piano player by painting—Winnipeg Art Gallery

3 Japanese ladies by pagoda—UBC campus, B.C.

man watering flowers—Stanley Park, Vancouver

bus crossing frame—southern Alberta

man hanging sign—Saint Andrews By the Sea, N.B.   Canada

house on cliff—Perce Rock, Gaspe, Quebec

girl at binoculars—Montreal

square dancers—Toronto

bull rider—Black Diamond, Alberta

pole vaulter—Toronto

Segwin Ship—Muskoka

Campobello Lighthouse—Campobello, N.B.

ballerina reflected in pool—Edmonton

neon of dragon—Toronto   Come to the World

neon Cinema de Paris—Quebec City

Chinese girl in head-dress—Vancouver

crowd applauding—Orpheum Theatre, Vancouver

Nanaksar Gurdwara Gurskh Temple—Richmond, B.C.   Next Door

SUPER: Canada The World Next Door sponsored by Tourism Canada

VIDEO **AUDIO**

TITLE PIONEER	Prairie Day steam train—near Winnipeg	music begins
ART DIRECTOR JOHN McINTYRE	farm windmill—High River Alberta	
CREATIVE DIRECTORS JOHN McINTYRE/ ARNOLD WICHT	skullers by Parliament—Ottawa	
PRODUCERS BOB KIRK/ CANDACE CONACHER	North West Mounted Police bugler—Winnipeg	
DIRECTOR STEPHEN YEATES	church cross as birds fly up—Quebec City	
PRODUCTION HOUSE THE DIRECTORS FILM CO. LTD.	little girl looking out window—Quebec City	
MUSIC/SOUND CRAWFORD-GOLDSMITH	pigeons flying by grain elevator—Claresholm, Alberta	
AGENCY CAMP ASSOCIATES ADVTG. LTD.	truck pulling up to gas station—Ukranian village, near Edmonton, Alberta Canada	
CLIENT TOURISM CANADA	2 kids in Halloween costume—Perkensfield, Ont.	

accordian player—Quebec City

4 Bavarians dancing—Toronto

3 women shoppers—Marine Building, Vancouver

little boy blowing bubbles—Quebec City

man leading haywagon across bridge—Les Eboulements, Quebec

Windermere Hotel—Muskoka

Shumka dancer—Vegreville, Alberta   Come to the World

Wagon wheel going by—Quebec City

Japanese girl with camera—UBC Campus, Vancouver

horse drawn carriage by Manege Militaire—Quebec City   Next Door

SUPER: Canada The World Next Door sponsored by Tourism Canada

CONSUMER COMMERCIAL, SINGLE

VIDEO   **AUDIO**

Open on sign "Ministry of Keeping Everything Absolutely the Same—Staff Canteen". Under is the "Today's Special" with "See Yesterday's Special" chalked on. A young man (#1), carrying "3 day instant photo" folder and lunch box runs by. Inside, about 20 employees all dressed in grey are sitting, eating their lunches and murmuring to each other. The canteen is furnished with an old snack machine, a wireless and other outdated remnants. #1 whistles to get everyone's attention.

#1: O.K. Guys, I've got today's surveillance pictures back...this thing is really big.

The pictures are passed around. Individuals shuffle the photos as they speak.

RANDOM: Look... Edmonton, Winnipeg... Toronto...it's everywhere.

Someone next to #1 holds up a photo.

#1 gives photo a superficial glance.

#1 opens lunch box. A look of utter terror appears on his face. Inside the lunch box is a bottle of Diet Pepsi. He slams the box shut before anyone else sees it, and forces a nervous smile.

#1: Now more than half the Diet Coke drinkers that received Taste Packs said they preferred the taste of Diet Pepsi.

#2: Gotta be that Diet Pepsi Taste Drive.

#3 (to #1): Say, this looks like your wife.

#1: What? My wife change?...to Diet Pepsi (laughs).

MUSIC: Sting

#1: Don't be ridiculous...

TITLE
CANTEEN

ART DIRECTORS
GRAY ABRAHAM/
COLIN PRIESTLY

WRITERS
BRENT PULFORD/
MARK SINGER

CREATIVE DIRECTOR
GRAY ABRAHAM

PRODUCER
ANDY WILLIAMSON

DIRECTOR
MARCO BRAMBILLA

PRODUCTION HOUSE
THE DIRECTORS FILM CO.

MUSIC/SOUND
ANDRE JAQUMIN-REDWOOD/
THE AIR CO.

AGENCY
J. WALTER THOMPSON

CLIENT
PEPSI-COLA LTD.

VIDEO

Open on tight two-shot of Paul and bartender with bar between them. Bartender is teaching Paul how to tilt a glass and pour a Foster's into it using only one hand. There are a couple of other people looking on, although we can't see them distinctly.

Paul begins to pour then looks to camera.

Paul continues to pour, looking back at his friend.

Friend indicates approval: There are sounds of scattered applause from watchers.

PAUL: G'day, I asked my friend Rick to teach me the bartender's art of pouring a perfect Foster's Lager single-handedly.

PAUL: How'm I doing, luv?

WOMAN: Not bad.
PAUL: (to camera) This technique lets you put the squeeze on the Golden Throat Charmer with one hand...

Widen frame to show that Paul has his other arm around the shoulder of his friend.

Just then, another attractive woman steps up to the bar on the other side of Paul (the side still holding the Foster's). Paul looks at her, looks at the first woman, then looks at the hand that's holding the Foster's. He then looks to camera.

Cut to product shot. (2 versions: 1 with drought tap handle, 1 without tap handle)

SUPER: The Golden Throat Charmer. Brewed in Canada.

...while you put the squeeze on a charming lady with the other. What more could a bloke ask for?

One more arm, maybe.

ALL: (laughter)

PAUL: Foster's. The Golden Throat Charmer.

TITLE
CHARMING LADY

ART DIRECTOR
PETER BARRON

WRITER
BARRY JONES

CREATIVE DIRECTOR
BARRY JONES

PRODUCER
PAT WHITE

DIRECTOR
DAVID ASHWELL

PRODUCTION HOUSE
DAVID ASHWELL FILM CO.

AGENCY
J. WALTER THOMPSON

CLIENT
CARLING O'KEEFE
BREWERIES OF CANADA LTD.

CONSUMER COMMERCIAL, SINGLE

44

VIDEO   **AUDIO**

TITLE
WINTER WALL

ART DIRECTOR
DAVID PURSER

WRITER
BARRY CHUDAKOV

CREATIVE DIRECTOR
BILL DURNAN

PRODUCER
CARL HARVEY

DIRECTOR
ALAR KIVILO

PRODUCTION HOUSE
PROPELLER

MUSIC/SOUND
THE AIR COMPANY—
RICK SHURMAN

AGENCY
MacLAREN ADVERTISING

CLIENT
IMPERIAL OIL LIMITED

With the camera locked off, we open on a stone wall—it's an early winters morning. Snow is falling. Two cars are parked silent, waiting for someone—natural SFX.

Suddenly, over the wall comes a string of bed-sheets tied together—followed quickly by two men dressed in black and white striped outfits—they look at each other in surprise as they drop to the ground. One being a little slower than the other, they both run to the waiting cars.

The car on the left starts instantly—the car on the right is having trouble—the left car drives off—the other car still won't start (SFX of car engine turning over).

The car finally starts after a while but we see it hesitating and running rough.

It starts to move just as two Mounties wearing snow shoes, run after him with police dogs.

SUPER: Esso Logo. No Trouble Gasoline. For Winter.

SFX UNDER THROUGHOUT.

ANNCR: If the Esso No Trouble Gasoline now helps you get away from gas line freeze-up and in cold damp weather, stalling and rough idling...

...Why get caught without it?

CONSUMER COMMERCIAL, CAMPAIGN

GOLD AWARD

LARGE FRAME	SMALL FRAME	AUDIO		
CU passport; Hong Kong being stamped on it.	CU girl on plane intercom.	VO INTERCOM: Please enjoy your stay in Hong Kong.		
Hero's hand picking up leather garment bag. Cathay Pacific tag is prominent in frame.	CU girls in flight. CU plane taking off.	MVO: When it's important		
Hero hefts bag onto his shoulder.	CU food on tray.	that your needs as a business person		
¾ overhead shot of hero walking through throng of people in airport.	CU girl turning, smiling.	be reconciled with your wants as a traveller...		
Hero walking purposefully toward camera (as in print shot)				
As hero passes by camera frame freezes and blows out to white. SUPER LOGO: Cathay Pacific. Arrive in better shape.		Cathay Pacific... Arrive in better shape.		

TITLE
RELIABILITY/SERVICE

ART DIRECTOR
MALCOLM MARCUS

WRITER
JANET KESTIN/BASIL MINA

CREATIVE DIRECTOR
TONY HOUGHTON

PRODUCER
JILL WADE

DIRECTOR
JIM SONZERO

PRODUCTION HOUSE
PARTNERS FILM CO.

MUSIC/SOUND
CONNIE VAN BEEK

AGENCY
LEO BURNETT COMPANY LTD.

CLIENT
CATHAY PACIFIC

LARGE FRAME	SMALL FRAME	AUDIO		
Open on airport door sliding open as traveller walks through. Written: Hong Kong International Airport in English and Chinese. It moves out of frame.	Flight engineer walking around plane doing final external flight check.	Airport Sounds	Hero and associate are seated in car talking. We see them through the window.	
			Car pulls away. Frame freezes and blows out to white. SUPER LOGO: Arrive in better shape. Cathay Pacific.	Cathay Pacific... Arrive in better shape.
Hero turns and recognizes Chinese business associate who has come to meet him in a chauffeur-driven Rolls.	ECU: Rolls-Royce engine.	MVO: When it's essential that you get		
Hero shakes hand with Chinese businessman.	Cut to airport video screen showing time of CX-801 departure. Changes to read "Departed".	where you're going precisely		
Hero casually tosses the bags into the trunk.	Plane is in motion. Wheels turn to camera.	when you have to be there...		
ECU: Cathay Pacific baggage tag as Hero's bag goes into trunk.	Cut to plane taking off.			

GOLD AWARD

AUDIO

MUSIC TRACK
THROUGHOUT

TITLE
SUNGLASSES/EIGHT BALL/
BELT BUCKLE

ART DIRECTOR
PAUL HAINS

WRITERS
BRUCE McCALLUM/
PAUL HAINS

CREATIVE DIRECTOR
BRUCE McCALLUM

PRODUCER
KAY BROWN

DIRECTOR
JIM SONZERO

PRODUCTION HOUSE
PARTNERS FILM CO.

MUSIC/SOUND
CONNIE VAN BEEK

AGENCY
PALMER BONNER BCP

CLIENT
CARLING O'KEEFE
BREWERIES OF CANADA LTD.

AUDIO

MUSIC TRACK
THROUGHOUT

CONSUMER COMMERCIAL, CAMPAIGN

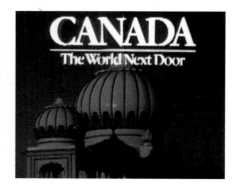

SILVER AWARD

VIDEO	AUDIO
winged statue — Mont Royal Park, Montreal	(music begins)
cruise ship at Canada Harbour Place — Vancouver	
sacred buffalo skull — Head Smashed In Buffalo Jump, Alberta	
Delta Police Band — Vancouver	
diddly boppers — Edmonton	
jammer bus — Waterdon National Park	
polo — Gormley, Ontario	
waterfall — Takkakaw Falls, Yoho National Park, B.C.	
little girl going down steps — Vancouver	
Vistadome train in tunnel — Field, B.C.	
people on beach — Wendake Beach, Ont.	

piano player by painting — Winnipeg Art Gallery

3 Japanese ladies by pagoda — UBC campus, B.C.

man watering flowers — Stanley Park, Vancouver

bus crossing frame — southern Alberta

man hanging sign — Saint Andrews By the Sea, N.B.   Canada

house on cliff — Perce Rock, Gaspe, Quebec

girl at binoculars — Montreal

square dancers — Toronto

bull rider — Black Diamond, Alberta

pole vaulter — Toronto

Segwin Ship — Muskoka

Campobello Lighthouse — Campobello, N.B.

ballerina reflected in pool — Edmonton

neon of dragon — Toronto   Come to the World

neon Cinema de Paris — Quebec City

Chinese girl in head-dress — Vancouver

crowd applauding — Orpheum Theatre, Vancouver

Nanaksar Gurdwara Gurskh Temple — Richmond, B.C.   Next Door

SUPER: Canada The World Next Door sponsored by Tourism Canada

TITLE
RODEO/PIONEER

ART DIRECTOR
JOHN McINTYRE

CREATIVE DIRECTORS
JOHN McINTYRE/
ARNOLD WICHT

PRODUCERS
BOB KIRK/
CANDACE CONACHER

DIRECTOR
STEPHEN YEATES

PRODUCTION HOUSE
THE DIRECTORS
FILM CO. LTD.

MUSIC/SOUND
CRAWFORD-GOLDSMITH

AGENCY
CAMP ASSOCIATES
ADVTG. LTD.

CLIENT
TOURISM CANADA

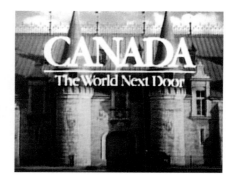

VIDEO	AUDIO
Prairie Day steam train — near Winnipeg	music begins
farm windmill — High River Alberta	
skullers by Parliament — Ottawa	
North West Mounted Police bugler — Winnipeg	
church cross as birds fly up — Quebec City	
little girl looking out window — Quebec City	
pigeons flying by grain elevator — Claresholm, Alberta	
truck pulling up to gas station — Ukranian village, near Edmonton, Alberta	Canada
2 kids in Halloween costume — Perkensfield, Ont.	

accordian player — Quebec City

4 Bavarians dancing — Toronto

3 women shoppers — Marine Building, Vancouver

little boy blowing bubbles — Quebec City

man leading haywagon across bridge — Les Eboulements, Quebec

Windermere Hotel — Muskoka

Shumka dancer — Vegreville, Alberta   Come to the World

Wagon wheel going by — Quebec City

Japanese girl with camera — UBC Campus, Vancouver

horse drawn carriage by Manege Militaire — Quebec City   Next Door

SUPER: Canada The World Next Door sponsored by Tourism Canada

CONSUMER COMMERCIAL, CAMPAIGN

SILVER AWARD

TITLE
RACE/CORVETTE/COPS

ART DIRECTOR
MARTIN SHEWCHUK

WRITER
JODY OVEREND

CREATIVE DIRECTOR
TONY HOUGHTON

PRODUCER
AGGIE BROOK

PRODUCTION HOUSE
BRATKOWSKI PRODUCTION

MUSIC/SOUND
AIR COMPANY

AGENCY
LEO BURNETT
COMPANY LTD.

CLIENT
PEPSI-COLA CANADA LTD.

VIDEO	AUDIO				
Open on busy beach scene. Young girl busy waxing red Corvette.	MUSIC TRACK: (Instrumental/ Rock 'N Roll) SFX: Natural CHORUS: She's so fine	SUPER: Suitable for carbohydrate/calorie reduced diets. Nutrasweet symbol. Close up on one handed opening. Muscle guy looks up at sound and starts to get up.	Summer's really humming And I feel a good time coming on. SFX: Pop Hiss MUSIC TRACK	Cut to Scott, looking surprised. Then to buddies laughing. Back to Scott, grinning and shrugging. SUPER: Are You Up For It? and Diet 7UP logo.	CHORUS: Are you up for it? Are you up for it? Diet 7UP.
Cut to Scott pulling up along side Corvette. She notices him, he notices her. They flirt. Buddies urge him on.	VOCALS: She's so fine What a pretty lady She's one of a kind A real beach baby	Cut to Scott drinking and back to muscle guy. Scott and the girl both look over at him.	MUSCLE GUY: Hey Pal!		
Scott gets out of his car and sits on hood. He continues flirting with the girl.	I'm gonna make her mine I'm gonna make her mine today CHORUS: Mine oh mine	Buddies look on nervously as muscle guy (filling the screen) walks over to Scott, finishes his Diet 7UP, crunches can in Scott's face and throws it in the garbage. Girl is looking on smiling.	MUSIC TRACK		
Cut to buddies. They notice muscle guy by tire. Scott doesn't.	MUSIC TRACK				
More flirting between Scott and girl. She gets a Diet 7UP and gives it to Scott.	VOCALS: Looks so cool Feeling hot and hazy Wanna drive my car Just drive me crazy	Cut to muscle guy with his arm around the girl.	MUSCLE GUY: Have you met my sister?		

VIDEO	AUDIO		
Open on Scott and buddy driving down highway. Two girls, driving in a car beside his, are flirting.	VOCALS: Are you up? Are you in? Are you ready to begin?	Scott and lady cop flirt. Scott does one handed opening of 7UP and takes a drink. Lady cop and Scott are still flirting as she writes out his ticket.	COP: What are you looking at? VOCALS: Are you up for it? Are you up for it? Are you up for it?
Scott hears siren and pulls over. Girls drive away.	Are you ready for the show? SFX: SIREN Come on baby, he let's go Alright.	Male cop rips ticket off her pad as lady cop looks on nervously. He gives ticket to Scott and the two cops walk off.	MUSIC TRACK COP: Have a nice day MUSIC TRACK
Scott gets out and leans against car. Two cops approach. Buddy is laughing and drinking 7UP.	MUSIC TRACK	Cut to Scott as he reads her phone number on the back of the ticket. Scott smiles. Cut away to two cops walking back to their cruiser.	VOCALS: Are you up for it? Are you up for it?
Big male cop stops by Scott.	COP: You're a real smart guy huh? Come down here with your fancy car...		
Lady cop gets license plate. She takes off her hat and lets her blond hair down as Scott watches.	VOCALS: You really want to go for it	Cut to Scott and buddy in car. Scott puts on his sunglasses. SUPER: Are you up for it? And 7UP logo.	BUDDY: See the way she looked at me?
Lady cop walks over to action. Buddy looking on longingly.	Rock and Roll Roll with it Having some fun with it Are you up for it?		SCOTT: Yeah VOCALS: 7UP 7UP

CONSUMER COMMERCIAL, CAMPAIGN

AUDIO

MUSIC TRACK
THROUGHOUT

TITLE
WATERWALKER/
MUSCLEMAN/BODY RUB/
HULA HOOP
DANCE/ROPE CLIMBER

ART DIRECTORS
LIAM McDONNELL

CREATIVE DIRECTOR
ROBERT MONK

AGENCY
NATHAN FRASER ROSS ROY

CLIENT
DURANGO BEER COOLER

AUDIO

MUSIC TRACK
THROUGHOUT

CONSUMER COMMERCIAL, CAMPAIGN

AUDIO

TITLE
KIM/KIM, GILLES/
KIDS, FOOD TABLE/PENGUIN

ART DIRECTOR
LIAM McDONNELL

CREATIVE DIRECTOR
ROBERT MONK

AGENCY
NATHAN FRASER ROSS ROY

CLIENT
CLUB MED

MUSIC TRACK
THROUGHOUT

AUDIO

MUSIC TRACK
THROUGHOUT

CONSUMER COMMERCIAL, CAMPAIGN

VIDEO	AUDIO
Open on Hogan at a typical backyard barbecue.	
Hogan speaks to camera. A man cooks in background.	HOGAN: G'day. My mates invited me over for a fine Canadian tradition —a Barby
Hogan speaks to cook.	(TO COOK): What's cookin' mate?
Cook turns to speak and throws a scrap to a dog.	COOK: Steak.
Hogan speaks again to camera as he takes a can of Foster's from a cooler.	HOGAN: Ace. Just like in Oz, when you're hungry enough to eat a Wallaby, and you'd like something while you're waitin', Foster's, the Golden Throat Charmer.
Hogan pours himself a can of Foster's.	

Cook turns to speak to Hogan and gestures to barbecue.	COOK: You know if you're that hungry I can throw a dog on for ya!
Hogan looks at dog. Dog looks at Hogan. Hogan speaks to man. Hogan speaks to dog. Hogan looks to camera.	HOGAN: No thanks mate. (TO DOG): If I was you I'd make me self scarce.
PRODUCT SHOT: Can, hot dog.	ANNCR (VO): Foster's. The Golden Throat Charmer.
SUPER: The Golden Throat Charmer. Brewed in Canada.	

TITLE
HOT DOG/KEG/
CHARMING LADY

ART DIRECTOR
DAVE KELSO/
PETER BARRON

WRITERS
BRAD RIDDOCH/
BARRY JONES

CREATIVE DIRECTORS
BRAD RIDOCH/
BARRY JONES

PRODUCER
PAT WHITE

DIRECTOR
DAVID ASHWELL

PRODUCTION HOUSE
DAVID ASHWELL FILM CO.

AGENCY
J. WALTER THOMPSON

CLIENT
CARLING O'KEEFE
BREWERIES
OF CANADA LTD.

VIDEO	AUDIO
Open on quiet Canadian bar.	
A man walks in and sits down at the bar. With a gesture to the bartender, he orders a Foster's.	
Beside him Hogan lowers his newspaper to reveal himself to the man and the camera for the first time.	
The man notices Hogan and speaks to him.	CDN: Hi.
	HOGAN: G'day.
	CDN: Can I buy ya' a can of Foster's?
Hogan slides a big 'un from out of frame.	HOGAN: Thanks mate but in Australia that ain't a can of Foster's. This is.
The bartender places a keg of Foster's on the bar.	BARTENDER: Well, in here, this is a can of Foster's.
Hogan smiles and speaks to camera.	HOGAN: Streuth. I could learn to like it here.
PRODUCT SHOT: Keg, draught glass and tap handle.	
SUPER: The Golden Throat Charmer. Brewed in Canada.	ANNCR: Foster's. The Golden Throat Charmer.

VIDEO	AUDIO		
TITLE COURIER/TRAIN **ART DIRECTOR** JOHN SPEAKMAN **WRITER** BILL MARTIN **CREATIVE DIRECTOR** GARY PROUK **PRODUCER** SUE HOXLEY **DIRECTOR** PETER MOSS **PRODUCTION HOUSE** PARTNERS FILM CO. LTD/ BILL HUDSON & ASSOC. **MUSIC/SOUND** THE AIR COMPANY **AGENCY** SCALI, McCABE, SLOVES (CANADA) LTD. **CLIENT** LABATT BREWING CO. LTD	Open on establishing shot of city street with female courier on bicycle. Quick shot of squash game in progress. Establishing shot of high school reunion focusing on two alumnists. Return to squash match. Establish a tree on a hot day. Dog and man sit in shade of tree. Female courier is finished for the day. Takes a bottle of Blue from the fridge. The squash game ends with the losing player pressed against the glass. Through the glass he sees people in the adjoining lounge having a Blue.	(music throughout) There's a heart in this land . . . . . . it's there in all you do. Man is it hot! I've never felt like this before.	Meanwhile, back at the reunion, our two heros are checking graduates using an old yearbook. Some attractive women are in evidence as is Blue. Female courier relaxing with a Blue. Back at the reunion, one of our men turns the yearbook on end as if to help identify another graduate. Female courier relaxing. Final shot of tree at late afternoon. It is now cool enough that the dog leaves its shade. Super-imposed over this shot is a CU of bottle of Blue. SUPER: That's why you call for the Blue.	That's why you call for the Blue.

VIDEO	AUDIO		
Open on couple kissing as train goes by. Establish different couple arguing in stair-well. The man is obviously leaving. 3 golfers waiting on green. Fourth is trying to get out of sand trap. CU of couple (in opening scene) by fence. Attractive waitress reaches for glass. Golfers still waiting. Back at the stairwell the man is returning with flowers. Ball soars over green. Friends help out in order to go to clubhouse.	Music throughout. VOCAL: It's true. That's why you call for it.	Waitress carries Blue through a crowded bar. Back at the stairwell, the man is leaving again; woman throws flowers after him. Waitress presents dart players with bill. Man at stairwell returns with larger bouquet of flowers. Neighbours applaud. Final shot of train and couple. Superimposed over this shot is a close-up of bottle of Blue. SUPER: That's why you call for the Blue.	That's why you call for the Blue. Hey, hey, hey . . . That's why you call for the Blue. That's why you call for the Blue.

CORPORATE COMMERCIAL, SINGLE

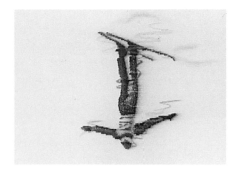  

VIDEO	AUDIO
Open on the base of a ski jump. We see mostly sky and the jump itself.	SUPER: Getting the Dream Off The Ground.
The shot moves slowly. Slow motion throughout.	VO: Training's a drag. Everyday I get up in the morning and something new hurts. Everyday you wonder why you took up Freestyle in the first place. But on the day of competition, you dig down and try to remember what you first liked about it. If you can do that...that's when you can pull off something magic...and you end up falling in love with free-style...all over again.
The jumper comes into frame, and begins his aerial. All the moves are seen as he completes a double back flip with a double twist.	
The intricate moves of this jump are spread throughout the course of the commercial so we can appreciate each individual move.	
The jumper lands successfully and raises his hands in exultation. The frame stops.	
SUPER: Proud sponsors of the Canadian Free-style Ski Team.	
LOGO: Fiberglas	

TITLE
WHEN THE MAGIC HAPPENS

ART DIRECTOR
JEFF KATZ

WRITER
T.J. HARRISON

CREATIVE DIRECTOR
TREVOR GOODGOLL

PRODUCER
CANDACE BOWES

DIRECTOR
MICHAEL MILLS

PRODUCTION HOUSE
MICHAEL MILLS
PRODUCTIONS

MUSIC/SOUND
HARRIS COLE
PRODUCTIONS

AGENCY
LOWE CANADA

CLIENT
FIBERGLAS CANADA INC.

PUBLIC SERVICE COMMERCIAL, SINGLE

GOLD AWARD

VIDEO	AUDIO
Open on a portrait shot of David with a drop cloth background. Throughout the spot alternate between medium close ups and tight close ups.	DAVID: Well, they would just come up to me and say—"you look different".
	They use words in the term of ...
SUPER: Do you have an open mind?	mongoloid...like mental case...or maybe retarded.
	Once they say it, I realize that they also have a handicap themselves.
SUPER: A question from the Ontario Office for Disabled Persons.	It would be great to be treated as anybody else...
Mortice effect with SUPER: (Trillium) Ontario Office for Disabled Persons Remo Mancini, Minister	as no different...as an individual.

TITLE
DAVID'S STORY

ART DIRECTOR
JIM GAULEY

WRITER
WENDY WONG

CREATIVE DIRECTOR
PAM FROSTAD

PRODUCER
SYLVIA MAGUIRE

DIRECTOR
GEORGE MORITA

PRODUCTION HOUSE
PARTNERS FILM CO.

AGENCY
VICKERS & BENSON

CLIENT
ONTARIO OFFICE FOR
DISABLED PERSONS

PUBLIC SERVICE COMMERCIAL, SINGLE

VIDEO

TITLE
THE OBJECT
OF THE GAME

ART DIRECTOR
JEFF KATZ

WRITER
T.J. HARRISON

CREATIVE DIRECTOR
TREVOR GOODGOLL

PRODUCER
SHEILA SONE

DIRECTOR
RICHARD UNRUH

PRODUCTION HOUSE
PARTNERS FILM CO.

MUSIC/SOUND
THE AIR COMPANY/
RICK SHURMAN

AGENCY
LOWE CANADA

CLIENT
SPORTCOM
INTERNATIONAL

The commercial opens up with a view of the corner of the rink low on the ice. There is a game going on. We hear it, but cannot see it. The sound of teams approaches and the puck comes into frame, bounces off the boards and rests in the middle of the frame. A couple of players come crashing into the boards, but continue on without the puck. It remains sitting there. We hear the sounds of players shouts, sticks, the crashing of boards and the fans cheering wildly. Again we do not see the violence that is going on all around. We still remain on the puck. So for the duration of the commercial the game goes on.

around us. But it seems to be carrying on without the puck. No one plays it. Finally we go to black with our message. LET'S GET BACK IN THE GAME. And the FAIRPLAY LOGO. There is a shrill whistle which ends the commercial.

AUDIO

TITLE
A MATTER OF OPINION

ART DIRECTOR
CHARLES EARP

WRITER
PAM FROSTAD

CREATIVE DIRECTOR
PAM FROSTAD

PRODUCER
BEV CORNISH

DIRECTOR
MICHAEL MILLS

PRODUCTION HOUSE
MICHAEL MILLS
PRODUCTIONS

MUSIC/SOUND
SYD KESSLER—THE AIR CO.

AGENCY
VICKERS & BENSON

CLIENT
CANADIAN ADVERTISING
FOUNDATION

Ambient SFX, music throughout

Our couch people react to a commercial.

1. I'm changing the channel now.
2. Why?

1. Because it was a stupid commercial and I don't like it.
2. It's funny.
1. It's insulting.
2. It's not funny?
1. It's sad to see things like that happen on the television. Watch this one.
2. Now that bothers me.
1. See and I love it.
2. It insults my intelligence.
1. It insults your intelligence.
2. Yeah.

1. Well, how about this ... PBBSSS

V.O.: Advertising. Talk to us about it.

SUPER: TOP: Advertising. Talk to us about it.

BOTTOM: The Canadian Advertising Foundation

Bring voices up:
1. Now that's interesting.
2. I don't know, I find, you know, it's boring and sometimes I find you boring ...

Fade voices; see super top, fade and replace with:
P.O. Box 2150, Station A, Toronto, Ontario. M5W 1H1.

BOTTOM: The C.A.F. logo

PUBLIC SERVICE COMMERCIAL, CAMPAIGN

Do you have
an open mind?

VIDEO	AUDIO	
Open on portrait shot of Les with drop cloth background. Throughout the spot, alternate between medium and tight close ups.	LES: I'm a pharmacist and I own and operate two retail pharmacies in Toronto. The biggest problem I have in dealing with the general public is probably one of image. I remember...	**TITLE** LES/DAVID/JONATHAN **ART DIRECTOR** JIM GAULEY **WRITER** WENDY WONG **CREATIVE DIRECTOR** PAM FROSTAD **PRODUCER** SYLVIA MAGUIRE **PRODUCTION HOUSE** PARTNERS FILM CO. **AGENCY** VICKERS & BENSON **CLIENT** ONTARIO OFFICE FOR DISABLED PERSONS
SUPER: A question from the Ontario Office for Disabled Persons.	when I first started working at the hospital ...I was wearing a uniform...I was wearing lab coats and identification and yet I ran into so many patients—even staff—who stopped and asked me which floor I belonged to...	
SUPER: Do you have an open mind?	and I should be returning to my room and all that.	
Mortice effect with SUPER: (Trillium) Ontario Office for Disabled Persons Remo Mancini, Minister	People see the wheelchair but not the person.	

Do you have
an open mind?

VIDEO	AUDIO
Open on a portrait shot of David with a drop cloth background. Throughout the spot alternate between medium close ups and tight close ups.	DAVID: Well, they would just come up to me and say—"you look different". They use words in the term of...
SUPER: Do you have an open mind?	mongoloid...like mental case...or maybe retarded. Once they say it, I realize that they also have a handicap themselves.
SUPER: A question from the Ontario Office for Disabled Persons.	It would be great to be treated as anybody else...
Mortice effect with SUPER: (Trillium) Ontario Office for Disabled Persons Remo Mancini, Minister	as no different...as an individual.

Publication
CITY AND
COUNTRY HOME

Art Director
MARIAN MUSTARD

Writer
ANITA DRAYCOTT

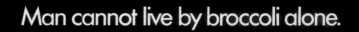

Art Director KAREN PRINCE	*Art Director* BRIAN HARROD
Writer BILL PARKER	*Writer* IAN MIRLIN
Creative Director MICHAEL PAUL	*Creative Director* BRIAN HARROD
3	**5**
Art Director GEORGES HAROUTIUN	*Art Director* DAVID SNIDER
	Writer PETER LANYON
	Creative Director PETER LANYON

Smoking creates all kinds of jobs.

PHYSICIANS FOR A SMOKE-FREE CANADA

Love 'em to bits.

LEVI'S
619's

CANADA'S CHOICE

6

Art Director
DIANNE EASTMAN
Writer
RICK BOOK

7

Art Director
BARRY CHEMEL
Writer
KURT HAGAN
Creative Director
WAYNE HILINSKI

8

Art Director
BRIAN HARROD
Writer
IAN MIRLIN
Creative Director
BRIAN HARROD

9

Art Director
COLIN PRIESTLEY
Writer
BRENT POLFORD
Creative Director
GRAY ABRAHAM

10

Art Director
BRIAN HANNIGAN
Writer
GEORGE ANKETELL
Creative Director
GEORGE ANKETELL

Once you've made a name
for yourself,
you need a good place to put it.

AMERICAN EXPRESS

NOT TRANSFERABLE INCESSIBLE

3112

VALID DATES/DATES DE VALID

Gold Card.

Hands by Oscar Peterson. Hands and face by Birks.

Timing... precise.
Performance... flawless.
All in the hands of the great
Oscar Peterson.
And, befitting such perfection,
a Swiss quartz watch from Birks.
Like The Master himself,
truly an original.
Birks' famous blue
box has been a
symbol of quality
and value for over a
hundred years.
A symbol too of the marvellous
variety of Birks' fine merchandise
and exclusive designs.
Because at Birks you're certain
to get the absolute best, no matter
how much or how little you pay.
That's the way it is.
That's the way it always will be.

Only at BIRKS

Ladies & gents $450. Pictured face also available: $425.

BELL

Agfa-Gevaert is the international
leader in reproduction systems
technology.
More than isolated products, Agfa-
Gevaert offers complete systems designed
and adapted for every field of use in the
graphic arts industry...systems that feature
an integrated line, from cameras and
processors, to specialized films, papers,
chemicals and more.

Together, they make up
the most innovative reproduction systems in the world.

AGFA-GEVAERT. SYSTEMS THAT
MAKE A WORLD OF DIFFERENCE.

AGFA *Agfa*

WINNING PARTNERSHIPS

Cathay Pacific Airlines · Tony Houghton, Malcolm Marcus, Janet Kestin, Jill Wade · Jim Sonzero
Gold Award · Consumer Commercial, Single

Carling Black Label Beer · Bruce McCallum, Paul Hains, Kay Brown · Jim Sonzero
Gold Award · Consumer Commercial, Campaign

Cathay Pacific Airlines · Tony Houghton, Malcolm Marcus, Janet Kestin, Jill Wade · Jim Sonzero
Gold Award · Consumer Commercial, Campaign

Ontario Office for Disabled Persons · Pam Frostad, Jim Gauley, Wendy Wong, Sylvia Maguire · George Morita
Gold Award · Public Service Commercial, Single

Loblaws Supermarkets Ltd. · Chuck Beisch, Phillippa Ewing, Dee Anderson · Bob Perks
Silver Award · Consumer Commercial, Single

Cathay Pacific Airlines · Tony Houghton, Malcolm Marcus, Janet Kestin, Jill Wade · Jim Sonzero
Silver Award · Consumer Commercial, Single

Ontario Office for Disabled Persons · Pam Frostad, Jim Gauley, Wendy Wong, Sylvia Maguire · George Morita
Certificate of Merit · Public Service Commercial, Campaign

Labatt Brewing Company Ltd. · Gary Prouk, John Speakman, Bill Martin, Pat Peat · Peter Moss
Certificate of Merit · Consumer Commercial, Campaign

Travel Alberta · Trevor McConnell, Bruce Walker, George Archer · David Smith
Certificate of Merit · Consumer Commercial, Single

Carling Black Label Beer · Bruce McCallum, Paul Hains, Kay Brown · Jim Sonzero
Certificate of Merit · Consumer Commercial, Single

We're proud of the partnerships we create.

The Partners' Film Company Limited

(416) 966-3500

N

WOW! As you can see, one word is all that we need to express our feelings about the quality of work that took the prizes at this year's ADCT Show. Our most sincere congratulations to all the winners. Provincial Papers is proud to help support the ADCT in the production of this Awards Annual. This book is printed on 200M Jenson Gloss, our own award winning No. 1 coated printing paper, manufactured in Canada.

PROVINCIAL
PAPERS

Typography for next year's ideas.

Techni Process Limited, Two Stewart Street,
Toronto, Canada. (416) 363-2493

EUREKA

Think of it as...

Great communication results from the perfect marriage of copy and art. It's what you strive for with every piece you design. But, after being printed, distributed, handled and manhandled, will your work still communicate as well as you intended?

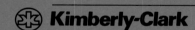

Armor for Art

Make the impression last. Print it on KIMDURA® Synthetic Paper from Kimberly-Clark. In a world where only the strong survive, KIMDURA stands alone. It's water and tear-resistant, and almost impervious to grease, oil and chemicals. KIMDURA also prints beautifully and can be easily punched, die-cut, folded, and glued to accommodate your design. Menu, map, manual or brochure...if it needs to last, specify KIMDURA® Synthetic Paper.

Think of it as armor for art.

Kimdura®
Synthetic Paper

Kimberly-Clark

AGENCY
HARROD & MIRLIN
CLIENT
CHESEBROUGH-POND'S
CREATIVE DIRECTOR
IAN MIRLIN

RADIO COMMERCIAL, CAMPAIGN

66

INTERVIEWER: I'm talking now with the Masked Marvel.

MASKED MARVEL: I'm not going to say I'm not and I'm not going to say I ain't.

INT: Did you ever wrestle the Moose?

MM: Well, I ain't sayin' I don't and I ain't sayin' I ain't.

INT: Well, tell me what you don't...tell me what you do know.

MM: The Moose has got this certain kind of quality that nobody has ever seen or heard of.

INT: You're very articulate for a wrestler.

MM: Guess I absorbed some brains (laughs).

SINGER: Moosehead Forever.

ANNOUNCER: Moosehead Beer. Come on. Get to know the Moose.

INTERVIEWER: These interviews are about me trying to understand the Moose a little bit better.

HIPPY GIRL: Your body's made up of 70% liquid.

INT: Isn't that fascinating...is he a water sign or something?

HG: Well, yeah? That makes sense, he probably is. Of course, he's a water sign because of the whole fluid thing.

INT: And what are you?

HG: I'm an air sign.

ANNOUNCER: Moosehead Beer. Come on. Get to know the Moose.

ANNOUNCER: I'm talking on the phone with the person who started the Moosehead Forever song. Can you give me a sort of rendition of how it goes.

COMPOSER: Bom, Bom, Ba, Ba, Bom, Bom, Ba, Ba, Ba, Bom, Dah, Dah, Dah, Dah, Dah, Dah, Dah, Dah, Dah, Dah, Hoot, Hoot, Hoot.

ANNR: Hold it, hold it, what is that "Hoot, Hoot" stuff, what does that mean?

COMP: It's a Moose call (laughs).

SINGER: Moosehead Forever.

ANNR: Moosehead Beer. Come on. Get to know the Moose.

TITLE
WRESTLER/HIPPY GIRL/COMPOSER
AGENCY
NATHAN FRASER ROSS ROY
CLIENT
MOLSON BREWERIES OF CANADA
CREATIVE DIRECTOR
ROBERT MONK

GOLD AWARD

RADIO COMMERCIAL, CAMPAIGN

DON: Hi folks, I'm here in downtown Ottawa, asking the ordinary man in the street how he feels about the coming of the Ottawa Sun. You sir?

JOHN TURNER: Well, I…I…I…I think…I…I… think it's an appropriate… question…a good question. I think, I think, I think I can say that I…I…I… ha-ha…I…

DON: (Impatiently) Mr. Turner, do you think it's just the news Ottawa's been waiting for? A simple yes or no.

JT: Well I…I…I… have to say that …I

DON: (cutting him off) Thank you very much, The Ottawa Sunday Sun. It's just the news you've been waiting for.

DON: Hi folks, I'm here in downtown Ottawa, asking the ordinary man in the street how he feels about the coming of the Ottawa Sunday Sun. You sir?

MULRONEY: Well, I feel very strongly, very definitely that I could state without equivocation or fear of contradiction that there will be no fence-sitting on this particular issue for me.

DON: (cutting him off) Mr. Mulroney. Do you feel the Ottawa Sun's just the news Ottawa's been waiting for. Yes or no.

M: Well yes…

DON: Thank you. Folks…

M: And no.

DON: The Ottawa Sunday Sun. It's just the news you've been waiting for.

TITLE
JOHN & BRIAN
AGENCY
AMBROSE CARR DEFOREST LINTON
CLIENT
OTTAWA SUN
CREATIVE DIRECTORS
DOUG LINTON/PETER BYRNE
PRODUCER
KATHY HENNIG
PRODUCTION HOUSE
SOUNDS INTERCHANGE

RADIO COMMERCIAL, CAMPAIGN

SFX: Office interior...

MAN: Are you the Davis who wrote these Arby's roast beef restaurant commercials?

DAVIS: For the 99¢ sale? Yeah. Who are you?

MAN: I'm Arby's lawyer. We have a problem with this script.

MAN: You call hamburgers "criminal, they leave one's mouth dying of boredom."

DAVIS: Yeah.

MAN: And "they should be charged with monotonous assault on the tastebuds."

DAVIS: Too strong?

MAN: We want to say "you really can taste the Arby's difference, that once people try Arby's roast beef sandwiches, they'll love them". Now, about the special offer...

DAVIS: Regular Arby's roast beef sandwich for only 99 cents?

MAN: You cannot say, "Buy a Lear jet with the money you'll save."

DAVIS: Why not?

MAN: Mr. Davis, to buy the cheapest Lear jet, a person would have to purchase 7 million five hundred thousand regular Arby's roast beef sandwiches at 99¢.

DAVIS: Yeah, so what's your point?

MAN: My point is, you cannot say that.

DAVIS: Weelll, why not have an announcer just say "Come to Arby's right now and get a delicious Arby's regular for only 99¢."

MAN: An excellent idea, Mr. Davis.

ANNOUNCER:
(10 second tag)

TITLE
LAWYER/YOU AGAIN

ART DIRECTOR
DAVID ADAMS

AGENCY
GRANT TANDY ADVERTISING

CLIENT
ARBY'S

CREATIVE DIRECTOR
DAVID ADAMS

PRODUCER
ANDY RICE

PRODUCTION HOUSE
GRIFFITH GIBSON

RADIO COMMERCIAL, CAMPAIGN

SFX: Office interior...

MAN: Mr. Davis?

DAVIS: Not you again!

MAN: That's right, the lawyer from Arby's.

DAVIS: What is it this time?

MAN: This latest commercial you've written for Arby's roast beef restaurants just won't do, Mr. Davis. It won't do at all.

DAVIS: All it says is that Arby's roast beef sandwiches are a great break from hamburgers, and that right now you can get a regular Arby's roast beef sandwich for 99 cents instead of up to two nineteen!

MAN: Not quite. You also say that Arby's is giving away a free satellite dish with each regular sandwich.

DAVIS: Yeah, so?

MAN: It's not true. Arby's isn't giving away anything.

DAVIS: Well why not?

MAN: Mr. Davis, think about it. A regular Arby's roast beef sandwich normally sells for up to $2.19. During this promotion participating Arby's are selling them for 99 cents. Is it likely that they would also give away a satellite dish worth over five thousand dollars?

DAVIS: Listen, nobody cares about a crummy $1.20. You gotta use modern marketing techniques if you want results.

MAN: Is that what you call this? "Each Arby's regular served piping hot by Walter Cronkite"?

DAVIS: Nice twist, hum? I figure he gives us great credibility.

MAN: But it isn't true!

DAVIS: So what are you saying? You expect me to stick to the truth?

MAN: Yes!

DAVIS: All right. But don't blame me if it doesn't work.

ANNOUNCER:

(10 second tag)

TITLE
LAWYER/YOU AGAIN

ART DIRECTOR
DAVID ADAMS

AGENCY
GRANT TANDY ADVERTISING

CLIENT
ARBY'S

CREATIVE DIRECTOR
DAVID ADAMS

PRODUCER
ANDY RICE

PRODUCTION HOUSE
GRIFFITH GIBSON

Our House
Is A Very Very Very Fine House . . .

511 King Street West is a proud architectural monument to an age when quality of design, attention to detail and integrity of construction were important. Today it is the home of **King West Communications**. And that's no accident.

King West Communications, formerly The Saturday Night Group, believes in the same principles that our house embodies: quality, care and imagination. That's why **King West Communications** is Canada's finest contract publisher.

King West Communications has built its unmatched reputation for excellence on the award-winning quality of its work. Behind the undeniable impact of the launching of the *Globe and Mail* family of magazines stood the **King West Communications** team, providing the best in editorial and design services. That's also true of *Wardair*, *The Royal Bank Reporter*, *Landmarks* and many others.

King West Communications has developed an industry-leading reputation founded upon care to detail, precision of execution and keen sensitivity to deadlines and budgets. No detail is too small when clients are looking for the very best typesetting, assembly and production management.

King West Communications offers professional marketing assistance to the publishing industry. Under one roof, you can find any service you need to support your publication: consulting on, and management of, your strategic business plans; the development of circulation and promotional campaigns — complete with full creative capabilities and state-of-the-art fulfillment services.

So when we say that our house is a very very very fine house, we're only telling you what the industry already knows.

To learn more about **King West Communications**, our services and how we can help you, contact Susan Linton, 511 King Street West, Toronto, Ontario M5V 2Z4 or call (416)591-8822.

Come on over to our house.

King West **Communications**

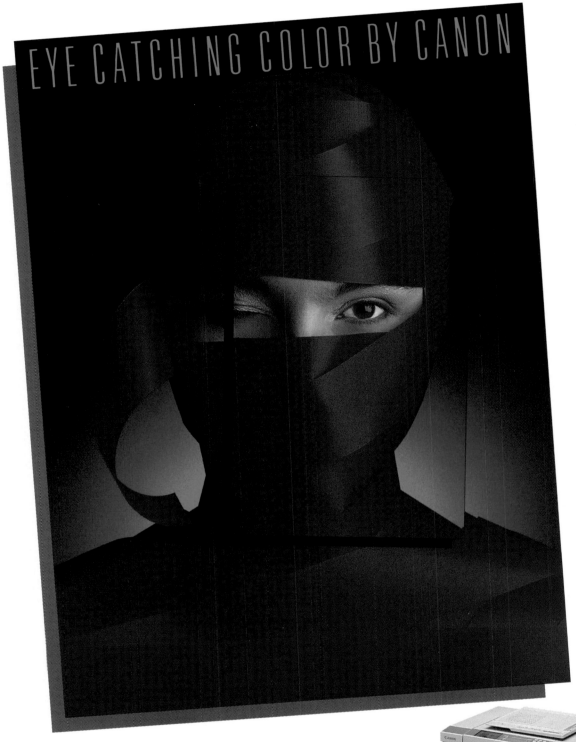

EYE CATCHING COLOR BY CANON

Seductive color. Creative editing. Laser sharp printing. That's the Canon Color Laser Copier.

This is the machine that set the standard in color copying overnight. Because it scans digitally, and prints by laser, colors are true to life.

But, you can change all that. Go to the copier's editing features. Turn blue skies green, green grass brown—if that's what you want. You can also delete parts of an image. Move images around on the page. Take type from one original and combine it with a picture from another.

Zoom can take you from 50% right up to 400%. Now you can make the minuscule massive. Or vice-versa.

There is so much this copier can do. All at a price that won't put you in the red. Call 1-800-387-1241 for an eye-opening demonstration.

Canon
COLOR LASER COPIER

"I WONDER HOW THEY FIXED THE RIF

Another chapter from The Empress Graphics Book of Wonders.

The men's briefs, hand-picked by client and art director, were ironed until wrinkle-free.

The small tuck and ripple, where the waistband is reinforced for strength, looked perfectly natural through the camera lens.

But on close examination of the transparencies, that tuck and ripple became a pain in the ass.

Even if there was time and money for dye transfers, and the best retoucher in the world, there was no chance of making the briefs look un-

retouched, because the fabric's fine continuous weave would be broken.

That's when Empress Graphics entered the picture, and while we were at it, we also cleaned up the waistband

ple WITHOUT BREAKING THE WEAVE."

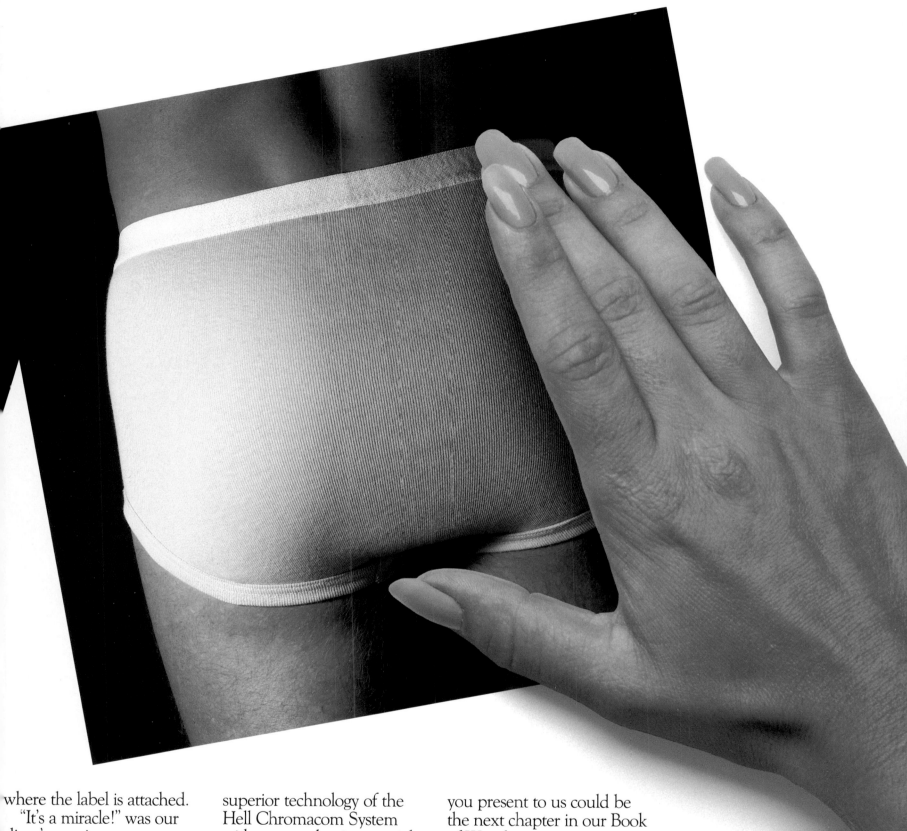

where the label is attached.

"It's a miracle!" was our client's reaction.

But we'd like you to be the judge.

Our wide range of image manipulation possibilities is truly incredible.

When we combine the superior technology of the Hell Chromacom System with our production specialists' experience, talent and dedication to excellence, you'll see the Empress Graphics' difference in your fine work. Every time.

The artistic challenge you present to us could be the next chapter in our Book of Wonders.

Empress Graphics Inc. Coming through with flying colours.

175 Midwest Road, Scarborough, Ontario M1P 3A7. (416) 751-0980.

Hot Colour!

WHAT YOU HAVE IN MIND, WE HAVE IN STOCK.

At The Image Bank, we now offer more than just the world's finest photography.

We now represent a wide range of illustrators, international talents that include Julius Ciss, Jerzy Kolacz, Michael Schwab, Don Weller and Bruce Wolfe.

Along with our library of over 350,000 photographs

(3 million worldwide), this new resource is the ideal solution for your advertising, publishing, editorial or corporate project.

The next time you're looking for that perfect visual — photography or illustration — give us a call. And look no further.

OUT OF VIETNAM

A young artist's road to freedom

BY CHAU PHAM

I was born near Hanoi, the day before Christmas, 1953. One of my grandfathers had worked for the Vietnamese government, then a colony of France, and had controlled several provinces of the country, but my parents were and are both artists. My father is a professional painter, having studied in the Vietnam Art School, a three-country (Cambodia, Laos and Vietnam) art school in Hanoi. He was born in 1918. My mother is a sculptor who studied at the same place and graduated with him, one year before the Communist Revolution took place in 1945.

PHOTOGRAPHY BY JOHN MASTROMONACO

SILVER AWARD

APPAREL PRODUCTION *management*

SILVER AWARD

1

TITLE
OUT OF VIETNAM

ART DIRECTORS
TERESA FERNANDES/DALE VOKEY

EDITOR
MARQ DE VILLIERS

PHOTOGRAPHER
JOHN MASTROMONACO

DESIGNER
DALE VOKEY

PUBLICATION
TORONTO LIFE MAGAZINE

PUBLISHER
KEY PUBLISHERS CO. LTD.

2

TITLE
APPAREL PRODUCTION MANAGEMENT

ART DIRECTOR
STEPHANIE POWER

EDITOR
LAURA ADAMS

ILLUSTRATOR
STEPHANIE POWER

DESIGNER
STEPHANIE POWER

PUBLICATION
MASS EXODUS

PUBLISHER
RYERSON SCHOOL OF FASHION/
4TH YEAR GRADUATING CLASS

BARE MINIMUM
STRIPPED-DOWN ACTIONWEAR

LESS IS DEFINITELY MORE IN THESE BARE ESSENTIALS
TO TAKE YOU FROM THE GYM TO THE BEACH AND
BACK ON TO THE STREET
PHOTOGRAPHY BY MONTALBETTI/CAMPBELL
PRODUCED BY TRACEY PINCOTT

30

WHEN WEARING VERY LITTLE, USE A LOT OF WIT, AS IN A FRONT-FASTEN BRA TOP BY TAYARI PAIRED
WITH STRIPED BEACH PANTS FROM GOTTEX, OR THE PROPHETIC BUBBLE SUIT, ALSO BY GOTTEX.
GLASSES BY MATSUDA.

31

1

BY WENDY DENNIS

THE GIRLS OF Summer

Our correspondent takes a heartwarming look and finds that the Boys of Summer really are larger than life

ILLUSTRATION BY BLAIR DRAWSON

2

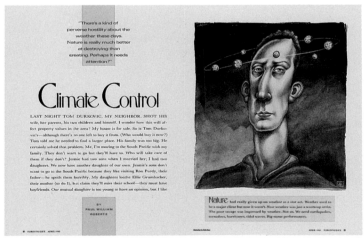

"There's a kind of perverse hostility about the weather these days. Nature is really much better at destroying than creating. Perhaps it needs attention."

Climate Control

LAST NIGHT TOM DURKOVIC, MY NEIGHBOR, SHOT HIS wife, her parents, his two children and himself. I wonder how this will affect property values in the area?

BY PAUL WILLIAM ROBERTS

Nature had really given up on weather as a star act. Weather used to be a major client but now it wasn't.

3

1

TITLE
BARE MINIMUM

ART DIRECTOR
SUSAN CASEY

EDITOR
TRACEY PINCOTT

PHOTOGRAPHER
DENIS MONTALBETTI

DESIGNER
SUSAN CASEY

PUBLICATION
V MAGAZINE

PUBLISHER
V MAGAZINE

2

TITLE
THE GIRLS OF SUMMER

ART DIRECTOR
TERESA FERNANDES

EDITOR
MARQ DE VILLIERS

ILLUSTRATOR
BLAIR DRAWSON

DESIGNER
TERESA FERNANDES

PUBLICATION
TORONTO LIFE MAGAZINE

PUBLISHER
KEY PUBLISHERS CO. LTD.

3

TITLE
CLIMATE CONTROL

ART DIRECTORS
TERESA FERNANDES/DALE VOKEY

EDITOR
MARQ DE VILLIERS

ILLUSTRATOR
ANITA KUNZ

DESIGNER
DALE VOKEY

PUBLICATION
TORONTO LIFE MAGAZINE

PUBLISHER
KEY PUBLISHERS CO. LTD.

1

TITLE
QUEEN BEES

ART DIRECTOR
SUSAN CASEY

EDITOR
ROBERT COLLISON

ILLUSTRATOR
PUBLIC EYE

DESIGNER
SUSAN CASEY

PUBLICATION
V MAGAZINE

PUBLISHER
V MAGAZINE

2

TITLE
CONTENTS—CLUB MONACO MAGAZINE

ART DIRECTOR
B.J. GALBRAITH

PHOTOGRAPHER
DON MILLER

DESIGNER
B.J. GALBRAITH

PUBLICATION
CLUB MONACO MAGAZINE

PUBLISHER
SOHO PUBLISHING CORP.

3

TITLE
CHIC TO CHIC

ART DIRECTOR
KAREN SIMPSON

PHOTOGRAPHER
JIM ALLEN

DESIGNER
KAREN SIMPSON

PUBLICATION
DOMINO MAGAZINE

PUBLISHER
THE GLOBE & MAIL

80

Why guys fight

*"Like most who have had a couple of fights, I don't like
to hit people in the face with my fists. I think of my fists as a bundle of
delicate bones, something like an ivory bird cage"*

I GOT OUT OF BED VERY SLOWLY
on the morning after my last fight. It took me
a while to reach the bathroom and when I did
I had to lean on the sink to hold myself up. It
was that luminous hour before sunrise, when
the mist is still in the trees out in the park,
and the earth seems to glow, and the east is
the color of skimmed milk and rose water.
There was a bruise on my left cheek and a
scratch on my nose. The right knee was gone
again, worse than before. My back muscles
were corded up. I couldn't close my right
hand, and the ribs all along my left side were
banged up and hurting. He must have caught
me there a couple of times when I brought up
my left arm. I tend to do that. I never seem to
learn. I get that left in his face, thinking
about a killing shot, to end it, and I get myself thumped. My wife was still asleep,
turned away from me and holding a pillow to
her. She'd stayed that way all night. She
thought I was an ass. I leaned on the bathroom sink, listening to the owl that lives in
the graveyard across the valley, and looked
at my face in the mirror, trying to feel like an
ass. It was no good. You'll be 41 soon, I said
to myself. This has got to stop. *Continued on page 101*

BY CARSTEN STROUD

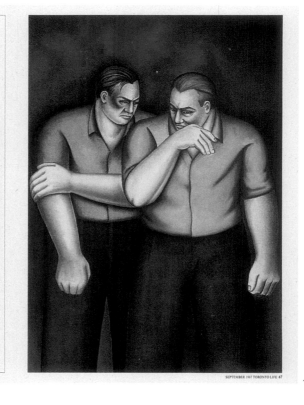

1

2

3

1

TITLE
WHY GUYS FIGHT

ART DIRECTOR
TERESA FERNANDES

EDITOR
MARQ DE VILLIERS

ILLUSTRATOR
SANDRA DIONISI

DESIGNER
TERESA FERNANDES

PUBLICATION
TORONTO LIFE MAGAZINE

PUBLISHER
KEY PUBLISHERS CO. LTD.

2

TITLE
WHAT'S HOT

ART DIRECTORS
TERESA FERNANDES/DALE VOKEY

EDITOR
MARQ DE VILLIERS

PHOTOGRAPHER
TAFFI ROSEN

FASHION STYLIST
DJANKA GAJDEL

DESIGNER
DALE VOKEY

PUBLICATION
TORONTO LIFE MAGAZINE

PUBLISHER
KEY PUBLISHERS CO. LTD.

3

TITLE
SERGE TALKS, PARIS LISTENS

ART DIRECTOR
KAREN SIMPSON

DESIGNER
KAREN SIMPSON

PUBLICATION
DOMINO MAGAZINE

PUBLISHER
THE GLOBE & MAIL

Who are these people who raise many of the city's children, and what do they think of their employers? Crib notes on the babysitting boom

BY LYNNE THOMAS

BUT THEIR HEARTS BELONG TO NANNY

FROM EARLY MONDAY MORNING to late Friday afternoon, from Harbourfront to Lawrence Park, from High Park to Rosedale through Riverdale, the parks and kitchens and playrooms, the markets and toy shops belong to them. So do the children. The babies sucking bottles in prams, the toddlers screaming down slides: their questions and tantrums and kisses, their tiny fists and pudgy feet and great gripping hugs, belong to the nannies. And from Monday to Friday, when the parents leave these children to their nannies—as they leave their homes to housekeepers, and gardens to gardeners, and clothes to cleaners— the soft belly of the city that holds half their lives settles into a world they never see. It is a quiet queendom of sorts, where the nannies, nearly 43,000 of them (including domestics), gently reign.

They gather over glasses of white wine in the airy sitting rooms of the tiny, turreted castles of Rosedale

with their babies and cookies and boxes of toys, like a pride of lionesses surrounded by cubs. These are "nannies' nannies," peaches and cream and properly pampered, with their spoons full of sugar and heads full of pedagogy, summoned to the colonies through ads in *The Lady*, the nannies' journal of London.

Downtown, tiny Filipino women, like exotic Asian flowers, connected by ropes to vines of children, fill the green parks that encircle the glass-and-granite condos. And across town, in the playroom of a west-end community centre, three Jamaican women sit as steady as islands in a sea of bobbing blond heads, living here on a faith that feeds their own kids back home.

In response to the campaign for domestics' rights, the Canadian Foreign Domestic Program (FDP) was put in place in 1981, resulting in about 5,000 immigrant women coming into the country every year. Still, this wasn't enough. This year, Statistics Canada figures

A STAR IS BORN (MAYBE)

While waiting to see whether his new role as He-Man would transform him into the next Stallone or Schwarzenegger, Swedish actor Dolph Lundgren returned to the city where he got his first Big Break.

BY ROBERT COLLISON

HELP WANTED

BY MARK CZARNECKI

1

TITLE
BUT THEIR HEARTS BELONG TO NANNY

ART DIRECTOR
TERESA FERNANDES

EDITOR
MARQ DE VILLIERS

ILLUSTRATOR
SANDRA DIONISI

DESIGNER
TERESA FERNANDES

PUBLICATION
TORONTO LIFE MAGAZINE

PUBLISHER
KEY PUBLISHERS CO. LTD.

2

TITLE
A STAR IS BORN (MAYBE)

ART DIRECTOR
SUSAN CASEY

EDITOR
ROBERT COLLISON

PHOTOGRAPHER
DENIS MONTALBETTI

DESIGNER
SUSAN CASEY

PUBLICATION
V MAGAZINE

PUBLISHER
V MAGAZINE

3

TITLE
HELP WANTED

ART DIRECTORS
DAVID WOODSIDE/CHRISTINE HIGDON/JAMES IRELAND

PHOTOGRAPHER
MIKE VISSER

DESIGNER
CHRISTINE HIGDON

PUBLICATION
CANADIAN BUSINESS MAGAZINE

PUBLISHER
C.B. MEDIA

82

PHOTOGRAPHY BY GEORGE WHITESIDE

THE YEN FOR JAPANESE DESIGN
What's available in Toronto — and who's making it available
BY ADELE FREEDMAN

OPPOSITE: BANRI NAKAMURA'S DIVIDER. BELOW,

LEFT: KETTLE FROM KAMIMURA BOWEN GALLERIES.

BELOW, RIGHT: MARTIN MYERS OF QUASI MODO

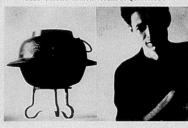

"JAPAN IS OUR FUTURE" IS A SLOGAN North Americans use to describe the country that, in only forty years, has transformed itself into an industrial and technological superpower. Japan, in this view, is a laboratory of modernism; and Tokyo the essence of a new urbanism. Overcrowding, astonishingly high property values, misuse of natural resources, accelerating social change, consumerism on a vast scale, pressured cultural values—it seems whatever Japan does to manage these problems must, sooner or later, apply here.

In Toronto, as in other cities around the world, Japan doubles as rearview mirror and crystal ball. If a certain degree of envy and mythmaking is involved, so be it. But there's another side to our collective fascination with Japan and things Japanese, which has to do with spirit, craft and the life of the imagination. We're talking artifacts—objects fashioned of clay, cloth, paper, wood, stone and mortar; old and new; worn, played, studied, bought, sold and collected; suddenly discovered, patiently rediscovered. And we're talking entrepreneurs—people born here or settled here, from Japan and elsewhere, who travel between Toronto and Tokyo in search of something special to bring back for sale or personal pleasure, or who've brought with them memories and skills that have enriched

1

For scholars and the art-minded, Japan equals wood-block prints—known generically as *ukiyo-e*, or pictures of the floating world

Since 1971, prices have zoomed: a print by Utamaro, a famous *ukiyo-e* artist, fetched £220,000 at Sotheby's last December

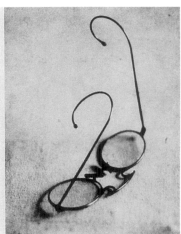

Continued on page 117

GOLD AWARD

1

TITLE
THE YEN FOR JAPANESE DESIGN

ART DIRECTOR
TERESA FERNANDES

EDITOR
MARQ DE VILLIERS

PHOTOGRAPHER
GEORGE WHITESIDE

DESIGNER
TERESA FERNANDES

PUBLICATION
TORONTO LIFE MAGAZINE

PUBLISHER
KEY PUBLISHERS CO. LTD.

1

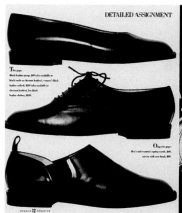   

SILVER AWARD

1

TITLE
DETAILED ASSIGNMENT

ART DIRECTOR
B.J. GALBRAITH

PHOTOGRAPHER
SHUN SASABUCHI

DESIGNER
B.J. GALBRAITH

PUBLICATION
CLUB MONACO MAGAZINE

PUBLISHER
SOHO PUBLISHING CORPORATION

84

Objets of Desire

Personal Details, Perfectly Crafted

PRODUCED BY TRACEY PINCOTT — PHOTOGRAPHY BY JOHN MASTROMONACO

SILVER AWARD

Hand-Painted

LEATHER HAT, DESIGNED BY MARY LEA WILSON
MAKE-UP BY MARIA VEREL — HAIR BY JOHN DONATO — LEOTARD AND BODY STOCKINGS BY SHAPES
FOR SHOPPING DETAILS SEE PAGE 78

1

Black and White

PLASTIC JEWELLERY BY MARTHA STURDY

1

TITLE
OBJECTS OF DESIRE

ART DIRECTOR
SUSAN CASEY

EDITOR
TRACEY PINCOTT

PHOTOGRAPHER
JOHN MASTROMONACO

DESIGNER
SUSAN CASEY

PUBLICATION
V MAGAZINE

PUBLISHER
V MAGAZINE

Hat tricks

Are hats hot? Is the chapeau apropos? If you let the world of couture be your guide, then they are the one essential accessory. On these pages we offer hats in all their wonder and whimsy. As someone somewhere once said, "A piece of magic is a hat." And what would a party be without one? Hair by Ginger Bains of Tuxedo. Makeup by Philippe Chansel of Cloutier/Ray Civello. Photographed by Michael Williams. Bowlerama! This one (above) by Anita Pineault. About $55. Alfred Sung's wool crepe jacket. $275. At Alfred Sung at Hazelton Lanes. Earrings from Fabrice. Ray-Bans from First Canadian Optical. Gloves from Euterpe. Feathered friends (opposite page): Golench Boudreau's ostrich feather cocktail hats and ostrich boas. Hats, $455 each. At Sublime and Holt Renfrew. Left: Wayne Clark's black velvet jacket. $275. At Alan Cherry, Danya, Meadows, and Your Choice. Right: Anne Klein's black velvet top. $272. Available at Brian Winston

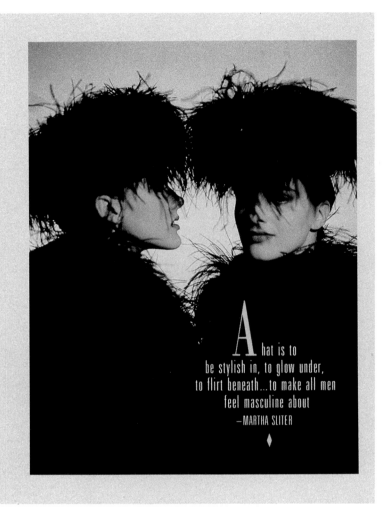

A hat is to be stylish in, to glow under, to flirt beneath...to make all men feel masculine about
— MARTHA SLITER

158 Toronto Life fashion Winter 1987

1

Hat tricks

Lover, gold-hatted, high-bouncing over, I must have you
— THOMAS PARKE D'INVILLIERS

Any old place I can hang my hat is home sweet home to me
— WILLIAM JEROME

Hat tricks

SILVER AWARD

1

TITLE
HAT TRICKS

ART DIRECTOR
BRAD MacIVER

EDITOR
JOHN MacKAY

PHOTOGRAPHER
MICHAEL WILLIAMS

PUBLICATION
TORONTO LIFE FASHION

PUBLISHER
KEY PUBLISHERS CO. LTD.

86

ALL ABOUT EVE •

NIGHT FLIGHTS

Creative

DIFFERENCES. WHEN EVERY DRESS HAS A ONE-OF-A-KIND FEELING. AND WHEN DRESSING FOR EVENING IS AS MUCH ABOUT FEELING AS IT IS ABOUT FASHION. IT'S THAT SUBTLE SOMETHING IN THE WAY YOU FEEL IN A DRESS, AND IT'S IN A DETAIL OR TWO – A CURVE, A LINE, A LENGTH, A CRINOLINE, A SPECIAL COLOR. TO IMPART THE SPECIAL NIGHT FEELING – A PORTFOLIO OF ONE-OF-A-KIND PHOTOGRAPHS BY BRUNO DAYAN

A TUBE OF BLACK VELVET, SKIRTED AND BOWED IN MIDNIGHT BLUE TAFFETA (OPPOSITE PAGE). BY ALFRED SUNG, $325. AT ALFRED SUNG AT HAZELTON LANES, LA FORET, HOLT RENFREW AND BOUTIQUE SILKWORM. SHOES, $300, AT BOUTIQUE QUINTO. HOSIERY BY CHRISTIAN DIOR. MAKEUP BY PHILIPPE CHANSEL OF CLOUTIER/RAY CIVELLO. HAIR THESE 14 PAGES BY DENIS BOUCHARD OF DENIS BOUCHARD HAIR INC. SHIRRED SCHERRER (THIS PAGE), INCANDESCENT BRONZE SILK VISCOSE, $2,000, AT SIMPSONS. EARRINGS BY DANNY POLLAK, GLOVES BY PLEASANT PHEASANT. MAKEUP BY PHILIPPE CHANSEL OF CLOUTIER/RAY CIVELLO

1

SILVER AWARD

1
TITLE
NIGHT FLIGHTS
ART DIRECTOR
BRAD MacIVER
EDITOR
JOHN MacKAY
PHOTOGRAPHER
BRUNO DAYAN
PUBLICATION
TORONTO LIFE FASHION
PUBLISHER
KEY PUBLISHERS CO. LTD.

BARE MINIMUM
STRIPPED-DOWN ACTIONWEAR

LESS IS DEFINITELY MORE IN THESE BARE ESSENTIALS
TO TAKE YOU FROM THE GYM TO THE BEACH AND
BACK ON TO THE STREET
PHOTOGRAPHY BY MONTALBETTI/CAMPBELL
PRODUCED BY TRACEY PINCOTT

30

WHEN WEARING VERY LITTLE, USE A LOT OF WIT, AS IN A FRONT-FASTEN BRA TOP BY TAYARI PAIRED
WITH STRIPED BEACH PANTS FROM GOTTEX, OR THE PROPHETIC BUBBLE SUIT, ALSO BY GOTTEX.
GLASSES BY MATSUDA.

31

1

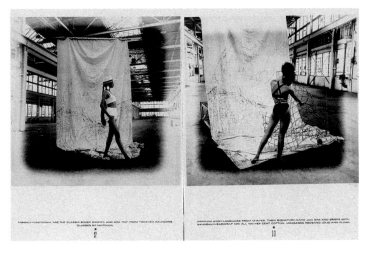

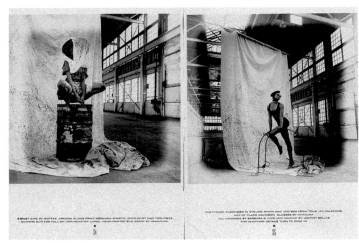

1

TITLE
BARE MINIMUM

ART DIRECTOR
SUSAN CASEY

EDITOR
TRACEY PINCOTT

PHOTOGRAPHERS
MONTALBETTI/CAMPBELL

DESIGNER
SUSAN CASEY

PUBLICATION
V MAGAZINE

BODY AND SEOUL

Who possesses the perfect body? A lithe and sensuous David encased in Carrara marble?
A pneumatic Ursula Andress rising from the waves? To an athlete, perfection depends upon purpose.
A marathon runner would have little use for the body of a wrestler; a sailor develops muscles
different to those of a diver. Our Olympic athletes seek the inimitable and display the impeccable.

BY VERONICA CUSACK

CHRIS WOODCROFT

WRESTLER

Wrestling is a total body sport,
therefore the body must be totally fit. Powerful
and dynamic, it must combine strength with speed.
A fifty-two-kilogram-class wrestler, he trains
four hours each day to perfect the explosive moves
required in Olympic competition.

ALLISON HIGSON

SWIMMER

They do not train by swimming alone.
To maintain her amazing speed, this world's-record
holder spends eighteen hours a week in the water, but
her regimen also contains ten hours of dry-land training. Rope climbing and weight training develop her
shoulders and triceps; running, both sprint and distance, gives power and thrust to her legs.

PHOTOGRAPHY BY JOHN MASTROMONACO

38 TORONTO LIFE AUGUST 1988   AUGUST 1988 TORONTO LIFE 37

1

BODY AND SEOUL

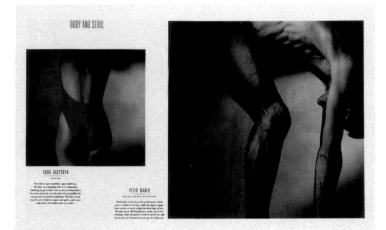

ANNA DACYSHYN

DIVER

PETER MADER

MARATHON RUNNER

BODY AND SEOUL

GAIL AND KAREN JOHNSON

SYNCHRO

CHRIS RIBBENS

GYMNAST

1

TITLE
BODY AND SEOUL

ART DIRECTORS
TERESA FERNANDES/DALE VOKEY

EDITOR
MARQ DE VILLIERS

PHOTOGRAPHER
JOHN MASTROMONACO

DESIGNER
DALE VOKEY

PUBLICATION
TORONTO LIFE MAGAZINE

PUBLISHER
KEY PUBLISHING

BEST OF CANADA

RICH BRITCHES

⟿

After seasons of ski pants and seamed-to-the-body leggings, the trouser reasserts itself for spring. Supple and flowing or crisp and snappy, pantlegs have gone wide enough to waken dreamy visions of Hollywood glamour. Here's sophistication in its most subtle, perfect form

SPELLBOUND
Grey and white stripe trousers (left) by Mariola Mayer, $185. Paired with her short sleeve blouse, $135. Mariola Mayer available at Your Choice, J. Michaels, Liptons and Cactus. Pearl stud earrings by Fabrice. Chair and tea set from 20th Century

INDISCREET
Dean and Dan's seductive silk satin palazzo pants and double-breasted gangster jacket (this page). Pants, $325. Jacket, $703. Both at Sublime. Shoes by Varda. Earrings from Fabrice. Silk rose, Dean and Dan. Hose by Phantom. Couch and lamp from Red Indian. Glass cocktail cart from 20th Century. Hair by Bill Angst. Makeup by Alan Milroy. Both of Cloutier/Ray Civello. For national availabilities, see Fashion File

1

RICH BRITCHES

RICH BRITCHES

1

TITLE
RICH BRITCHES

ART DIRECTOR
BRAD MacIVER

EDITOR
TIM BLANKS

PHOTOGRAPHER
MONIC RICHARD

PUBLICATION
TORONTO LIFE FASHION

PUBLISHER
KEY PUBLISHING

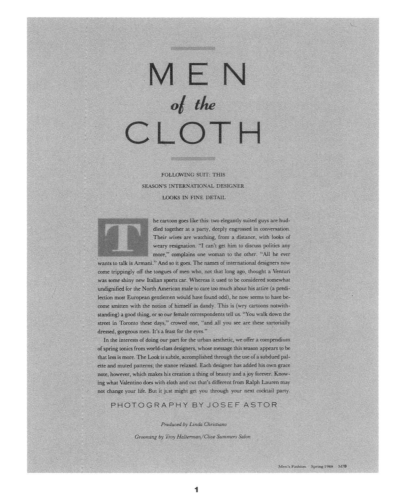

MEN
of the
CLOTH

FOLLOWING SUIT: THIS
SEASON'S INTERNATIONAL DESIGNER
LOOKS IN FINE DETAIL.

The cartoon goes like this: two elegantly suited guys are huddled together at a party, deeply engrossed in conversation. Their wives are watching, from a distance, with looks of weary resignation. "I can't get him to discuss politics any more," complains one woman to the other. "All he ever wants to talk is Armani." And so it goes. The names of international designers now come tripping off the tongues of men who, not that long ago, thought a Venturi was some shiny new Italian sports car. Whereas it used to be considered somewhat undignified for the North American male to care too much about his attire (a predilection most European gentlemen would have found odd), he now seems to have become smitten with the notion of himself as dandy. This is (wry cartoons notwithstanding) a good thing, or so our female correspondents tell us. "You walk down the street in Toronto these days," crowed one, "and all you see are these sartorially dressed, gorgeous men. It's a feast for the eyes."

In the interests of doing our part for the urban aesthetic, we offer a compendium of spring tonics from world-class designers, whose message this season appears to be that less is more. The Look is subtle, accomplished through the use of a subdued palette and muted patterns; the stance relaxed. Each designer has added his own grace note, however, which makes his creation a thing of beauty and a joy forever. Knowing what Valentino does with cloth and cut that's different from Ralph Lauren may not change your life. But it just might get you through your next cocktail party.

PHOTOGRAPHY BY JOSEF ASTOR

Produced by Linda Christano

Grooming by Troy Halterman/Close Summers Salon

1

  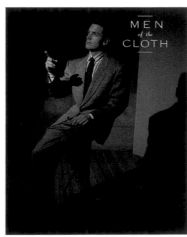 

1

TITLE
MEN OF THE CLOTH

ART DIRECTOR
TERESA FERNANDES

EDITOR
MARQ DE VILLIERS

PHOTOGRAPHER
JOSEF ASTOR

DESIGNER
TERESA FERNANDES

PUBLICATION
TORONTO LIFE MAGAZINE

PUBLISHER
KEY PUBLISHERS CO. LTD.

the SOFT PARADE

In a season of unambiguously sexy skirts and sharp suits, romance holds its head high. Fashion makes pretty pictures with flowing skirts, sheer fabrics and enchanting floral prints. When bare-it-all worldliness palls, there's always the sweet seduction of the fairy tale. Hair by Anne, Cloutier/Montreal. Makeup by Alex Borovoy. Thoroughly romantic but thoroughly modern, a blue linen dress from Emily Zarb. $195. At Your Choice, Sublime and Atomic Age. Earrings by Garbo

Mariola Mayer's pink and white candy-striped confection layers ruffle on ruffle. Mariola Mayer available at Your Choice, J. Michaels, Liptons and Cactus. White hose from Phantom

Festival 1988 Toronto Life fashion **171**

1

1

TITLE
THE SOFT PARADE

ART DIRECTOR
BRAD MacIVER

EDITOR
TIM BLANKS

PHOTOGRAPHER
MONIC RICHARD

PUBLICATION
TORONTO LIFE FASHION

PUBLISHER
KEY PUBLISHERS CO. LTD.

THE WILD ONES

Furs In Flight In The High Country

Photography by Montalbetti/Campbell
Produced by Tracey Pincott

SILVER FOX TROTTER WITH SCALLOP CUT BOTTOM BY BALENCIAGA OF PARIS, HAT BY AKUBRA, LEATHER PANTS BY NETO, MOCK TURTLE NECK BY ROMEO GIGLI

1

BLACK CHERRY SHEARED BEAVER WITH PERSIAN LAMB TRIM BY CHRISTIAN DIOR, LAMB'S WOOL HAT AND MUFF BY JAEGER, LEATHER PANTS BY NETO, SWEATER BY ZONDA NELLIS

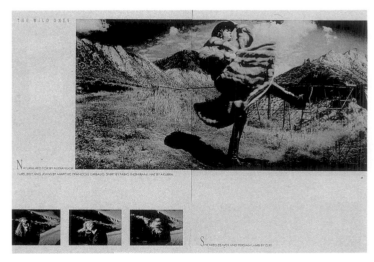

NATURAL RED FOX BY ALEXANDOR, FURS, BELT AND JEANS BY MARTINE FRANCOIS GIRBAUD, SHIRT BY FABIO INGHIRAMI, HAT BY AKUBRA

SHEARED BEAVER AND PERSIAN LAMB BY ZUKI

1

TITLE
THE WILD ONES

ART DIRECTOR
SUSAN CASEY

EDITOR
TRACEY PINCOTT

PHOTOGRAPHERS
MONTALBETTI/CAMPBELL

DESIGNER
SUSAN CASEY

PUBLISHER
V MAGAZINE

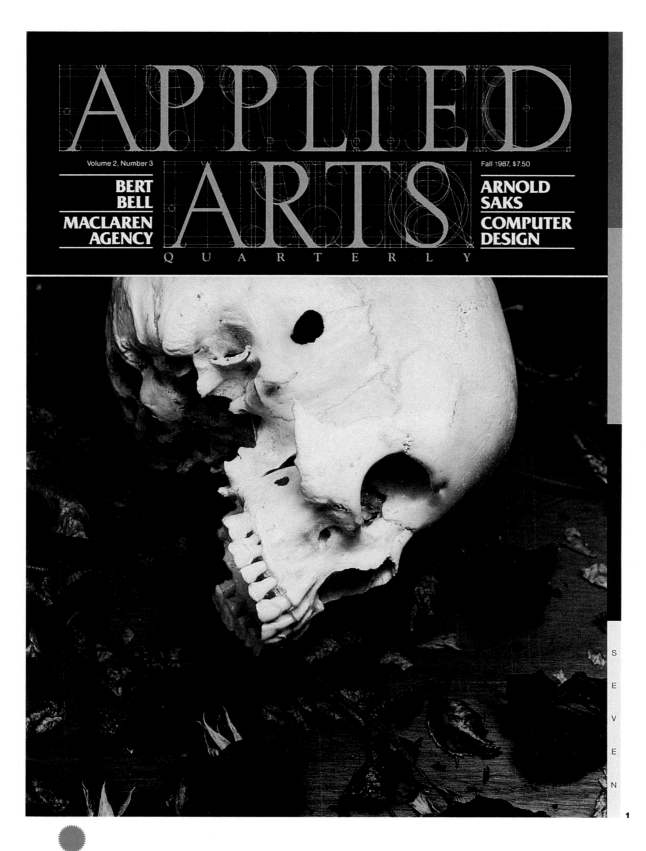

APPLIED ARTS

Volume 2, Number 3

Fall 1987, $7.50

BERT BELL

MACLAREN AGENCY

ARNOLD SAKS

COMPUTER DESIGN

QUARTERLY

S E V E N

1

SILVER AWARD

1

TITLE
APPLIED ARTS QUARTERLY FALL 1987

ART DIRECTOR
GEORGES HARCUTIUN

EDITOR
VALERIE THOMPSON

PHOTOGRAPHER
BERT BELL

DESIGNER
BONITA BOCANEGRA-COLLINS

PUBLICATION
APPLIED ARTS QUARTERLY

MAGAZINE COVERS

94

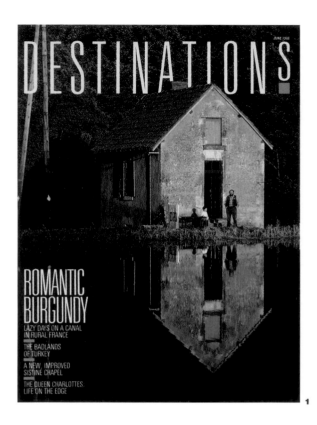

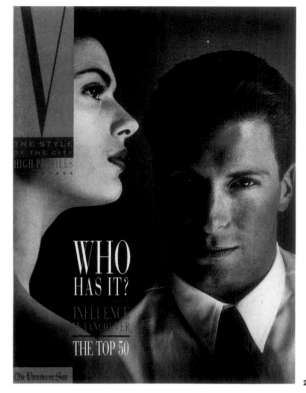

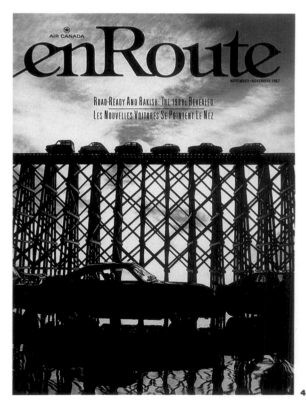

1

TITLE
DESTINATIONS JUNE 1988

ART DIRECTORS
PETER ENNESON/ANNA JANES

EDITOR
JACK McIVER

PHOTOGRAPHER
DIDIER DORVAL

DESIGNER
ANNA JANES

PUBLICATION
DESTINATIONS

PUBLISHER
THE GLOBE & MAIL

2

TITLE
WHO HAS IT?

ART DIRECTOR
SUSAN CASEY

EDITOR
ROBERT COLLISON

PHOTOGRAPHER
CHICK RICE

DESIGNER
SUSAN CASEY

PUBLICATION
V MAGAZINE

3

TITLE
CALGARY 88

ART DIRECTOR
ARTHUR NIEMI

EDITOR
MURRAY CAMPBELL

PHOTOGRAPHER
JOHN MASTROMONACO

DESIGNER
ARTHUR NIEMI

PUBLICATION
CALGARY 88

PUBLISHER
THE GLOBE & MAIL

4

TITLE
ROAD READY AND RAKISH

ART DIRECTOR
EVELYN STOYNOFF

EDITOR
CAROLYN JACKSON

PHOTOGRAPHER
YURI DOJC

DESIGNERS
EVELYN STOYNOFF/AUDREY GOTO

PUBLICATION
ENROUTE MAGAZINE

MAGAZINE COVERS

96

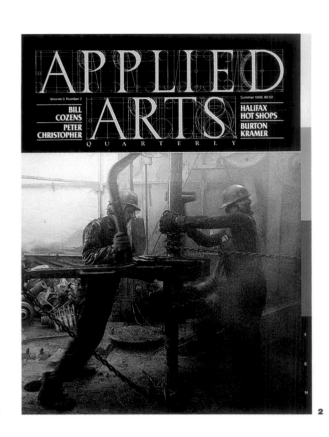

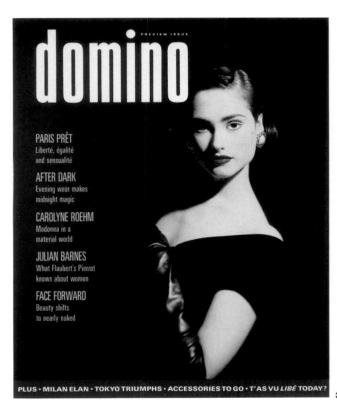

Think of it as...

There comes a time in every designer's life when you're asked to do the impossible. The client wants a piece that's warm, rich and artfully printed in deep colors…but, if it's left out in the rain, it should be none the worse for wear.

Make the improbable a reality, on PREVAIL® Fiber Reinforced Paper from Kimberly-Clark. With a richly textured surface backed by a street-tough core of synthetic fibers, it prints like paper and wears like fabric. Folded, grommetted, die-cut or glued, when the going gets tough, PREVAIL outperforms other papers and synthetics.

Canvas That Prints

Prevail®
Fiber Reinforced Paper

Think of it as canvas that prints.

Kimberly-Clark

DIRECTIONS | 88

MAGAZINE COVERS

98

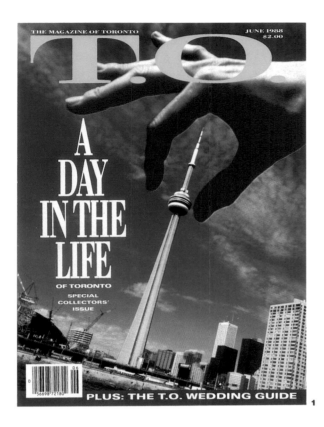

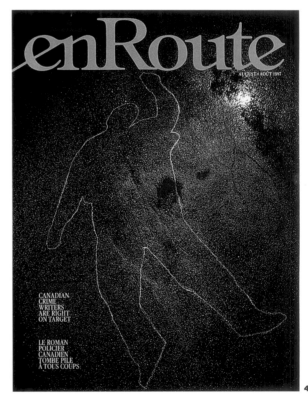

1	**2**	**3**	**4**
TITLE A DAY IN THE LIFE	**TITLE** CLUB MONACO MAGAZINE	**TITLE** THE TOP 50	**TITLE** MYSTERY & MAHEM
ART DIRECTORS PAUL HURREN/MANUEL RODENKIRCHEN	**ART DIRECTOR** B.J. GALBRAITH	**ART DIRECTOR** TERESA FERNANDES	**ART DIRECTOR** EVELYN STOYNOFF
EDITORS KIM GREENE/BOBBY ROTENBERG	**PHOTOGRAPHER** ANDREW MACPHERSON	**EDITOR** MARQ DE VILLIERS	**EDITOR** CAROLYN JACKSON
PHOTOGRAPHER PAUL BARDEN	**PUBLICATION** CLUB MONACO MAGAZINE	**PHOTOGRAPHER** JOHN MASTROMONACO	**PHOTOGRAPHER** JIM ALLEN
PUBLICATION T.O. MAGAZINE	**PUBLISHER** SOHO PUBLISHING CORPORATION	**ILLUSTRATOR** JAMIE BENNETT	**DESIGNERS** EVELYN STOYNOFF/AUDREY GCTO
PUBLISHER SOHO PUBLISHING CORPORATION		**DESIGNER** TERESA FERNANDES	**PUBLICATION** ENROUTE MAGAZINE
		PUBLICATION TORONTO LIFE MAGAZINE	
		PUBLISHER KEY PUBLISHERS CO. LTD.	

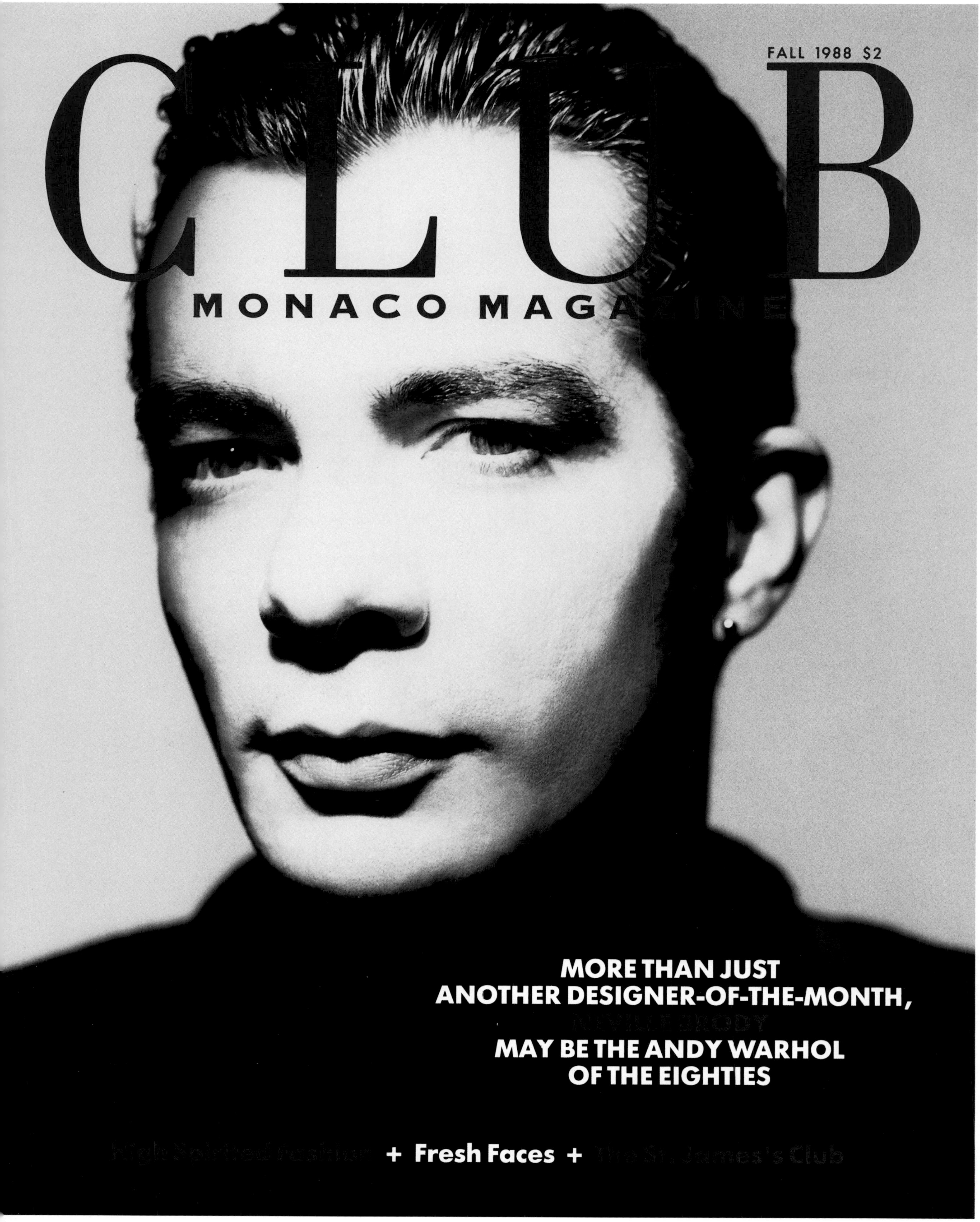

FALL 1988 $2
CLUB
MONACO MAGAZINE
MORE THAN JUST
ANOTHER DESIGNER-OF-THE-MONTH,
NEVILLE BRODY
MAY BE THE ANDY WARHOL
OF THE EIGHTIES
High Spirited Fashion + Fresh Faces + The St. James's Club

GOLD AWARD

1

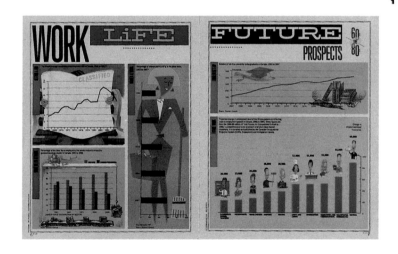

1

TITLE
ROYAL BANK REPORTER/WINTER '88

ART DIRECTOR
NADIA MARYNIAK

EDITOR
WINSTON COLLINS

PHOTOGRAPHER
VARIOUS

ILLUSTRATOR
VARIOUS

DESIGNERS
NADIA MARYNIAK/PETER ENNESON

PUBLICATION
ROYAL BANK REPORTER/WINTER '88

PUBLISHER
THE ROYAL BANK OF CANADA

SILVER AWARD

1

TITLE
MASS EXODUS

ART DIRECTOR
STEPHANIE POWER

EDITOR
LAURA ADAMS

PHOTOGRAPHERS
ALLEN HASLINGER/CLAIRE FISHER

DESIGNERS
CHRIS HOY/CHRIS ARMSTRONG
FIONA McKERROW/STEPHANIE POWER

PUBLICATION
MASS EXODUS

PUBLISHER
RYERSON SCHOOL OF FASHION/
4TH YEAR GRADUATING CLASS

COMPLETE MAGAZINE DESIGN

SILVER AWARD

1

1

TITLE
ROYAL BANK REPORTER/FALL '88

ART DIRECTOR
NADIA MARYNIAK

EDITOR
WINSTON COLLINS

ILLUSTRATORS
SAN MURATA/ANDREW PLEWES/JANICE GOLDBERG

DESIGNER
NADIA MARYNIAK

PUBLICATION
ROYAL BANK REPORTER/FALL '88

PUBLISHER
THE ROYAL BANK OF CANADA

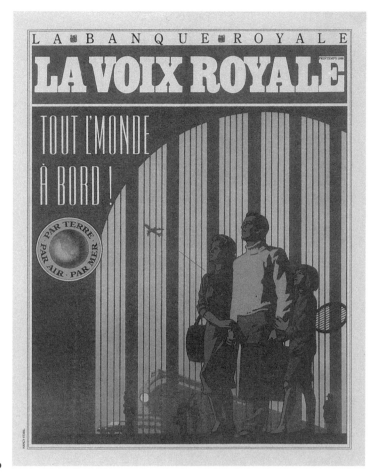

SILVER AWARD

1

1

TITLE
ROYAL BANK REPORTER/SPRING '88

ART DIRECTOR
NADIA MARYNIAK

EDITOR
WINSTON COLLINS

DESIGNER
NADIA MARYNIAK

PUBLICATION
ROYAL BANK REPORTER/SPRING '88

PUBLISHER
THE ROYAL BANK OF CANADA

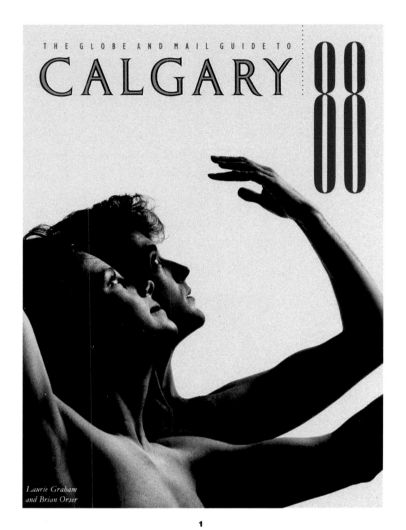

THE GLOBE AND MAIL GUIDE TO
CALGARY 88

*Laurie Graham
and Brian Orser*

1

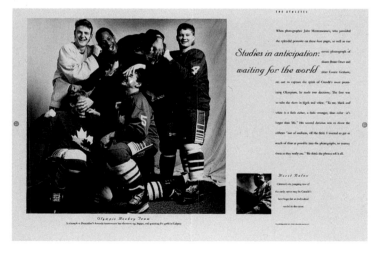

Ski jumping

1

TITLE
GLOBE & MAIL GUIDE TO CALGARY '88

ART DIRECTOR
ARTHUR NIEMI

EDITOR
MURRAY CAMPBELL

PHOTOGRAPHER
JOHN MASTROMONACO

DESIGNERS
VIVIAN OZOLS/ARTHUR NIEMI/MARK KOUDYS

PUBLICATION
GLOBE & MAIL

PUBLISHER
GLOBE & MAIL

1

1

TITLE
V—OCTOBER 1987

ART DIRECTOR
SUSAN CASEY

EDITOR
ROBERT COLLISON

DESIGNER
SUSAN CASEY

PUBLICATION
V MAGAZINE

ISSUE

THE VOICE OF THE ART DIRECTORS CLUB OF TORONTO

INSIDE
A MATTER OF OPINIONS

VISUAL ESSAY
ROBIN KOBRYN — BEING THERE

COMMENTARY
THE CRUX OF KRONE

TRENDS
A NEW TUBE OF PAINT

NUMBER THREE

1

PRESIDENT'S MESSAGE

A NEW TUBE OF PAINT

In praise of video paint systems, now playing at a screen near you

THE CRUX OF KRONE

A few thoughts on paper, from the master of the page

BEING THERE

*The reel world invites Robin Kobryn in,
and he's good enough to take us with him*

BY DON SNYDER

1

TITLE
ISSUE

ART DIRECTOR
TERESA FERNANDES

EDITOR
T.W. COLE

PHOTOGRAPHER
ED GAJDEL

PUBLICATION
ISSUE

PUBLISHER
ART DIRECTORS CLUB OF TORONTO

HOUSE ORGAN DESIGN

1

TITLE
LAWSON MARDON NEWS

ART DIRECTOR
ARTHUR NIEMI

EDITOR
DEJA RODECK

PHOTOGRAPHER
MICHAEL KOHN

ILLUSTRATOR
BLAIR DRAWSON

DESIGNERS
ART NIEMI/MARK KOUDYS

PUBLICATION
LAWSON MARDON NEWS

PUBLISHER
LAWSON MARDON

HOUSE ORGAN DESIGN

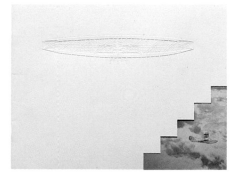

1

Les premières machines volantes

Le premier aéronef que rencontre le visiteur en entrant dans le Musée est le *Silver Dart*, premier « plus lourd que l'air » qui ait donné certains résultats au Canada. L'histoire du *Silver Dart* commence en 1907, lorsque le célèbre inventeur du téléphone, Alexander Graham Bell, réunit quatre jeunes gens – dont deux diplômés en génie canadiens fraîs émoulus de l'Université de Toronto, John A. D. McCurdy et Frederick W. « Casey » Baldwin – pour former l'Aerial Experiment Association (AEA).

Le but poursuivi par l'AEA était fort ambitieux, puisqu'elle ne visait rien de moins que de construire « un aérodrome efficace, ou une machine volante capable de se déplacer dans les airs par sa propre puissance et portant un homme ». Elle réalisera d'ailleurs son programme avec brio, puisqu'elle construira et mettra à l'essai successivement, à très brève échéance, 4 aéroplanes.

Le dernier de ces aéroplanes sera précisément le *Silver Dart*, considéré comme le plus perfectionné de son époque. Le 23 février 1909, son concepteur John McCurdy l'utilisera pour réaliser le premier vol en avion au Canada : après avoir décollé sur la glace à Baddeck Bay, près de la propriété de Bell, à l'Île du Cap-Breton (Nouvelle-Écosse), le *Silver Dart* franchira une distance de 0,8 km (0,5 mille) environ.

Voulant réunir des fonds pour poursuivre leurs expériences, McCurdy et Baldwin organiseront, le 2 août 1909, une démonstration de l'aéroplane devant les autorités militaires canadiennes du camp de Petawawa (Ontario) mais, au quatrième atterrissage, le *Silver Dart* capotera, subissant des dommages irréparables.

Le 23 février 1959, soit le jour même du cinquantième anniversaire de l'historique premier vol du *Silver Dart*, le lieutenant-colonel Paul Hartman pilotera à Baddeck Bay, en présence de John McCurdy

lui-même, une réplique de cet aéronef, construite par l'Aviation royale canadienne (ARC). C'est d'ailleurs cette réplique qui est exposée au Musée.

Si nombre d'autres Canadiens ont construit et piloté des avions avant la première guerre mondiale, le Musée n'a pourtant qu'un aéronef authentique de cette période de l'aviation au Canada, le monoplan McDowall. Construit par un ingénieur municipal d'Owen Sound, Robert McDowall, il est le seul appareil de fabrication canadienne de cette époque qui existe encore. Ce monoplan, qui parviendra bien à faire quelques « bonds » mais qui ne réussira jamais vraiment à voler, demeure toutefois une fascinante illustration des efforts déployés par les premiers passionnés de l'aviation.

LE MONOPLAN MCDOWALL, QUI NE RÉUSSIRA JAMAIS VRAIMENT À VOLER, SERVIRA DE MONTRE, PRÈS DE DURHAM (ONTARIO), DANS LES ANNÉES 20.

Ces Canadiens qui ont volé pour les Alliés pendant la première guerre mondiale

Après l'accrochage, à Petawawa, du *Silver Dart*, McCurdy, Baldwin et Bell lui-même multiplieront leurs appels auprès du gouvernement, à Ottawa, pour lui demander d'aider financièrement l'aviation. Mais ces demandes demeureront vaines. Le Canada n'aura donc pas encore de corps d'aviation lorsqu'il s'engagera dans la première guerre mondiale, à laquelle il contribuera surtout en fournissant des hommes et en fabriquant des avions d'entraînement.

Il s'agira toutefois là d'une généreuse et respectable contribution, puisque plus de 22 000 Canadiens serviront dans le Royal Flying Corps (RFC) et les Royal Naval Air Services (RNAS) ou, après l'unification de ces deux services, dans la Royal Air Force (RAF). Plus de 1 500 d'entre eux y périront, et non moins de 750 seront décorés. Des 27 pilotes de l'aviation britannique qui enregistreront 50 victoires ou plus, 4 seront des Canadiens, dont notamment les 2 as de l'Empire qui survivront à la guerre : W. A. « Billy » Bishop et Raymond Collishaw, avec respectivement 72 et 60 victoires. Collishaw aura, de sa part, dirigé le Black Flight, une équipe de 5 Canadiens considérée comme la meilleure unité de combat des Alliés dans la guerre aérienne, avant de devenir vice-maréchal de l'air dans la RAF.

Nombre des avions qu'ont pilotés les canadiens de la première guerre mondiale sont exposés au Musée, dont un Sopwith Snipe du genre de celui que pilotera le major W. G. Barker, qui recevra la croix de Victoria, et un triplan Sopwith, qu'utilisera le Black Flight pour abattre 87 aéronefs ennemis entre mai et juillet 1917.

LE TRIPLAN SOPWITH, BLACK PRINCE, PILOTÉ PAR W. M. ALEXANDER, D.F.C., L'UN DES MEMBRES DU FAMEUX BLACK FLIGHT, UNE ÉQUIPE FORMÉE EXCLUSIVEMENT DE CANADIENS, TEL QU'ILLUSTRÉ DANS CE TABLEAU. TABLEAU DE ROBERT W. BRADFORD, DIRECTEUR ASSOCIÉ DU MUSÉE.

Bradford juge, pour sa part, que la découverte de l'appareil *La Vigilance* – le Curtiss HS-2L qui, en 1919, sera le premier aéronef de brousse commercial – demeure l'un des faits marquants des années qu'il a passées au Musée. Une rumeur, à l'effet qu'un HS-2L gisait quelque part en forêt près de Kapuskasing (Ontario), courait déjà depuis plusieurs années lorsque, en 1968, le pilote Don Campbell découvrira le HS-2L au fond d'un lac sans nom de cette région. Et, dès l'année suivante, une équipe formée d'employés du Musée, de plongeurs bénévoles et de cadets de l'air repêchera l'appareil.

Lorsqu'il apprendra que l'aéronef n'était pas un simple HS-2L, mais bien *La Vigilance*, Bradford sera transporté de joie : « Comment pouvions-nous espérer, nous qui étions partis à la recherche de quelques vestiges d'un des premiers avions de brousse canadiens, tomber sur l'aéronef qui avait accompli le premier vol de brousse enregistré dans toute notre histoire de l'aviation? »

Le Musée continue aujourd'hui d'enrichir sa collection, et, comme par le passé, il doit compter sur les dons d'aéronefs et l'aide financière de nombreux particuliers et organismes pour compléter les maigres ressources dont il dispose. Son mandat englobe toutefois aussi l'exposition et l'aviation des Forces armées canadiennes, et il acquiert ainsi également certains aéronefs militaires canadiens dès qu'ils sont retirés du service.

Les aéronefs d'importance historique sont souvent en mauvais état lorsqu'ils arrivent au Musée. Sa politique est de préserver l'authenticité des aéronefs figurant dans sa collection et de les remettre

en état de voler en utilisant les méthodes de construction, les pièces et les matériaux de l'époque. Tout se fait donc suivant le mot d'ordre : Préserver plutôt que restaurer, restaurer plutôt que remplacer et ne remplacer que lorsque cela s'avère indispensable.

Constamment en quête d'éléments qui permettront d'élucider l'histoire, les spécialistes du Musée ont une collection de plus de 40 000 photographies à leur disposition, ainsi que la meilleure bibliothèque du Canada qui soit consacrée à l'aviation. Le conservateur Fred Shortt et les conservateurs adjoints Barry MacKeracher et Ed Patten, qui apportent au Musée l'expérience de toute une vie dans le domaine de l'aviation, dirigent les travaux de restauration, qui exigent une très forte dose de patience et de méticulosité.

Le Musée a décidé de rétablir le fort populaire programme itinérant de démonstration d'aéronefs historiques qu'il a dispensé de 1930 à 1982 dans toutes les provinces à l'exception de Terre-Neuve, et la première démonstration aura lieu au moment de l'ouverture du nouvel établissement, le 17 juin 1988. Le pilote en chef du Musée, George Neal, s'envolera alors dans le Sopwith Pup de la première guerre mondiale.

Kenneth M. Molson, le premier conservateur du Musée et l'un des principaux historiens de l'aviation du Canada, reconnaît qu'il y a encore beaucoup à faire pour enrichir la collection. Il considère toutefois avec fierté le progrès qui ont été accomplis depuis la fondation du Musée, il y a plus de vingt-cinq ans : « Aucun de ceux qui étaient là à la première heure, affirme-t-il, n'aurait pu imaginer ni l'essor qu'allait connaître notre établissement, ni les immenses lacunes que l'on réussirait à combler dans la collection. »

1

TITLE
AVIATION HOUSE ORGANS

ART DIRECTOR
NEVILLE SMITH

DESIGNERS
NEVILLE SMITH/AVIVA FURMAN

PUBLICATION
AVIATION HOUSE ORGANS

PUBLISHER
THE NATIONAL AVIATION MUSEUM

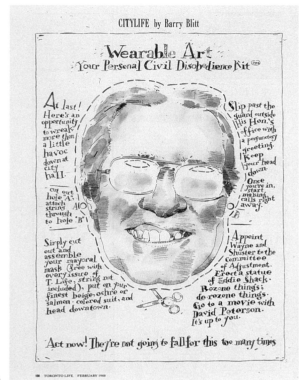

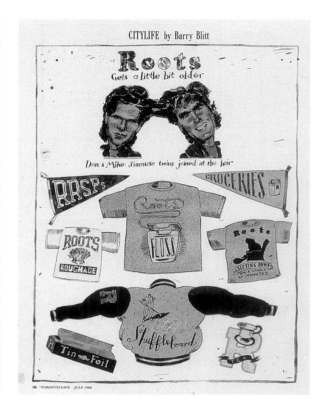

GOLD AWARD

1

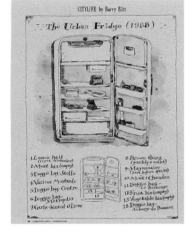

1

TITLE
CITY LIFE

ART DIRECTOR
TERESA FERNANDES

EDITOR
MARQ DE VILLIERS

ILLUSTRATOR
BARRY BLITT

DESIGNER
LINA McPHEE

PUBLICATION
TORONTO LIFE MAGAZINE

PUBLISHER
KEY PUBLISHERS CO. LTD.

EDITORIAL ILLUSTRATION

GOLD AWARD

SILVER AWARD

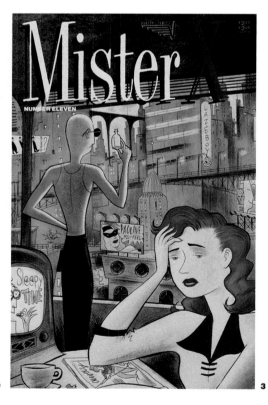

SILVER AWARD

1	2	3
TITLE THE CRASH OF '88	**TITLE** LIGHTWEIGHT BRIGADE	**TITLE** MISTER X
ART DIRECTOR PETER ENNESON	**ART DIRECTOR** FRED WOODWARD	**ART DIRECTOR** DEAN MOTTER
EDITOR MARGARET WENTE	**ILLUSTRATOR** BARRY BLITT	**ILLUSTRATOR** MAURICE VELLEKOOP
ILLUSTRATOR MAURICE VELLEKOOP	**DESIGNER** JOLENE CUYLER	**PUBLISHER** VORTEX COMIC INC.
DESIGNER PETER ENNESON	**PUBLICATION** ROLLING STONE	
PUBLICATION REPORT ON BUSINESS MAGAZINE		
PUBLISHER GLOBE & MAIL		

EDITORIAL ILLUSTRATION

SILVER AWARD

1

TITLE
THE MYSTERIOUS REICHMANNS

ART DIRECTOR
TERESA FERNANDES

EDITOR
MARQ DE VILLIERS

ILLUSTRATOR
BLAIR DRAWSON

DESIGNER
TERESA FERNANDES

PUBLICATION
TORONTO LIFE MAGAZINE

PUBLISHER
KEY PUBLISHERS CO. LTD.

1

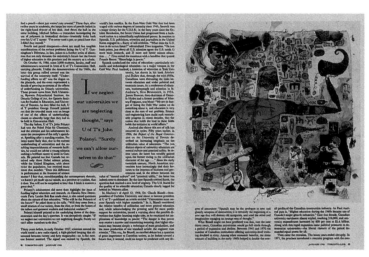

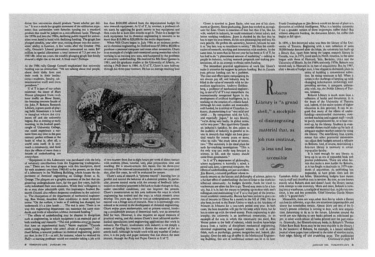

1

TITLE
SCHOOL OF HARD KNOCKS

ART DIRECTOR
TERESA FERNANDES

EDITOR
MARQ DE VILLIERS

ILLUSTRATOR
HENRIK DRESCHER

DESIGNER
TERESA FERNANDES

PUBLICATION
TORONTO LIFE MAGAZINE

PUBLISHER
KEY PUBLISHERS CO. LTD.

LEADERS OF THE FREE AND WESTERN WORLDS IN PRESUMMIT CAUCUS

JUNE 1988 TORONTO LIFE

1

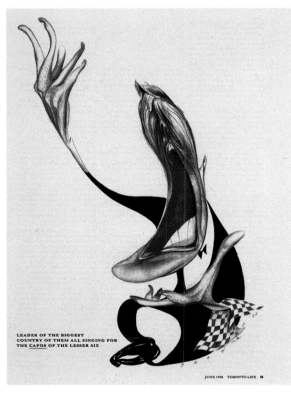

LEADER OF THE BIGGEST
COUNTRY OF THEM ALL SINGING FOR
THE CAPOS OF THE LESSER SIX

JUNE 1988 TORONTO LIFE

LEADER OF THE GROUP'S SECOND BIGGEST COUNTRY IN NOON REPOSE

JUNE 1988 TORONTO LIFE

1

TITLE
G7 DOSSIER

ART DIRECTORS
TERESA FERNANDES/MARTHA WEAVER

EDITOR
MARQ DE VILLIERS

ILLUSTRATOR
STEVE BRODNER

DESIGNER
MARTHA WEAVER

PUBLICATION
TORONTO LIFE MAGAZINE

PUBLISHER
KEY PUBLISHERS CO. LTD.

TITLE
THE GIRLS OF SUMMER

ART DIRECTOR
TERESA FERNANDES

EDITOR
MARQ DE VILLIERS

ILLUSTRATOR
BLAIR DRAWSON

DESIGNER
TERESA FERNANDES

PUBLICATION
TORONTO LIFE MAGAZINE

PUBLISHER
KEY PUBLISHERS CO. LTD.

EDITORIAL ILLUSTRATION

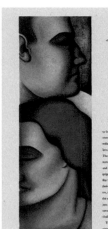

1

2

3

4

1
TITLE
BUT THEIR HEARTS BELONG TO NANNY
ART DIRECTOR
TERESA FERNANDES
EDITOR
MARQ DE VILLIERS
ILLUSTRATOR
SANDRA DIONISI
DESIGNER
TERESA FERNANDES
PUBLICATION
TORONTO LIFE MAGAZINE
PUBLISHER
KEY PUBLISHERS CO. LTD.

2
TITLE
OZONE WINTER
ART DIRECTOR
TERESA FERNANDES
EDITOR
MARQ DE VILLIERS
ILLUSTRATOR
GENE GREIF
DESIGNER
TERESA FERNANDES
PUBLICATION
TORONTO LIFE MAGAZINE
PUBLISHER
KEY PUBLISHERS CO. LTD.

3
TITLE
RICHARD GEPHARDT
ART DIRECTOR
RIP GEORGES
ILLUSTRATOR
JAMIE BENNETT
PUBLISHER
REGARDIE'S MAGAZINE

4
TITLE
MONEY FROM HOME
ART DIRECTOR
JAMES IRELAND
EDITOR
PENNY WILLIAMS
ILLUSTRATOR
MAURICE VELLEKOOP
DESIGNER
FERNANDA PISANI
PUBLICATION
YOUR MONEY
PUBLISHER
C.B. MEDIA

1

TITLE
SEPTEMBER SONG/NEW YORK

ART DIRECTOR
FRANCIS TREMBLAY

EDITOR
DIANA CARR

ILLUSTRATOR
NINA BERKSON

DESIGNER
FRANCIS TREMBLAY

PUBLICATION
MTL MAGAZINE

PUBLISHER
CANAM PUBLICATIONS

2

TITLE
COUNTRY REVIVAL

ART DIRECTOR
DARWYN COOKE

EDITOR
DIANNE COLLINS

ILLUSTRATOR
RICK SEALOCK

DESIGNER
DARWYN COOKE

PUBLICATION
ROCK EXPRESS

PUBLISHER
ROCK EXPRESS COMMUNICATIONS

3

TITLE
SPECTRUM

ART DIRECTOR
CATE COCHRAN

EDITOR
MARGARET WENTE

ILLUSTRATOR
BARRY BLITT

DESIGNER
GEORGE KARABOTSOS

PUBLICATION
REPORT ON BUSINESS MAGAZINE

PUBLISHER
THE GLOBE & MAIL

4

TITLE
LYING

ART DIRECTOR
MICHAEL WALSH

ILLUSTRATOR
ANITA KUNZ

PUBLICATION
THE WASHINGTON POST MAGAZINE

PUBLISHER
THE WASHINGTON POST MAGAZINE

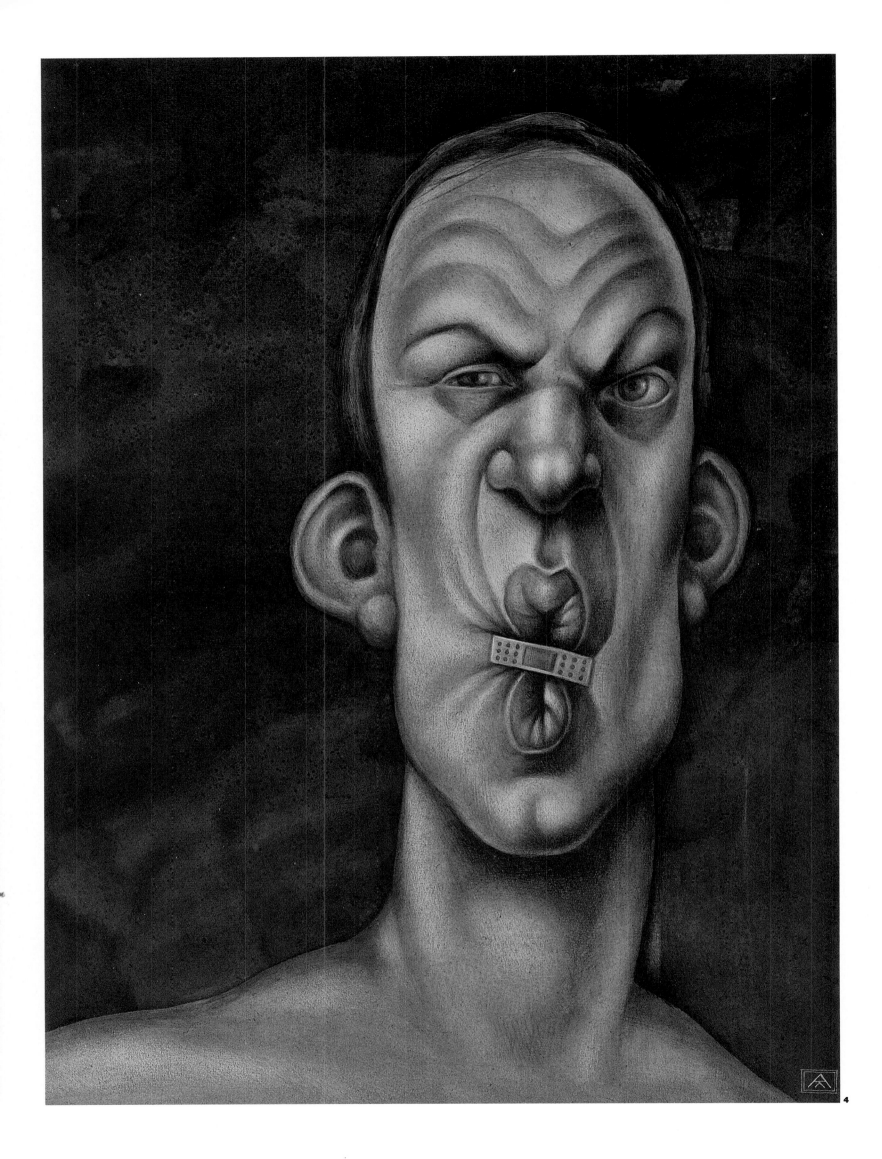

4

EDITORIAL ILLUSTRATION

THE GAMBLER AND THE HEIRESS

With the unwitting aid of his client, a 24-year-old assistant bank manager named Brian Molony engineered the biggest fraud in Canadian banking history. It was ridiculously easy.

By Gary Ross

Sherry Brydson's charm was lost in the private dining room of the CIBC. Senior bankers did not sprinkle their conversation with references to astrology, karma or vitamin B6. They were not "into" anything

A TRAIN TRIP

By ERNEST HEMINGWAY

1
TITLE
THE GAMBLER AND THE HEIRESS

ART DIRECTOR
CATE COCHRAN

EDITOR
MARGARET WENTE

ILLUSTRATOR
SIMON NG

DESIGNER
CATE COCHRAN

PUBLICATION
REPORT ON BUSINESS MAGAZINE

PUBLISHER
THE GLOBE & MAIL

2
TITLE
A TRAIN TRIP

ART DIRECTOR
WENDALL K. HARRINGTON

ILLUSTRATOR
ROSS MacDONALD

PUBLISHER
ESQUIRE MAGAZINE

1

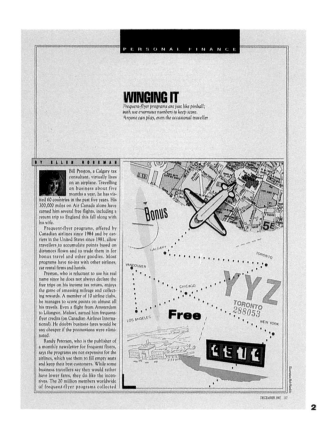

2

3

1

TITLE
THE NEW PROPHETS OF PROFIT

ART DIRECTOR
JUDY MARGOLIS

ILLUSTRATOR
JAMIE BENNETT

DESIGNER
CHRIS STOCKBAUER

PUBLICATION
CA MAGAZINE

PUBLISHER
CA MAGAZINE

2

TITLE
WINGING IT

ART DIRECTOR
CATE COCHRAN

ILLUSTRATOR
BOB HAMBLY

DESIGNER
PETER ENNESON

PUBLICATION
REPORT ON BUSINESS MAGAZINE

PUBLISHER
THE GLOBE & MAIL

3

TITLE
CITYLIFE—MARCH

ART DIRECTOR
TERESA FERNANDES

EDITOR
MARQ DE VILLIERS

ILLUSTRATOR
BARRY BLITT

DESIGNER
LINA MCPHEE

PUBLICATION
TORONTO LIFE MAGAZINE

PUBLISHER
KEY PUBLISHERS CO. LTD.

1

TITLE
WHY GUYS FIGHT

ART DIRECTOR
TERESA FERNANDES

EDITOR
MARQ DE VILLIERS

ILLUSTRATOR
SANDRA DIONISI

DESIGNER
TERESA FERNANDES

PUBLICATION
TORONTO LIFE MAGAZINE

PUBLISHER
KEY PUBLISHERS CO. LTD.

EDITORIAL ILLUSTRATION

THE TORONTONIAN

TRADING PLACES

When the crunch hits the free trade negotiations, don't expect the resolute Canadians to blink

BY MATTHEW HART

MUSIC

STOP THE MUSIC

A British band thought it could come over here and play whatever punk tunes it liked. But this is Canada – where vigilant politicians stand on guard

By BRUCE HEADLAM

"There's a kind of perverse hostility about the weather these days. Nature is really much better at destroying than creating. Perhaps it needs attention."

Climate Control

LAST NIGHT TOM DURKOVIC, MY NEIGHBOR, SHOT HIS

BY
PAUL WILLIAM
ROBERTS

Nature had really given up on weather as a nice art.

SPECIAL REPORT

SHOPPING FOR MONEY

MONEY IS A COMMODITY LIKE EVERYTHING ELSE, SO DO YOUR COMPARISON SHOPPING. THE BETTER YOUR PREPARATION, THE CHEAPER YOUR PURCHASE

BY NANCY JEANNINE SMITH

SMART BORROWING

1

TITLE
TRADING PLACES

ART DIRECTOR
LISA M LLER

ILLUSTRATOR
BARRY BLITT

PUBLICATION
TORONTO MAGAZINE

PUBLISHER
GLOBE & MAIL

2

TITLE
STOP THE MUSIC

ART DIRECTOR
BRUCE RAMSAY

EDITOR
JOHN FRASER

ILLUSTRATOR
BRIAN CRONIN

PUBLICATION
SATURDAY NIGHT MAGAZINE

PUBLISHER
PETER WHITE

3

TITLE
CLIMATE CONTROL

ART DIRECTORS
TERESA FERNANDES/DALE VOKEY

EDITOR
MARQ DE VILLIERS

ILLUSTRATOR
ANITA KUNZ

DESIGNER
DALE VOKEY

PUBLICATION
TORONTO LIFE MAGAZINE

PUBLISHER
KEY PUBLISHERS CO. LTD.

4

TITLE
SHOPPING FOR MONEY

ART DIRECTOR
JAMES IRELAND

EDITOR
PENNY WILLIAMS

ILLUSTRATOR
MAURICE VELLEKOOP

DESIGNER
FERNANDA PISANI

PUBLICATION
YOUR MONEY

PUBLISHER
C.B. MEDIA

124

Objects of Desire

Personal Details, Perfectly Crafted

PRODUCED BY TRACEY PINCOTT — PHOTOGRAPHY BY JOHN MASTROMONACO

GOLD AWARD

1

Hand-Painted

LEATHER HAT, DESIGNED BY MARY LEA-WILSON
MAKE-UP BY MARIA VEREL — HAIR BY JOHN DONATO — LEOTARD AND BODY STOCKINGS BY SHAPES
FOR SHOPPING DETAILS SEE PAGE 79

Black and White

PLASTIC JEWELLERY BY MARTHA STURDY

1

TITLE
OBJECTS OF DESIRE

ART DIRECTOR
SUSAN CASEY

EDITOR
TRACEY PINCOTT

PHOTOGRAPHER
JOHN MASTROMONACO

DESIGNER
SUSAN CASEY

PUBLICATION
V MAGAZINE

ART DIRECTOR
SUSAN CASEY

PHOTOGRAPHER
JOHN MASTROMONACO

Hat tricks

Are hats hot? Is the chapeau apropos? If you let the world of couture be your guide, then they are the one essential accessory. On these pages we offer hats in all their wonder and whimsy. As someone somewhere once said, "A piece of magic is a hat." And what would a party be without one? Hair by Ginger Bains of Tuxedo. Makeup by Philippe Chansel of Cloutier/Ray Civello. Photographed by Michael Williams. Bowlerama! This one (above) by Anita Pineault. About $55. Alfred Sung's wool crepe jacket: $275. At Alfred Sung at Hazelton Lanes. Earrings from Fabrice. Ray-Bans from First Canadian Optical. Gloves from Euterpe. Feathered friends (opposite page): Golench Boudreau's ostrich feather cocktail hats and ostrich boas. Hats, $450 each. At Sublime and Holt Renfrew. Left: Wayne Clark's black velvet jacket. $275. At Alan Cherry, Danya, Meadows, and Your Choice. Right: Anne Klein's black velvet top. $272. Available at Brian Winston

158   Toronto Life fashion Winter 1987

A hat is to be stylish in, to glow under, to flirt beneath...to make all men feel masculine about
— MARTHA SLITER

1

SILVER AWARD

1

TITLE
HAT TRICKS

ART DIRECTOR
BRAD MacIVER

EDITOR
JOHN MacKAY

PHOTOGRAPHER
MICHAEL WILLIAMS

PUBLICATION
TORONTO LIFE FASHION

PUBLISHER
KEY PUBLISHERS CO. LTD.

EDITORIAL PHOTOGRAPHY

128

PHOTOGRAPHY BY GEORGE WHITESIDE

THE YEN FOR JAPANESE DESIGN

What's available in Toronto — and who's making it available

BY ADELE FREEDMAN

OPPOSITE: BANRI NAKAMURA'S DIVIDER. BELOW,
LEFT: KETTLE FROM KAMIMURA BOWEN GALLERIES.
BELOW, RIGHT: MARTIN MYERS OF QUASI MODO

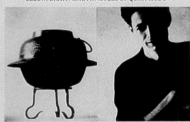

"JAPAN IS OUR FUTURE" IS A SLOGAN North Americans use to describe the country that, in only forty years, has transformed itself into an industrial and technological superpower. Japan, in this view, is a laboratory of modernism; and Tokyo the essence of a new urbanism. Overcrowding, astonishingly high property values, misuse of natural resources, accelerating social change, consumerism on a vast scale, pressured cultural values—it seems whatever Japan does to manage these problems must, sooner or later, apply here.

In Toronto, as in other cities around the world, Japan doubles as rearview mirror and crystal ball. If a certain degree of envy and mythmaking is involved, so be it. But there's another side to our collective fascination with Japan and things Japanese, which has to do with spirit, craft and the life of the imagination. We're talking artifacts—objects fashioned of clay, cloth, paper, wood, stone and mortar; old and new; worn, played, studied, bought, sold and collected; suddenly discovered, patiently rediscovered. And we're talking entrepreneurs—people born here or settled here, from Japan and elsewhere, who travel between Toronto and Tokyo in search of something special to bring back for sale or personal pleasure, or who've brought with them memories and skills that have enriched

132 : Homes : Summer 1988

1

For scholars and the art-minded, Japan equals wood-block prints—known generically as *ukiyo-e*, or pictures of the floating world

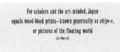

our environment. Some go to find their roots, others take their own with them, while keen to explore another culture. Toronto Japan is a clutter with variations, comprised of many different stories. Here are ways of them.

For scholars and the art-minded, Japan equals wood-block prints. Between generically as *ukiyo-e*, or pictures of the floating world, these floating *ukiyo-e*, ice and landscape, were published in quantity from the seventeenth to nineteenth century, designated for an increasingly powerful merchant class. But their popularity went beyond the bourgeois marketplace. Much collected them, and so did son Gogh, Frank Lloyd Wright, the most Japanese of American architects, bought (and sold) them, too.

Stuart Jackson, who runs a gallery on Yorkville Avenue, fell into wood-love while a psychology major in Minneapolis. He purchased while he thought was a Chinese print, took it to the Boston Museum of Fine Arts for verification and was informed he'd acquired an example of *ukiyo-e* that was all it took. Through day life he collected, meanwhile quoting through college writing essays on "The psychology of languages as seen through Japanese and Indian art" and the like. ("No one knew what I was talking

128 Homes : Summer 1988

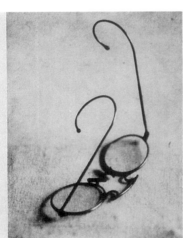

Since 1971, prices have zoomed: a print by Utamaro, a famous *ukiyo-e* artist, fetched $220,000 at Sotheby's last December

OPPOSITE: ARCHITECT MILIA VALASAKIS FROM STUDIO.
BELOW, LEFT: GREY VASE FROM MANY BOUTIQUE. BELOW,
BELOW, RIGHT: PORCELAIN VASE FROM KADA KADA

about," he cheerfully admits.) *Ukiyo-e* were cheap then, and costlier live. "I paid twenty-two dollars for Rainlandle and twenty-five dollars for Hiroshige," says Jackson, of works by two celebrated print artists which now sell, on average, for $200 to $500 (or more) apiece.

After graduation, Jackson wrangled himself into numerous work with Japanese artists. He headed for Toronto in 1978, lured by reports of the city—but notably to see the Chinese exhibition at the Royal Ontario Museum. He also curated a trip, opened a gallery on Bedford Street and turned to his present premises in 1975. Here, he says, he does "enough buying and selling outside to warflant the timing up." Jackson now finds it too expensive to buy at auction: since 1971, where Japanese dealers began to release in their heritage, prices have zoomed: 24 print by Utamaro, another famous *ukiyo-e* artist, fetched $220,000 at Sotheby's in London last December, breaking the world's record for a single Japanese woodcut.) But even, insists Jackson, "doesn't necessarily equal expensive or great" design and sandblast are the servants of quality.

To which Kaoru Kimimura, co-proprietor of the Kamimura Bowen Galleries on Bedford Street, adds a third indicator: a name artist. Kamimura reached art history in

Continued on page 137

SILVER AWARD

1

TITLE
THE YEN FOR JAPANESE DESIGN

ART DIRECTOR
TERESA FERNANDES

EDITOR
MARQ DE VILLIERS

PHOTOGRAPHER
GEORGE WHITESIDE

DESIGNER
TERESA FERNANDES

PUBLICATION
TORONTO LIFE MAGAZINE

PUBLISHER
KEY PUBLISHERS CO. LTD.

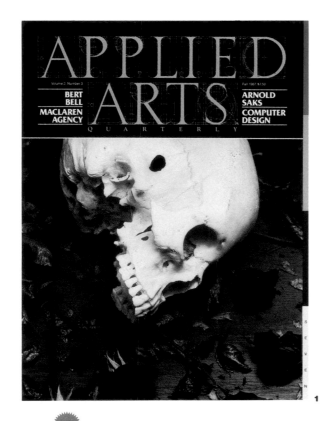

SILVER AWARD

SILVER AWARD

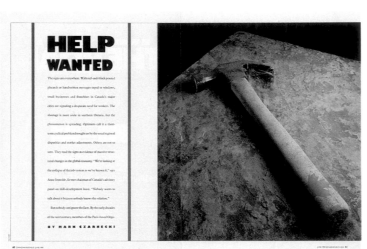

SILVER AWARD

1	**2**	**3**
TITLE STILL LIFE	**TITLE** LAW AND DISORDER	**TITLE** HELP WANTED
ART DIRECTOR GEORGES HAROUTIUN	**ART DIRECTOR** THERESE SHECHTER	**ART DIRECTORS** DAVID WOODSIDE/CHRISTINE HIGDON/JIM IRELAND
EDITOR VALERIE THOMPSON	**EDITOR** SARAH MURDOCH	**PHOTOGRAPHER** MIKE VISSER
PHOTOGRAPHER BERT BELL	**PHOTOGRAPHER** NIGEL DICKSON	**DESIGNER** CHRISTINE HIGDON
DESIGNER BONITA BOCANEGRA-COLLINS	**DESIGNER** ANGLE DESIGN	**PUBLICATION** CANADIAN BUSINESS
CLIENT APPLIED ARTS QUARTERLY	**PUBLICATION** THE FINANCIAL TIMES OF CANADA	**PUBLISHER** C.B. MEDIA

NEW ATTITUDES ON
AGING

This summer Holt Renfrew organized a ground-breaking seminar on the physical and psychological realities of aging. The issue couldn't be more timely. On these eight pages, *Fashion* magazine, co-sponsor of the event, presents an exclusive report

We live. We age. It's that simple, that inescapable. So the issue isn't *if*, but how we grow older. And the simplicity doesn't make it any less pressing. In fact, there's more involved than just the greying of the baby boomers. There was also a population explosion after the First World War. And that generation is now closing in on 70. The latest census figures show there are already twice as many people 75 years old and over as there were a mere 10 years ago (1,470,490 in 1986 compared to 747,810 in 1976). The impact is already obvious, and it can only continue to grow. New social pressures demand new attitudes toward aging. The cosmetics industry has taken the most aggressive stance. Anti-aging is its battle cry. The cosmetic arsenal includes all sorts of products that promise to ameliorate the march of time. But it is (and will be for the foreseeable future) growing old naturally – with as much grace as possible – that is of more concern to the vast majority of us. And that was the issue addressed by the Holt Renfrew Seminar. A range of across-the-board experts offered advice on everything from sensible diet and fitness, to spas and cosmetic surgery, sophisticated side-products of a society freed by its medical advances to focus on the quality of life. And in just about every instance, the experts boiled their philosophies down to one stark, simple concept: Life is what you make it. Such a conclusion sounds tailor-made for a Hallmark card, but that doesn't mean it's any less valid. Look at it this way – with more life to live than ever before, it follows that we can be making much more of every year. The choice is ours – and that's a reassuring thought as we face the future.

PHOTOGRAPHED BY SHIN SUGINO

REPORTED BY ARLENE BYNON, BARBARA RIGHTON, WENDY WALSH AND TIM BLANKS

1

1

TITLE
NEW ATTITUDES ON AGING

ART DIRECTOR
BRAD MacIVER

EDITOR
JOHN MacKAY

PHOTOGRAPHER
SHIN SUGINO

PUBLICATION
TORONTO LIFE FASHION

PUBLISHER
KEY PUBLISHERS CO. LTD.

ALL
ABOUT
EVE
•

NIGHT
FLIGHTS

*C*REATIVE
DIFFERENCES. WHEN EVERY DRESS HAS A
ONE-OF-A-KIND FEELING. AND WHEN
DRESSING FOR EVENING IS AS MUCH ABOUT
FEELING AS IT IS ABOUT FASHION. IT'S THAT
SUBTLE SOMETHING IN THE WAY YOU FEEL IN A
DRESS, AND IT'S IN A DETAIL OR TWO – A
CURVE, A LINE, A LENGTH, A CRINOLINE, A
SPECIAL COLOR. TO IMPART THE SPECIAL
NIGHT FEELING – A PORTFOLIO OF
ONE-OF-A-KIND PHOTOGRAPHS
BY BRUNO DAYAN

A TUBE OF BLACK
VELVET, SKIRTED AND
BOWED IN MIDNIGHT
BLUE TAFFETA
(OPPOSITE PAGE). BY
ALFRED SUNG. $325. AT
ALFRED SUNG AT
HAZELTON LANES, LA
FORET, HOLT
RENFREW AND
BOUTIQUE SILKWORM.
SHOES, $300. AT
BOUTIQUE QUINTO.
HOSIERY BY
CHRISTIAN DIOR.
MAKEUP BY PHILIPPE
CHANSEL OF
CLOUTIER/RAY
CIVELLO. HAIR THESE
14 PAGES BY DENIS
BOUCHARD OF DENIS
BOUCHARD HAIR INC.
SHIRRED SCHERRER
(THIS PAGE).
INCANDESCENT
BRONZE SILK VISCOSE.
$2,000. AT SIMPSONS.
EARRINGS BY DANNY
POLLAK. GLOVES BY
PLEASANT PHEASANT.
MAKEUP BY PHILIPPE
CHANSEL OF
CLOUTIER/RAY
CIVELLO

1

ALL
ABOUT
EVE

1

TITLE
NIGHT FLIGHTS

ART DIRECTOR
BRAD MacIVER

EDITOR
JOHN MacKAY

PHOTOGRAPHER
BRUNO DAYAN

PUBLICATION
TORONTO LIFE FASHION

PUBLISHER
KEY PUBLISHERS CO. LTD.

EDITORIAL PHOTOGRAPHY

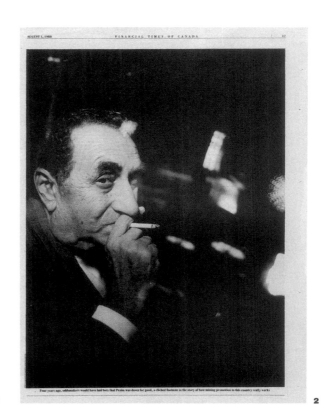

1

TITLE
DIFFERENT STROKES

ART DIRECTOR
BRUCE RAMSAY

EDITOR
ROBERT FULFORD

PHOTOGRAPHER
DEBORAH SAMUEL

PUBLICATION
SATURDAY NIGHT MAGAZINE

PUBLISHER
JOHN MacFARLANE

2

TITLE
THE PEZ

ART DIRECTOR
THERESE SHECHTER

EDITOR
SARAH MURDOCH

PHOTOGRAPHER
DENIS MONTALBETTI

PUBLICATION
THE FINANCIAL TIMES OF CANADA

3

TITLE
UNDER SURVEILLANCE

ART DIRECTOR
BRUCE RAMSAY

EDITOR
JOHN FRASER

PHOTOGRAPHER
BRIAN SMALE

PUBLICATION
SATURDAY NIGHT MAGAZINE

PUBLISHER
PETER WHITE

4

TITLE
AT A LOSS FOR WORDS

ART DIRECTOR
BRUCE RAMSAY

EDITOR
JOHN FRASER

PHOTOGRAPHER
EDWARD GAJDEL

DESIGNER
KASPAR deLINE

PUBLICATION
SATURDAY NIGHT MAGAZINE

PUBLISHER
PETER WHITE

THE WILD ONES

Furs In Flight In The High Country

Photography by Montalbetti/Campbell
Produced by Tracey Pincott

SILVER FOX TROTTER WITH SCALLOP CUT BOTTOM BY BALENCIAGA OF PARIS, HAT BY AKUBRA, LEATHER PANTS BY NETO, MOCK TURTLE NECK BY ROMEO GIGLI.

1

BLACK CHERRY SHEARED BEAVER WITH PERSIAN LAMB TRIM BY CHRISTIAN DIOR, LAMB'S WOOL HAT AND MUFF BY JAEGER, LEATHER PANTS BY NETO, SWEATER BY ZONDA NELLIS.

THE WILD ONES

NATURAL RED FOX BY AUSTRALIAN OR TURTLE BELT AND JEANS BY MARTINE FRANCOIS GIRBAUD, SHIRT BY FABIO INGHIRIBAG, HAT BY AKUBRA

SHEARED BEAVER AND PERSIAN LAMB BY ZUKI

1

TITLE
THE WILD ONES

ART DIRECTOR
SUSAN CASEY

EDITOR
TRACEY PINCOTT

PHOTOGRAPHERS
MONTALBETTI/CAMPBELL

DESIGNER
SUSAN CASEY

PUBLISHER
V MAGAZINE

BARE MINIMUM
STRIPPED-DOWN ACTIONWEAR

LESS IS DEFINITELY MORE IN THESE BARE ESSENTIALS
TO TAKE YOU FROM THE GYM TO THE BEACH AND
BACK ON TO THE STREET
PHOTOGRAPHY BY MONTALBETTI/CAMPBELL
PRODUCED BY TRACEY PINCOTT

30

WHEN WEARING VERY LITTLE, USE A LOT OF WIT. AS IN A FRONT-FASTEN BRA TOP BY TAYARI PAIRED
WITH STRIPED BEACH PANTS FROM GOTTEX, OR THE PROPHETIC BUBBLE SUIT, ALSO BY GOTTEX.
GLASSES BY MATSUDA.

31

1

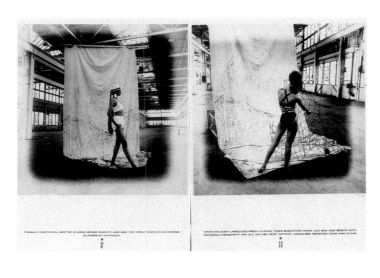

FRANKLY FUNCTIONAL ARE THE CLASSIC BOXER SHORTS AND BRA TOP FROM TOUS LES GARÇONS.
GLASSES BY MATSUDA.

32

DRIVING BODY LANGUAGE FROM SHAPES: THEIR SIGNATURE-SHAPED JOG BRA AND BRIEFS WITH
BANDEAU HEADWRAP ARE ALL 100 PER CENT COTTON. MESSAGES RECEIVED LOUD AND CLEAR.

33

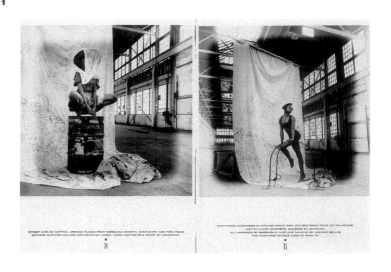

STREET CHIC BY GOTTEX. AFRICAN FLAME PRINT SIGNATURE GHERTO, OVER-SHIRT AND TWO-PIECE
BATHING SUIT FOR FULLISH HOT-WEATHER LIVING. HAND-PAINTED SILK SCARF BY VALENTINA.

34

FAST-TRACK SLEEKNESS IN CYCLING PANTS AND JOG BRA FROM TOUS LES GARÇONS.
HAT BY CLARK DAVIDSON. GLASSES BY MATSUDA.
ALL EARRINGS BY BARBARA D. IVER AND MAKEUP BY JOHNNY BELLUE.
FOR SHOPPING DETAILS TURN TO PAGE 241.

35

1

TITLE
BARE MINIMUM

ART DIRECTOR
SUSAN CASEY

EDITOR
TRACEY PINCOTT

PHOTOGRAPHERS
MONTALBETTI/CAMPBELL

DESIGNER
SUSAN CASEY

PUBLICATION
V MAGAZINE

1	2	3	4
TITLE	**TITLE**	**TITLE**	**TITLE**
THE GUEST STAR	DEAL OF THE DECADE	DOUBLE TAKE	BINGO
ART DIRECTOR	**ART DIRECTOR**	**ART DIRECTOR**	**ART DIRECTOR**
BRUCE RAMSAY	THERESE SHECHTER	BRUCE RAMSAY	BRUCE RAMSAY
EDITOR	**EDITOR**	**EDITOR**	**EDITOR**
ROBERT FULFORD	SARAH MURDOCH	ROBERT FULFORD	JOHN FRASER
PHOTOGRAPHER	**PHOTOGRAPHER**	**PHOTOGRAPHER**	**PHOTOGRAPHER**
EDWARD GAJDEL	ELAINE ELLMAN	CHICK RICE	EDWARD GAJDEL
PUBLICATION	**PUBLICATION**	**PUBLICATION**	**PUBLICATION**
SATURDAY NIGHT MAGAZINE	THE FINANCIAL TIMES OF CANADA	SATURDAY NIGHT MAGAZINE	SATURDAY NIGHT MAGAZINE
PUBLISHER		**PUBLISHER**	**PUBLISHER**
PETER WHITE		PETER WHITE	PETER WHITE

ISSUE

THE VOICE OF THE ART DIRECTORS' CLUB OF TORONTO

INSIDE
A MATTER OF OPINIONS

VISUAL ESSAY
ROBIN KOBRYN — BEING THERE

COMMENTARY
THE CRUX OF KRONE

TRENDS
A NEW TUBE OF PAINT

NUMBER THREE

1

2

3

1

TITLE
ISSUE

ART DIRECTOR
TERESA FERNANDES

EDITOR
T.W. COLE

PHOTOGRAPHER
EDWARD GAJDEL

PUBLISHER
ART DIRECTORS CLUB OF TORONTO

2

TITLE
CALCULATED SUCCESS

ART DIRECTOR
BRUCE RAMSAY

EDITOR
ROBERT FULFORD

PHOTOGRAPHER
JIM ALLEN

HAND COLOURING
RICK ZOLKOWER

PUBLICATION
SATURDAY NIGHT MAGAZINE

PUBLISHER
PETER WHITE

3

TITLE
GLOBE & MAIL GUIDE TO CALGARY '88

ART DIRECTOR
ARTHUR NIEMI

EDITOR
MURRAY CAMPBELL

PHOTOGRAPHER
JOHN MASTRONOMACO

DESIGNERS
VIVIAN OZOLS/ARTHUR NIEMI/MARK KOUDYS

PUBLISHER
GLOBE & MAIL

EDITORIAL PHOTOGRAPHY

140

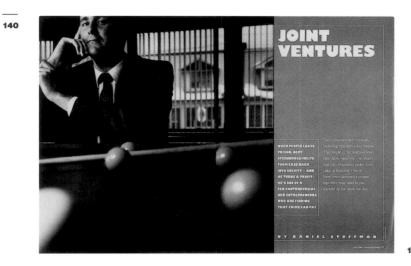

JOINT VENTURES

LEST WE FORGET

1

1

TITLE
JOINT VENTURES

ART DIRECTORS
CHRISTINE HIGDON/JIM IRELAND

PHOTOGRAPHERS
BOB KARPA
JOHN MASTROMONACO

DESIGNER
CHRISTINE HIGDON

PUBLICATION
CANADIAN BUSINESS

PUBLISHER
C.B. MEDIA

2

TITLE
LOOK, UP IN THE SKY

ART DIRECTORS
TERESA FERNANDES/MARTHA WEAVER

EDITOR
MARQ DE VILLIERS

PHOTOGRAPHER
DOUG FORSTER

DESIGNER
TERESA FERNANDES

PUBLICATION
TORONTO LIFE MAGAZINE

PUBLISHER
KEY PUBLISHERS CO. LTD.

3

TITLE
LEST WE FORGET

ART DIRECTOR
LINDA STEPHENSON

EDITOR
PATRICK WALSH

PHOTOGRAPHER
ROBERT L. DODA

PUBLICATION
FOCUS ON YORK

PUBLISHER
SUSAN CAMENZINO

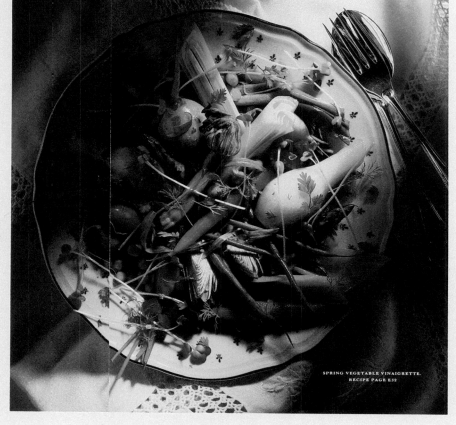

1

TITLE
FRENCH EVOLUTIONS

ART DIRECTORS
TERESA FERNANDES/MARTHA WEAVER

EDITOR
MARQ DE VILLIERS

PHOTOGRAPHER
ROBERT WIGINGTON

DESIGNER
MARTHA WEAVER

PUBLICATION
TORONTO LIFE MAGAZINE

PUBLISHER
KEY PUBLISHERS CO. LTD.

JACK COCKWELL

BERNARD SHAPIRO

THE NEWCOMERS
Why They Made It to The Top 50

PETER COLE. "A rascal," says one observer. "Charismatic," say others. Without a doubt a major new financial player in our Top 50. Under Cole's stewardship, Central Capital has made thirty-eight acquisitions in eighteen months and has grown to $23 billion from $6.25 billion in 1986. Cole's importance is chiefly that he's the WASP front man for Central's controlling shareholders, Leonard Ellen and Reuben Cohen. Cole, who was recruited from the Canadian Imperial Bank of Commerce (where his talents were persistently undervalued), has zillions of contacts in the blue-blood Toronto Establishment—a boon to Cohen and Ellen, who are perceived as mysterious

figures (hailing from Moncton and Montreal, respectively). Cole has recruited Bay Street's best and brightest to this otherwise unglamorous firm.

MICHAEL MACKENZIE. The big bang has increased the influence of the country's chief regulator of banks, trusts and insurance companies. So has the collapse of certain financial institutions. The four pillars are shaking, and Mackenzie, who this year is paired with Ontario Securities Commission chairman Stanley Beck, has the task of steadying them. His biggest goal now—and a spectre to bankers—is to meddle with how the banks deal with mergers they've arranged with brokers. Mackenzie's very worried about the co-mingling of depositors' funds with the monies handled by the newly acquired brokerages' "cowboy" traders. If they don't tread respectfully, the bankers

could find Mackenzie something of a nemesis; most steps they take will have to meet with his approval. Mackenzie also played a key role in getting the banks to deal with Third World debts.

GORDON ASHWORTH. The low-profile, highly regarded adviser to Premier Peterson. He joins our list this year because a consensus is emerging that Hershell Ezrin, Heather Peterson and Ashworth are interchangeably influential with their very influential boss.

PETER MANSBRIDGE. By turning down highly commercial CBS, he becomes public broadcasting's most important symbol. Will he use his influence to aid in shoring up a faltering CBC? Stay tuned.

ALLAN GREGG. There will be a federal election this year (most likely) or next.

Either way, the Tories are preparing now (one mole says that the jingle is already recorded), and whatever pollster Gregg finds out will shape the party's campaign.

DOUG CREIGHTON. This was the year of trading *Posts*—daily *Houston* for daily *Financial*—Creighton's biggest gamble since the *Sun* rise. (Plans are also afoot for new *Suns*, in Washington, D.C., and elsewhere.) Success may mean the waning of the *Globe*'s ROB. Failure may mean the waning of Creighton.

ELINOR CAPLAN AND DR. HUGH SCULLY. Abortion. Midwives. Skyrocketing costs. The aftermath of extra-billing. The minister of health—successfully revived after a well-publicized case of conflict-of-interestitis—has her hands full. It helps that she "has a lot of credibility outside

government" and that she's "powerful, wise and respected in the legislature." Paired with Caplan this year is Ontario Medical Association head Hugh Scully, who's making sure the doctors' interests are kept at the forefront of the various debates.

WILLIAM THORSELL AND JOHN HONDERICH. The free-trade warriors. They represent the country's great economic debate. Thorsell marshals the *Globe*'s editorials in favor; Honderich directs the *Star*'s "anti-" beat.

A. ROY MEGARRY. A latecomer to his calling (stints in accounting and management consulting went before). He is, nonetheless, more possessed by the traditional publisher's proprietorial instinct than his peers in the Thomson newspaper empire—owing to the *Globe*'s edito-

rial clout and his own entrepreneurial successes (the *Report on Business Magazine*, for instance). A major business force in the city and the country, he has the task of protecting the money-making ROB from *The Financial Post*'s frontal assault, one of the big breaking stories of the year.

ARDEN HAYNES. Imperial Oil had a very good year and so did its corporate leader. Haynes is busy (like Bill Dimma [see page 75]) championing the cause of corporate ethical reform. His company bid unsuccessfully for Dome Petroleum, but did luck out with a bid for another major western Canadian gas producer (Sulpetro). Most important, Haynes maintains tradition whereby at least this branch plant (controlled by EXXON) operates with overt autonomy from head office; in addition to its policy of very attractive

48 TORONTO LIFE MAY 1988

MAY 1988 TORONTO LIFE 41

Photography by John Mastromonaco

1

ELINOR CAPLAN

ATOM EGOYAN

FRANCESCA VALENTE

DR. BUDHENDRA DOOBAY

1

TITLE
THE TOP 50

ART DIRECTOR
TERESA FERNANDES

EDITOR
MARQ DE VILLIERS

PHOTOGRAPHER
JOHN MASTROMONACO

DESIGNER
TERESA FERNANDES

PUBLICATION
TORONTO LIFE MAGAZINE

PUBLISHER
KEY PUBLISHERS CO. LTD.

TAKE IT TO THE limit

Cutting-edge fashion by designers who dare

Warning. This dramatic apparel is not for the faint of heart. Wear it at your own risk, for you will not go un-noticed. Created by some of the most daring Canadian and international designers, the fashion on the following pages demands a sense of drama, and a taste for living at the edge.

Foreground: Gianfranco Ferre grey wool suit, $1,450, and charcoal wool coat, $1,675. Alcione silk tie, $65. All at Classica Uomo. White cotton shirt from Alan Goouch, $65. Lorenzo Banfi shoes from Boutique Quinto, $425.
Background: Gianmarco Venturi wool jacket in black-and-white check, $990, and black wool trousers, $440. Alcione silk tie, $65. All at Classica Uomo. Reporter white cotton shirt from Alan Goouch, $55. Cesare Paciotti shoes from Boutique Quinto, $325. Glasses from Josephson Opticians. Umbrella from Holt Renfrew. For **her clothing** in the following photographs, see Index to Shops, page M60.

Photographs by George Whiteside
Styling by Anne Nikolajevich
Makeup by Philippe Chansel-Cloutier
Hair by Steven Rose-Cloutier

1

1

TITLE
TAKE IT TO THE LIMIT

ART DIRECTOR
TERESA FERNANDES

EDITOR
WENDY DENNIS

PHOTOGRAPHER
GEORGE WHITESIDE

DESIGNER
TERESA FERNANDES

PUBLICATION
TORONTO LIFE MAGAZINE

PUBLISHER
KEY PUBLISHERS CO. LTD.

BODY AND SEOUL

Who possesses the perfect body? A lithe and sensuous David encased in Carrara marble?
A pneumatic Ursula Andress rising from the waves? To an athlete, perfection depends upon purpose.
A marathon runner would have little use for the body of a wrestler; a sailor develops muscles
different to those of a diver. Our Olympic athletes seek the inimitable and display the impeccable.

BY VERONICA CUSACK

CHRIS WOODCROFT

WRESTLER

Wrestling is a total body sport,
therefore the body must be totally fit. Powerful
and dynamic, it must combine strength with speed.
A fifty-two-kilogram-class wrestler, he trains
four hours each day to perfect the explosive moves
required in Olympic competition.

ALLISON HIGSON

SWIMMER

They do not train by swimming alone.
To maintain her amazing speed, this world's-record
holder spends eighteen hours a week in the water, but
her regimen also contains ten hours of dry-land training. Rope climbing and weight training develop her
shoulders and triceps; running, both sprint and distance, gives power and thrust to her legs.

PHOTOGRAPHY BY JOHN MASTROMONACO

36 TORONTO LIFE AUGUST 1988

AUGUST 1988 TORONTO LIFE 37

BODY AND SEOUL

ANNE OGRZSHYN

DIVER

PETER MAHER

MARATHON RUNNER

BODY AND SEOUL

GAIL AND KAREN JOHNSON

SYNCHRONIZED SWIMMERS

CHRIS HIBBERT

OARSMAN

1

TITLE
BODY AND SEOUL

ART DIRECTORS
TERESA FERNANDES/DALE VOKEY

EDITOR
MARQ DE VILLIERS

PHOTOGRAPHER
JOHN MASTROMONACO

DESIGNER
DALE VOKEY

PUBLICATION
TORONTO LIFE MAGAZINE

PUBLISHER
KEY PUBLISHING

146

FOCUS ON ME!
FOCUS ON ME!
Nine Politicians Snap The Shutter On Themselves

ANDREW DANSON'S IDEA WAS SIMPLE. Place a politician in his (or her) place, take one test shot, turn the remote shutter release over to the subject, and leave the room until the pol has exposed the rest of the roll. Then print 'em, and see what the pols perpetrated on themselves.

This ingenious notion of taking the politician's preoccupation with self (Focus on Me! Focus on Me!) and making it self-conscious through the cool and unwinking eye of the camera finds in the nine following pages some of its best expression. Politicians, after all, live by the image; manipulation of image is the blood of their being. But few of them have any training in self-scrutiny, and when the intervening intelligence of the Media Person is removed, there is left only . . .what? In hollow people, a hollowness, in men and women of self-regard a preening affection, in brittle people a series of nervous tics, in people of good humor a playfulness, in confident people a willingness to fool with image. . . . But, as you will see, there are few truly confident people in those we picture here.

These nine pictures were drawn from the fifty-nine in the book *Unofficial Portraits: Canadian Politicians Photographed by Themselves*, by Andrew Danson, published this month by Doubleday Canada Ltd./York University. An exhibition of the full set will be on display at the Art Gallery of York University throughout October.

PRODUCED BY
ANDREW DANSON

SINCLAIR STEVENS
MP FOR YORK-PEEL

66 TORONTO LIFE OCTOBER 1987

OCTOBER 1987 TORONTO LIFE 67

1

SILVER AWARD

1

TITLE
FOCUS ON ME

ART DIRECTORS
TERESA FERNANDES/DALE VOKEY

EDITOR
MARQ DE VILLIERS

PHOTOGRAPHER
ANDREW DANSON

DESIGNER
DALE VOKEY

PUBLICATION
TORONTO LIFE MAGAZINE

PUBLISHER
KEY PUBLISHERS CO. LTD.

WHEN WORKERS TURN BOSSES

Once Lamford was just another lumber mill on the verge of extinction. Now it's a testament to the power of worker ownership, with 250 people calling the shots and sharing the profits

In the six weeks that 17-year-old Chris Haines packed a lunch every day to wait in line for his first job at the local lumber mill in New Westminster, B.C., he never imagined himself as a director of the company. But then again he never thought he would have to buy the mill just to keep his job.

When Haines hired on back in 1976 at Lamford Cedar, his first job was pulling boards off the green chain, the conveyor that spews out lengths of lumber from rough-cut logs. In just a few years, he worked his way up to apprentice millwright. Then came the economic recession of the early 1980s. The bearded young lumber grader remembers vividly the

BY JOHN FAUSTMANN ■ PHOTOGRAPHY BY ZORAN MILICH

1

1

TITLE
WHEN WORKERS TURN BOSSES

ART DIRECTOR
CATE COCHRAN

EDITOR
MARGARET WENTE

PHOTOGRAPHER
ZORAN MILICH

DESIGNER
CATE COCHRAN

PUBLICATION
REPORT ON BUSINESS MAGAZINE

PUBLISHER
THE GLOBE & MAIL

EDITORIAL PHOTOJOURNALISM

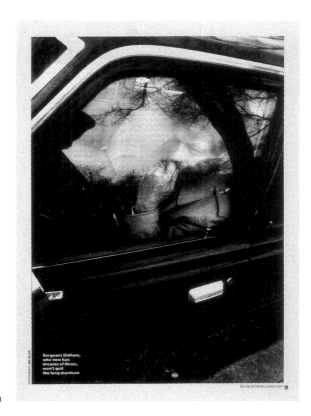

1

1

TITLE
STRANGER IN THE PARK

ART DIRECTOR
BRUCE RAMSAY

EDITOR
BARBRA MOON

PHOTOGRAPHER
JIM ALLEN

DESIGNER
BRUCE RAMSAY

PUBLICATION
SATURDAY NIGHT MAGAZINE

PUBLISHER
SATURDAY NIGHT

1

1

off

TITLE
DAY IN THE LIFE OF A FLOWER

ART DIRECTORS
DAVID WOODSIDE/JIM IRELAND/CHRISTINE HIGDON

PHOTOGRAPHER
JIM ALLEN

DESIGNER
DAVID WOODSIDE

PUBLICATION
CANADIAN BUSINESS MAGAZINE

PUBLISHER
C.B. MEDIA

SHOTS IN THE

DARK

Toronto at night: an 8-page portfolio

PHOTOGRAPHS BY TOM SKUDRA

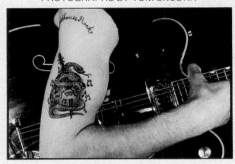

TEXT BY GARY MICHAEL DAULT

Night town. When the shadows are long and aspirations have a short fall and the city is fuelled by music. Where taking care of business means playing doctor to the beat, pumping up the city's rhythmic heart until the music is one big, heavy, sonic pacemaker that gets everyone through to morning.

In the jungle of cities, the nights last longer than the days. City days are broken up into lunches and dinners, conferences, taxis and flight departures. The city's night, on the other hand, is a long, dark matrix of hope and illusion, punctuated by the people in it—people who, for some reason, all look like Time itself. Take this woman at the bar. She is an hourglass. Perhaps she is beautiful. Whatever else she is, she is a possibility. Her companion is trying to make time.

42 TORONTO LIFE MARCH 1988

MARCH 1988 TORONTO LIFE 43

1

SHOTS IN THE

DARK

SHOTS IN THE

DARK

1

TITLE
SHOTS IN THE DARK

ART DIRECTOR
TERESA FERNANDES

EDITOR
MARQ DE VILLIERS

PHOTOGRAPHER
TOM SKUDRA

DESIGNER
TERESA FERNANDES

PUBLICATION
TORONTO LIFE MAGAZINE

PUBLISHER
KEY PUBLISHERS CO. LTD.

2

SILVER AWARD

3

1	2	3
TITLE	**TITLE**	**TITLE**
BOPHA, RESIST, ARREST	GIZELLA'S DREAM ROLE	CTV
EDITOR	**EDITOR**	**ART DIRECTOR**
PAT McCORMICK	PAT McCORMICK	THERESE SHECHTER
PHOTOGRAPHER	**PHOTOGRAPHER**	**EDITOR**
DICK LOEK	BERNARD WEIL	MICHAEL POSNER
DESIGNER	**DESIGNER**	**PHOTOGRAPHERS**
KAM WAI YU	KAM WAI YU	DAVID STREET/SHANE KELLY
PUBLICATION	**PUBLICATION**	**DESIGNER**
WHAT'S ON	WHAT'S ON	THERESE SHECHTER
PUBLISHER	**PUBLISHER**	**PUBLICATION**
THE TORONTO STAR	THE TORONTO STAR	THE FINANCIAL TIMES OF CANADA

Earn your living on borrowed time.

Smart image making professionals know that expensive photographic and video equipment is worthless if it isn't in constant use. It creates overhead and cuts into your bottom line. That's why pros like Deborah Samuel rent. And all the equipment Deborah used to create this image, you can rent from Studio Centre. Because at Studio Centre we're dedicated to renting, so we rent what we sell and more. Much more. Everything from drive-in sound staged studios, darkrooms and lab facilities, to the most exotic of panoramic cameras and video equipment. Plus everything in between.

In fact we rent so much gear we wrote a book about it: 'The Black Book'. And you can get it free by calling our rental department at 391-5500 locally or fax your requirements to 1-416-391-5555. Better yet, if you'd like to see what a little time can earn you, visit the new Studio Centre at 58 Scarsdale Road in Don Mills, Ontario M3B 2R7.

The man on the left
was wearing blue
briefs until Empress
undressed him.
(Note the skin tone!
You'd swear he's
wearing nothing.)

Then we dressed
him up again in smart
red Stanfield's, before
anyone could mutter
tsk-tsk.

We know most every-
one claims to perform
incredible feats with
colour separation
and state-of-the-art
equipment.

Maybe yes, maybe no.

Just because Empress
has the largest and
the most advanced
installation of the
Hell Chromacom

system in all of North
America, and despite
Hell's technological
superiority over
competition, when
all is said and done,
it is the experience,
the talent and the
dedication to excel-
lence in our Empress
people that makes
all the difference to
your fine work.

When it comes to
colour separation,
high-tech without
high-touch will go
nowhere. On the
other hand, you'll
appreciate the visible
difference when
synergism is at work.

Empress Graphics Inc.

Coming through
with flying colours.

Empress Graphics Inc.
175 Midwest Road, Scarborough,
Ontario, Canada M1P 3A7
(416) 751-0980

Photography by:
Ireland Graphics Photography.

We hope you enjoyed our portfolio.

THEY MAY BE A GREAT BUNCH OF COMPUTER GUYS, BUT WILL THEY ALWAYS WORK WELL TOGETHER?

While some computer salesmen may be great fun during a sale, not all display the same good humour when it comes to interrupting their busy schedules to help a co-worker with a service call.

Not so at Blumer-LeVon.

Because we're in the business, we know how important reliable service is. And so, to service our Macintosh™ customers even better, we've put together a full support team of graphics, technical and presentation experts.

What that guarantees is this.

THERE WILL BE NO FUNNY STUFF WHEN IT COMES TO KEEPING OUR PROMISES.

Seriously.

Because no one's expected to be a jack-of-all-trades, each member of our team is a master at their specialty. Which means indepth answers to your most pressing questions.

And speaking of which, a member of our service team will always be in the office to take your calls. If that person can't help you out, they'll put you onto the right person right away.

And that's not all.

WHEN IT COMES TO THE CHANGING NEEDS OF THE BUSINESS, WE'RE A BUNCHA WISE GUYS.

Already our team is very proficient on the amazing Lightspeed Color Layout System for the Macintosh II. With one call, you can be too.

In fact, whatever software is designed to make your job easier tomorrow, we're working on today.

Because at Blumer-LeVon we think the best test of service is after you buy the product.

Anything less and we'd sure feel like fools.

Give us a call today.

Blumer-LeVon
WE SPEAK YOUR LANGUAGE

Authorized Dealer

25 Prince Andrew Place, Don Mills, Ontario M3C 2H2 (416) 444-8431

Apple, the Apple logo and Macintosh are trademarks of Apple Computer Inc.   The Three Stooges ©1988 Norman Maurer Productions Inc. / Columbia Pictures Industries Inc. All rights reserved

A BRUSH WITH

The Aztek 3000-S Airbrush is revolutionary.
It's not a modification, it's brand new. Some say that with the Aztek 3000-S we've
re-invented the airbrush. But why not judge for yourself?

- The range of nozzles, which incorporate needles unique to the Aztek 3000-S, are interchangeable literally in seconds by inserting them directly into the airbrush body and are virtually impossible to clog in normal use.

- Nozzles are stored in their own protective cases.

- The revolutionary design means that the air hose enters at the rear of the 3000-S body, keeping it well away from the artist's work. Artists can work single-handed.

- Lightweight yet sturdy body.

- The 1cc, 2.5cc and 8cc color cups are interchangeable and can be mounted on the left or right of the airbrush in seconds.

- The angle of the color cups can be varied, and the lids further reduce the risk of paint spillage.

- Full range of fine line, general purpose, high flow and spatter nozzles.

- The double-action 'floating' control lever ensures that artist retains full, precise control of air and color.

- Aztek 3000-S is capable of producing just air for drying areas of work.

- Unique roller control enables artist to vary the proportion of color in the spray.

- Roller control enables selection of single action, double action or fixed double action all in one airbrush.

- Incredibly quick to clean — minimum downtime. Unscrew nozzle and place in own capsule with solution. Cups come apart for wipe-easy cleaning.

- Aztek hi-tech box makes a stable, convenient work station with everything to hand.

- Full warranty — just ask your stockist for details.

A Kodak Company

3000-S
Aztek is a trademark

NOW THE FUTURE IS IN YOUR HANDS!

15 Connie Crescent,
12, Concord, Ontario L4K 1L3
(416) 736-6324

PiCo Design

STATIONERY

GOLD AWARD

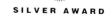

SILVER AWARD

SILVER AWARD

SILVER AWARD

1	2	3	4
TITLE BIBS & BUBBLES	**TITLE** ELLMAN BONIC INC.	**TITLE** PATRICIA HUMPHREYS	**TITLE** HANGAR 13 CORPORATE ID
ART DIRECTOR PETER BAKER	**ART DIRECTOR** DAVID SHELLY	**ART DIRECTOR** RICHARD CLEWES	**ART DIRECTOR** MICHEL ROULEAU/GLENN TORRESAN
DESIGNER PETER BAKER	**DESIGNER** DAVID SHELLY	**DESIGNER** RICHARD CLEWES	**ILLUSTRATOR** MICHEL ROULEAU
DESIGN FIRM TAYLOR & BROWNING ASSOCIATES	**DESIGN FIRM** GRAPHISPHERE INC.	**DESIGN FIRM** RICHARD CLEWES	**DESIGNERS** GLENN TORRESAN/MICHEL ROULEAU
CLIENT ELIZABETH SHERGOLD	**CLIENT** ELLMAN BONIC INC.	**CLIENT** PATRICIA HUMPHREYS	**DESIGN FIRM** HANGAR 13
PRINTER LUNAR CAUSTIC PRESS			**CLIENT** HANGAR 13

STATIONERY

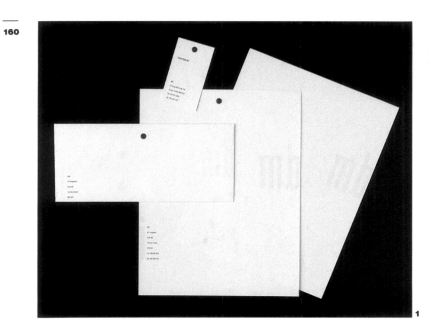

1

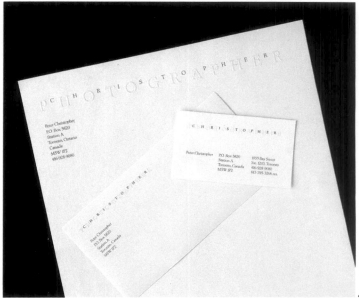

2

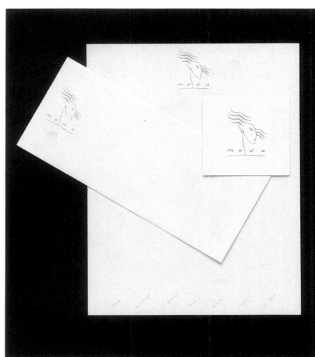

3

4

1
TITLE
MBI STATIONERY

ART DIRECTOR
STEVE MYKOLYN

DESIGNERS
STEVE MYKOLYN/DAVE REDSHAW/CHRISTINE HOUDE

DESIGN FIRM
MBI

CLIENT
MBI

2
TITLE
PETER CHRISTOPHER STATIONERY

ART DIRECTOR
ROBERT HYLAND

DESIGNER
ROBERT HYLAND

DESIGN FIRM
ROBERT HYLAND DESIGN

CLIENT
PETER CHRISTOPHER

PRINTER
McCHARTERS & CO. LTD.

3
TITLE
MODA

ART DIRECTOR
NEVILLE SMITH

ILLUSTRATOR
NEVILLE SMITH

DESIGNER
NEVILLE SMITH

DESIGN FIRM
NEVILLE SMITH GRAPHIC DESIGN

4
TITLE
JOHN ORMSBY STATIONERY

ART DIRECTOR
JOHN ORMSBY

DESIGNER
JOHN ORMSBY

DESIGN FIRM
JOHN ORMSBY DESIGN

STATIONERY

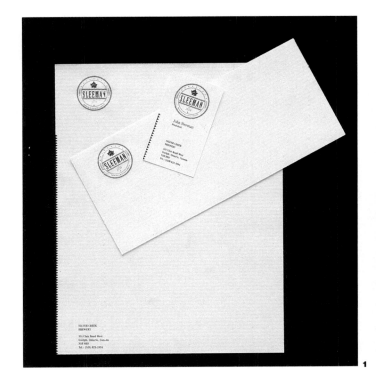

COMPLETE IDENTITY PROGRAM

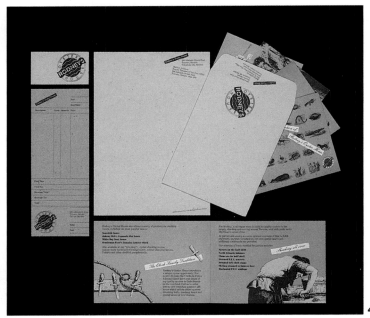

1

TITLE
SLEEMAN STATIONERY

ART DIRECTORS
PAUL BROWNING/JOANNE VERONNEAU

DESIGNER
JOANNE VERONNEAU

DESIGN FIRM
TAYLOR & BROWNING DESIGN ASSOCIATES

CLIENT
THE SLEEMAN BREWERY & MALTING COMPANY

2

TITLE
NATIONAL GALLERY OF CANADA

ART DIRECTOR
IAN C. TUDHOPE

DESIGNERS
BOB BOUTILIER/DON DOOL

DESIGN FIRM
TUDHOPE ASSOCIATES INC.

CLIENT
NATIONAL GALLERY OF CANADA

3

TITLE
MARATHON

ART DIRECTOR
TED LARSON

WRITER
LAUREN VINEBERG

PHOTOGRAPHER
PHILIP GALLARD

DESIGNER
TED LARSON

DESIGN FIRM
OASIS CREATIVE GROUP

CLIENT
MARATHON SHOPPING CENTRES

4

TITLE
RODNEY'S OYSTER HOUSE

WRITER
JANE FRENCH

DESIGNERS
RICHARD KERR/LES HOLLOWAY/NITA WALLACE

DESIGN FIRM
DESIGNSOURCE

CLIENT
RODNEY'S OYSTER HOUSE

PRINTER
C.J. GRAPHICS INC.

GOLD AWARD   1

GOLD AWARD   2

1

TITLE
MENKES

ART DIRECTOR
JEAN PAGE

ILLUSTRATOR
PETER BAKER

DESIGNER
PETER BAKER

DESIGN FIRM
TAYLOR & BROWNING DESIGN ASSOCIATES

CLIENT
MENKES DEVELOPMENT CORPORATION

2

TITLE
MODA WORD MARK

ART DIRECTOR
NEVILLE SMITH

ILLUSTRATOR
NEVILLE SMITH

DESIGNER
NEVILLE SMITH

DESIGN FIRM
NEVILLE SMITH GRAPHIC DESIGN

CLIENT
MODA HAIR DESIGN, OTTAWA

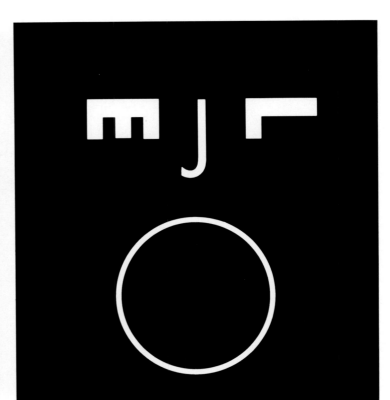

1

GOLD AWARD

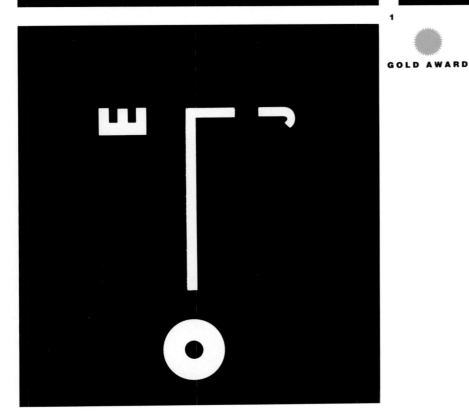

College Park.₂

1

TITLE
JOEL BENARD LOGOTYPE

ART DIRECTOR
PAUL HASLIP

DESIGNER
PAUL HASLIP

DESIGN FIRM
HYNES, HASLIP & PARTNERS

CLIENT
JOEL BENARD, PORTRAIT PHOTOGRAPHER

2

TITLE
COLLEGE PARK LOGO

ART DIRECTOR
BEV W. TUDHOPE

DESIGNER
MARTHA BRITTON

DESIGN FIRM
TUDHOPE ASSOCIATES INC.

CLIENT
COLLEGE PARK

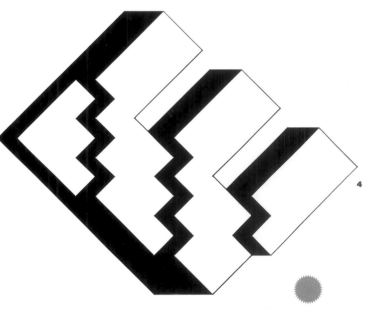

SILVER AWARD

SILVER AWARD

1	2	3	4
TITLE PALUSKI BOATS LTD.	**TITLE** ELLMAN BONIC INC.	**TITLE** PEREZ CORPORATION	**TITLE** EMMESS LOGO
ART DIRECTOR PETER BAKER	**ART DIRECTOR** DAVID SHELLY	**DESIGNER** GARY LUDWIG	**ART DIRECTOR** MALCOLM WADDELL
ILLUSTRATOR PETER BAKER	**DESIGNER** DAVID SHELLY	**DESIGN FIRM** THE SPENCER FRANCEY GROUP	**DESIGNER** MALCOLM WADDELL
DESIGNER PETER BAKER	**DESIGN FIRM** GRAPHISPHERE INC.	**CLIENT** PEREZ CORPORATION	**DESIGN FIRM** ESKIND WADDELL
DESIGN FIRM TAYLOR & BROWNING DESIGN ASSOCIATES	**CLIENT** ELLMAN BONIC INC.		**CLIENT** EMMESS EQUITIES INC.
CLIENT MANUFACTURER OF ROWING SHELLS AND KAYAKS			

THE NEW SYMBOLS •

An integral feature of the new identity is the series of graphic devices to communicate the services we offer to our customers.

These will appear across a broad range of applications from depot signage including pole signs, company stationery and on promotional items. On depots, the symbols will be featured which make the services available at that particular depot.

Pictures can often communicate more immediately than words, especially when people are passing by at speed in their car or truck.

These symbols have been specially created for ATS and will become as much a part of our identity as our name.

TYRES •

EXHAUSTS •

BATTERIES •

SHOCKS •

MOT TESTING •

1

2

3

1	**2**	**3**
TITLE	**TITLE**	**TITLE**
ATS	THE PLANET TYPOGRAPHIC ART LTD. LOGO	FUSION CANADA LOGO
ART DIRECTOR	**ART DIRECTOR**	**ART DIRECTOR**
GLENN TUTSSEL	ROBBIE GOULDEN	IAN C. TUDHOPE
ILLUSTRATOR	**ILLUSTRATOR**	**DESIGNER**
COLIN FREWIN	BOB MEECHAM	DON DOOL
DESIGNER	**DESIGNER**	**DESIGN FIRM**
GLENN TUTSSEL	MIRO CHASTVEN	TUDHOPE ASSOCIATES INC.
DESIGN FIRM	**DESIGN FIRM**	**CLIENT**
MICHAEL PETERS GROUP	ZEPPELIN GRAPHICS INC.	FUSION CANADA
CLIENT	**CLIENT**	
ATS	THE PLANET TYPOGRAPHIC ART LTD.	

166

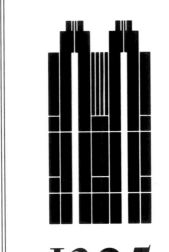

1	**2**	**3**	**4**
TITLE	**TITLE**	**TITLE**	**TITLE**
1325 AVENUE OF THE AMERICAS LOGO	INTERLINK—AN INTERGENERATIONAL PROGRAMME	MACFORUM	CITY CENTRE PLAZA
ART DIRECTOR	**ART DIRECTOR**	**DESIGNER**	**ART DIRECTOR**
IAN C. TUDHOPE	TERRY O'CONNOR	JEANNETTE HANNA	WILL NOVOSEDLIK
DESIGNER	**DESIGNER**	**DESIGN FIRM**	**DESIGNER**
YIN HOSKINS	TERRY O'CONNOR	THE SPENCER FRANCEY GROUP	BRYAN MORRIS
DESIGN FIRM	**DESIGN FIRM**	**CLIENT**	**DESIGN FIRM**
TUDHOPE ASSOCIATES INC.	TERRY O COMMUNICATIONS INC.	MACFORUM	BOULEVARD
CLIENT	**CLIENT**		**CLIENT**
EDWARD J. MINSKOFF EQUITIES	INTERLINK		INDUCON

SYMBOLS AND LOGOTYPES

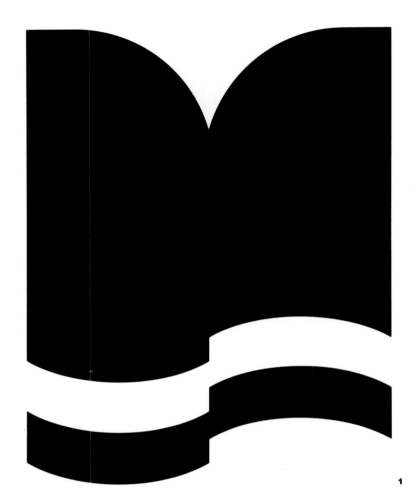

1

2

OPTIONS

3

1

TITLE
McCLELLAND & STEWART

ART DIRECTOR
ROBERT BURNS

DESIGNER
ROBERT BURNS

DESIGN FIRM
BURNS & COMPANY

CLIENT
McCLELLAND & STEWART

2

TITLE
GORD GRANT ELECTRIC IDENTITY

ART DIRECTOR
ALEX MacLEOD

DESIGNER
ALEX MacLEOD

DESIGN FIRM
TYPEFACES

CLIENT
GORD GRANT ELECTRIC (SUDBURY)

3

TITLE
OPTIONS LOGOTYPE

ART DIRECTOR
ALEX MacLEOD

WRITER
ALEX MacLEOD

DESIGNER
ALEX MacLEOD

DESIGN FIRM
ALEX MacLEOD DESIGN SOLUTIONS

CLIENT
WILLIAM M. MERCER LIMITED

COMPLETE DESIGN PROGRAM

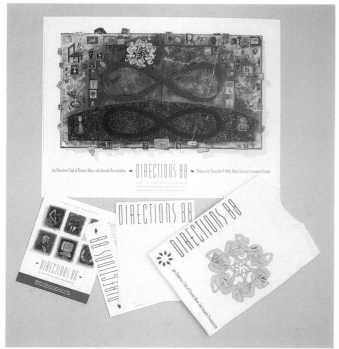

1	2	3
TITLE	**TITLE**	**TITLE**
AUCTION '88	DIRECTIONS 88	CENTRAL PARK LODGES
ART DIRECTOR	**ART DIRECTOR**	**ART DIRECTOR**
CARMEN DUNJKO	LOUIS FISHAUF	JEANNETTE HANNA
WRITER	**PHOTOGRAPHER**	**WRITER**
ELLIOTT COLLINS	SEE SPOT RUN	HELEN BATTERSBY
ILLUSTRATOR	**ILLUSTRATOR**	**PHOTOGRAPHERS**
JILL CHEN	HENRIK DRESCHER & FRIENDS	JIM PANOU/CHRISTOPHER DEW
DESIGNER	**DESIGNER**	**DESIGNER**
JILL CHEN	LOUIS FISHAUF	BARBARA WOOLLEY
DESIGN FIRM	**DESIGN FIRM**	**DESIGN FIRM**
CARMEN DUNJKO ASSOCIATES	REACTOR ART & DESIGN	THE SPENCER FRANCEY GROUP
CLIENT	**CLIENT**	**CLIENT**
ART DIRECTORS CLUB OF TORONTO	ART DIRECTORS CLUB OF TORONTO	CENTRAL PARK LODGES

COMPLETE DESIGN PROGRAM

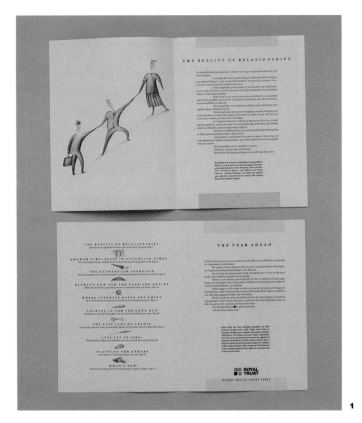

1

2

3

1

TITLE
ROYAL TRUST PERSONAL FINANCE ADVISOR

ART DIRECTOR
ROBERT BURNS

WRITER
JOHN STEWART

ILLUSTRATOR
FRANK VIVA

DESIGNERS
PAMELA STRADWICK/GREGORY HALAS

DESIGN FIRM
BURNS AND COMPANY

CLIENT
ROYAL TRUSTCO LTD.

2

TITLE
1st ANNUAL HAUGHTON BRAZEAU AIR SHOW
& FAMILY PICNIC

ART DIRECTORS
PHILIP BRAZEAU/CATHERINE HAUGHTON

WRITER
CECIL MORRIS

ILLUSTRATOR
PAULA MUNCK/REACTOR

DESIGNER
DERWYN GOODALL

DESIGN FIRM
HAUGHTON BRAZEAU

CLIENT
HAUGHTON BRAZEAU

3

TITLE
ICSC TRUSTEE SPOUSES LUNCHEON

ART DIRECTOR
URSULA KAISER

WRITER
VALERIE CLARK

ILLUSTRATOR
JEFF JACKSON

DESIGNER
URSULA KAISER

DESIGN FIRM
URSULA KAISER

CLIENT
ICSC—INTERNATIONAL COUNCIL OF SHOPPING CENTRES

PRINTER
LUNAR CAUSTIC PRESS

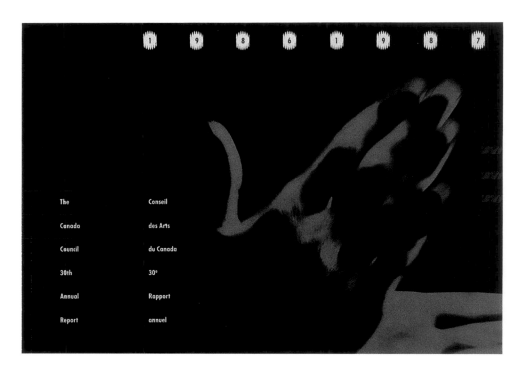

GOLD AWARD

1

TITLE
THE CANADA COUNCIL 30TH ANNUAL REPORT 1986/87

ART DIRECTOR
MALCOLM WADDELL

WRITER
MARY-ANNE DALKOWSKI

DESIGNER
PETER SCOTT

DESIGN FIRM
ESKIND WADDELL

CLIENT
THE CANADA COUNCIL

ANNUAL REPORTS

1

1

TITLE
GROUPE DMR INC.

ART DIRECTOR
MONIQUE DUPRAS

WRITER
BURSON-MARSTELLER

PHOTOGRAPHER
NORMAND GRÉGOARE

ILLUSTRATORS
NORMAND COUSINEAU/VIVIENNE FLESCHER
STEWART BRIERS/JEFFREY FISHER

DESIGNERS
MONIQUE DUPRAS/DIANE PRIMEAU

DESIGN FIRM
BURSON-MARSTELLER

CLIENT
GROUPE DMR INC.

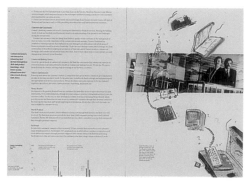

1

TITLE
THE TORONTO DOMINION BANK 132nd ANNUAL REPORT

ART DIRECTOR
ROSLYN ESKIND

WRITERS
SUE DE STEIN/LINDA BINNS

PHOTOGRAPHER
BERNARD BOHN

ILLUSTRATOR
JEFF JACKSON

DESIGNERS
PETER SCOTT/GLENDA RISSMAN

DESIGN FIRM
ESKIND WADDELL

CLIENT
THE TORONTO DOMINION BANK

DIRECTIONS|88

ANNUAL REPORTS

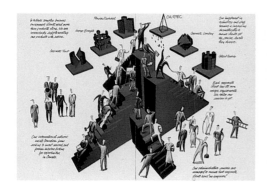

1

TITLE
ROYAL TRUST ANNUAL REPORT

ART DIRECTOR
ROBERT BURNS

WRITER
GAYLE STEWART-GRAY

PHOTOGRAPHER
PHILIP ROSTRON

ILLUSTRATOR
FRANK VIVA

DESIGNER
PAMELA STRADWICK

DESIGN FIRM
BURNS AND COMPANY

CLIENT
ROYAL TRUSTCO LTD.

1986/87
ANNUAL
REPORT

YMCA

THE YMCA
OF
METROPOLITAN
TORONTO

1

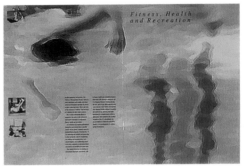

1

TITLE
YMCA 86/87 REPORT

ART DIRECTORS
PAUL HODGSON/BRIAN TSANG

WRITER
HILTON TUDHOPE

PHOTOGRAPHER
RUTH KAPLAN

IMAGE PROCESSING
IAN JAFFREY

DESIGNERS
PAUL HODGSON/BRIAN TSANG

DESIGN FIRM
THE SPENCER FRANCEY GROUP

CLIENT
YMCA OF METROPOLITAN TORONTO

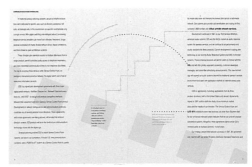

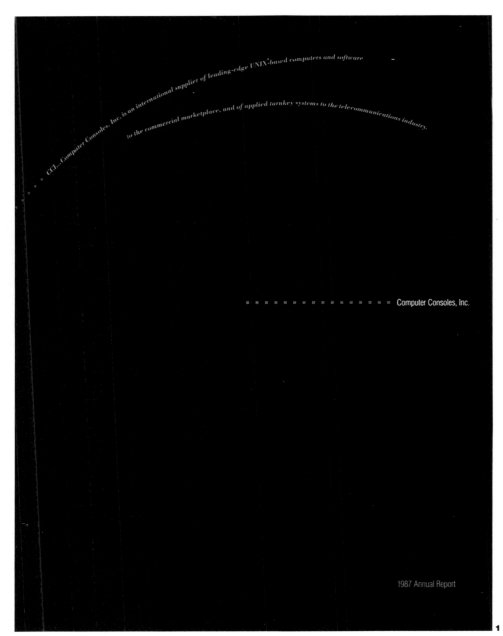

1

TITLE
C.C.I 1987

ART DIRECTOR
JEAN PAGE

WRITERS
WAYNE DONNELLY/WILLIAM THOMAS

PHOTOGRAPHER
TED KAWALERSKI

DESIGNER
CATHY HENDREN

DESIGN FIRM
TAYLOR & BROWNING DESIGN ASSOCIATES

CLIENT
COMPUTER CONSOLES, INCORPORATED

ANNUAL REPORT 1987

TransCanada PipeLines

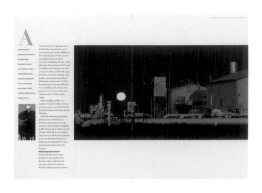

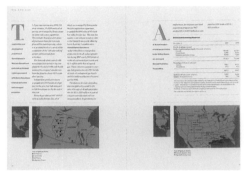

1

1

TITLE
T.C.P.L. 1987

ART DIRECTOR
SCOTT TAYLOR

WRITER
CHARLES WYATT

PHOTOGRAPHER
PETER CHRISTOPHER

DESIGNER
JEAN PAGE

DESIGN FIRM
TAYLOR & BROWNING DESIGN ASSOCIATES

CLIENT
TRANSCANADA PIPELINES

Think of it as...

Often, the best way to capture the printed image you want is to use a coated paper. But, every once in a while, you probably wish that coated papers were just a little more durable...and a little less affected by moisture and repeated folding.

Paper In A Raincoat

Get a little more "last" to the lustre of coated papers—with LASTING IMAGES® Specialty Coated Paper from Kimberly-Clark.

Smooth and bright, latex-coated LASTING IMAGES prints like standard coated papers, but maintains a high degree of moisture resistance, stain resistance and fold endurance. From manuals to menus, your work will keep looking good on LASTING IMAGES.

Think of it as paper in a raincoat.

Lasting Images®
Specialty Coated Paper

✻ **Kimberly-Clark**

ONEX CORPORATION

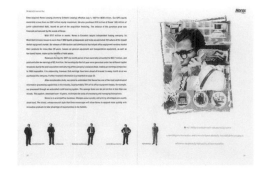

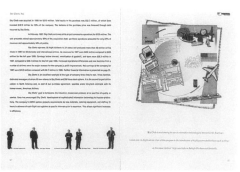

ANNUAL REPORT 1987

1

1

TITLE
ONEX CORPORATION 1987

ART DIRECTOR
PAUL BROWNING

WRITER
HILTON TUDHOPE

ILLUSTRATORS
JEFF JACKSON/BOB HAMBLY/JAY BELMORE
BILL BOYKO/LINDA MONTGOMERY/DOUG MARTIN
ROSS MacDONALD

DESIGNERS
JOE DRVARIC/LISA MILLER

DESIGN FIRM
TAYLOR & BROWNING DESIGN ASSOCIATES

CLIENT
ONEX CORPORATION

DIRECTIONS | 88

ANNUAL REPORTS

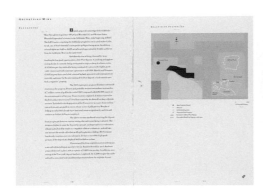

1

TITLE
AMERICAN BARRICK

ART DIRECTOR
SCOTT TAYLOR

PHOTOGRAPHER
JAY MAISEL

DESIGNERS
WILLIAM LAM/JOHN SHENG

DESIGN FIRM
TAYLOR & BROWNING DESIGN ASSOCIATES

CLIENT
AMERICAN BARRICK RESOURCES CORPORATION

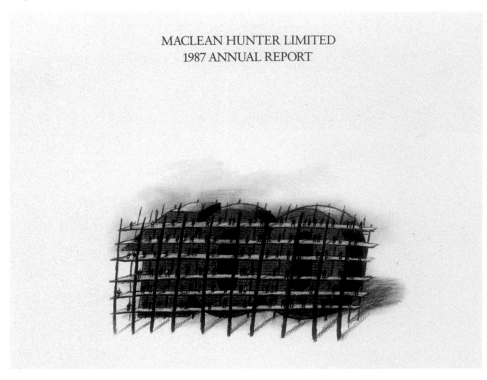

MACLEAN HUNTER LIMITED
1987 ANNUAL REPORT

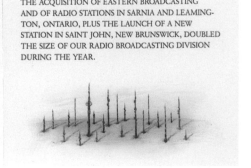

THE ACQUISITION OF EASTERN BROADCASTING AND OF RADIO STATIONS IN SARNIA AND LEAMINGTON, ONTARIO, PLUS THE LAUNCH OF A NEW STATION IN SAINT JOHN, NEW BRUNSWICK, DOUBLED THE SIZE OF OUR RADIO BROADCASTING DIVISION DURING THE YEAR.

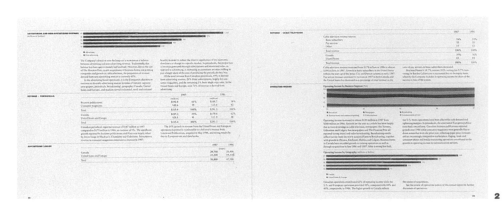

1

TITLE
THE REPORTER/ANNUAL REPORT FOR EMPLOYEES

ART DIRECTOR
ARTHUR NIEMI

ILLUSTRATORS
RENÉ ZAMIC/MIKE CHERKAS

DESIGNERS
ARTHUR NIEMI/VIVIAN OZOLS/MARK KOUDYS

DESIGN FIRM
ATLANTA ART & DESIGN

CLIENT
IMPERIAL OIL

2

TITLE
MACLEAN HUNTER 1987

ART DIRECTOR
SCOTT TAYLOR

WRITER
COLLEEN FLOOD

PHOTOGRAPHER
PAUL ORENSTEIN

ILLUSTRATOR
JERZY KOLACZ

DESIGNER
JOHN PYLYPCZAK

DESIGN FIRM
TAYLOR & BROWNING DESIGN ASSOCIATES

CLIENT
MACLEAN HUNTER LTD.

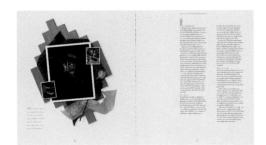

1

1

TITLE
CAMPEAU 1987

ART DIRECTORS
SCOTT TAYLOR/PAUL CAMPBELL

WRITER
VALERIE CLARK

PHOTOGRAPHERS
RON BAXTER SMITH/HEDRICH-BLESSING

DESIGNER
PAUL CAMPBELL

DESIGN FIRM
TAYLOR & BROWNING DESIGN ASSOCIATES

CLIENT
CAMPEAU CORPORATION

MERIDIAN TECHNOLOGIES INC.

ANNUAL REPORT 1988

1

1

TITLE
MERIDIAN TECHNOLOGIES INC.

ART DIRECTOR
LAWRENCE FINN

PHOTOGRAPHER
SHIN SUGINO

DESIGNER
LAWRENCE FINN

DESIGN FIRM
LAWRENCE FINN & ASSOCIATES LTD.

CLIENT
MERIDIAN TECHNOLOGIES

BROCHURES

1

GOLD AWARD

2

1

TITLE
SIGNATURE

ART DIRECTOR
MALCOLM WADDELL

WRITERS
B.W. POWE/GEORGE HOUK

PHOTOGRAPHER
IMAGE BANK CANADA

ILLUSTRATORS
JAN WADDELL/KATE WADDELL

DESIGNERS
MALCOLM WADDELL/MERCEDES ROTHWELL

DESIGN FIRM
ESKIND WADDELL

CLIENT
EMPRESS GRAPHICS INC., MEAD PAPER

2

TITLE
LA SCALA

ART DIRECTOR
WILL NOVOSEDLIK

DESIGNER
MICHAEL STOKELY

DESIGN FIRM
BOULEVARD

CLIENT
SELECT PAPERS

BROCHURES

1

CLIENT MORIYAMA & TESHIMA PLANNERS LTD. ON BEHALF OF THE CANADIAN EMBASSY, TOKYO WITH THE SUPPORT OF SHIMIZU CORPORATION AND THE MITSUBISHI TRUST AND BANKING CORPORATION, TOKYO, JAPAN

GOLD AWARD

2

1	**2**
TITLE	**TITLE**
CANADIAN EMBASSY REDEVELOPMENT	REINHART McMILLAN BROCHURE
ART DIRECTOR	**ART DIRECTOR**
PAUL HODGSON	CARMEN DUNJKO
WRITER	**PHOTOGRAPHER**
MORIYAMA & TESHIMA PLANNERS LTD.	DEBORAH SAMUEL
PHOTOGRAPHER	**DESIGNER**
CHRISTOPHER DEW	CARMEN DUNJKO
ILLUSTRATORS	**DESIGN FIRM**
LISA SMITH/RICK DAKIN	CARMEN DUNJKO ASSOCIATES
DESIGNERS	**CLIENT**
BARBARA WOOLLEY/MAUREEN NISHIKAWA	REINHART McMILLAN HAIR
DESIGN FIRM	
THE SPENCER FRANCEY GROUP	

BROCHURES

SILVER AWARD

1

2

1	2
TITLE IMPRESSIONS	**TITLE** PARILUX
ART DIRECTOR CARMEN DUNJKO	**ART DIRECTORS** JEAN PAGE/KEN KASKIN
WRITER RITA YUNGER LINDER/ELLIOT COLLINS	**WRITER** TONY LEIGHTON
DESIGNERS CARMEN DUNJKO/JENNIFER COGHILL	**PHOTOGRAPHERS** MATTHEW WILEY/GARTH GROSJEAN PHILIP ROSTRON/MICHAEL KOHN/DEBORAH SAMUEL
DESIGN FIRM CARMEN DUNJKO ASSOCIATES	**DESIGNER** JEAN PAGE
CLIENT GRENVILLE PRINTING & MANAGEMENT LTD.	**DESIGN FIRM** TAYLOR & BROWNING DESIGN ASSOCIATES
	CALLIGRAPHY KAREN CHEESEMAN
	CLIENT GRAPHIC PAPERS

BROCHURES

SILVER AWARD

1

2

1

TITLE
MENKES

ART DIRECTORS
JEAN PAGE/SCOTT TAYLOR

WRITER
VALERIE CLARK

PHOTOGRAPHER
HEDRICH-BLESSING

DESIGNER
JEAN PAGE

DESIGN FIRM
TAYLOR & BROWNING DESIGN ASSOCIATES

CLIENT
MENKES DEVELOPMENT INC.

2

TITLE
BULLOCH DISC BROCHURE

ART DIRECTORS
DELA KILIAN/BRIAN MOORE

WRITER
KELVIN BROWNE

PHOTOGRAPHER
DEBORAH SAMUEL

DESIGNER
DELA KILIAN

DESIGN FIRM
DESIGN FORCE INC.

CLIENT
BULLOCH DISC ENTERTAINMENT SERVICES

BROCHURES

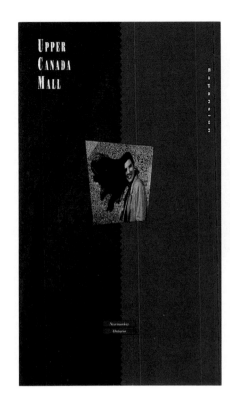

1

SILVER AWARD

2

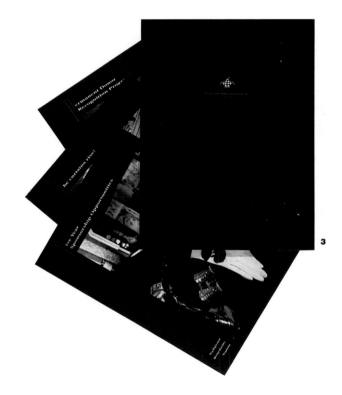

3

1	2	3
TITLE UPPER CANADA MALL	**TITLE** ORR & BOSS BROCHURE	**TITLE** ELGIN WINTER GARDEN
ART DIRECTOR PAUL HODGSON	**ART DIRECTOR** PAUL HASLIP	**ART DIRECTOR** CARMEN DUNJKO
WRITER HELEN BATTERSBY	**WRITER** JAMES HYNES	**WRITER** JUDITH JOHN
PHOTOGRAPHER JIM ALLEN	**PHOTOGRAPHERS** M. RAFELSON/S. EVANS	**DESIGNER** JILL CHEN
DESIGNERS PAUL HODGSON/BARBARA WOOLLEY	**ILLUSTRATOR** ACORN ART & ILLUSTRATION	**DESIGN FIRM** CARMEN DUNJKO ASSOCIATES
DESIGN FIRM THE SPENCER FRANCEY GROUP	**DESIGNER** PAUL HASLIP	**CLIENT** ONTARIO HERITAGE FOUNDATION
CLIENT CAMBRIDGE SHOPPING CENTRES	**DESIGN FIRM** HYNES, HASLIP & PARTNERS	
	CLIENT ORR & BOSS INC.	

CATALOGUES

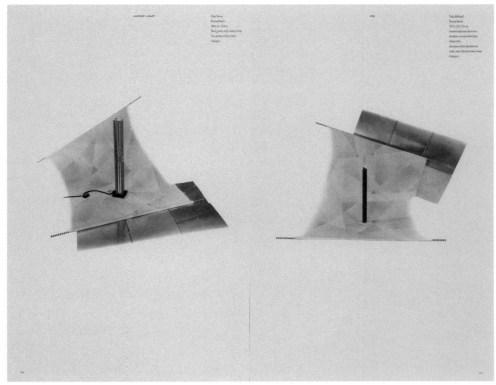

1

3

2

1

TITLE
VIRTU 3

ART DIRECTOR
DEL TERRELONGE

WRITERS
ALLAN KLUSACEK/ESTHER SHIPMAN

PHOTOGRAPHER
RON BAXTER SMITH

DESIGNER
DEL TERRELONGE

DESIGN FIRM
TERRELONGE DESIGN INC.

CLIENT
FORUM AND FUNCTION
DIRECTIONS IN CANADIAN DESIGN

2

TITLE
ART FOR THE MASSES

ART DIRECTOR
LOUIS FISHAUF

DESIGNER
LOUIS FISHAUF

DESIGN FIRM
REACTOR ART & DESIGN

CLIENT
REACTOR ARTWEAR

3

TITLE
BLISS

ART DIRECTORS
LOUIS FISHAUF/DITI KATONA

DESIGNER
DITI KATONA

DESIGN FIRM
REACTOR ART & DESIGN

CLIENT
FEMCOM

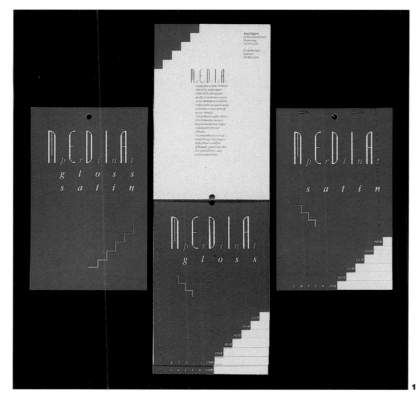

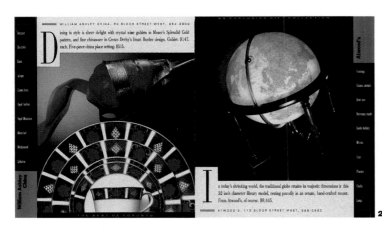

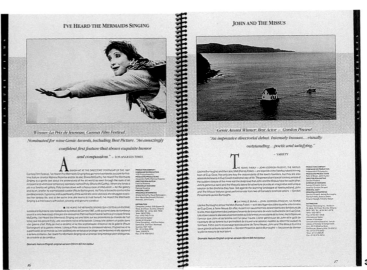

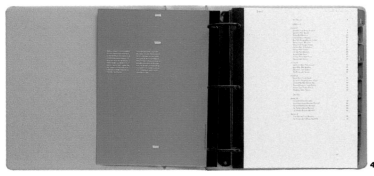

1	2	3	4
TITLE MEDIAPRINT	**TITLE** BEST OF TORONTO CATALOGUE	**TITLE** OFDC	**TITLE** CADILLAC FAIRVIEW SHOPPING GUIDE
ART DIRECTOR ROBERT HYLAND	**ART DIRECTOR** PAUL HASLIP	**ART DIRECTOR** SHARI SPIER	**ART DIRECTORS** MICHAEL MALLOY/PAUL BROWNING
WRITER JENNIFER VOPNI	**WRITER** JAMES HYNES	**ILLUSTRATOR** RENE ZAMIC	**WRITERS** CHRISTINE SMITH/JOHN GARNER
DESIGNERS ROBERT HYLAND/GEORGE KAY	**PHOTOGRAPHER** RON TANAKA	**DESIGNER** SHARI SPIER	**ILLUSTRATOR** ACORN ILLUSTRATION & ART STUDIO
DESIGN FIRM ROBERT HYLAND DESIGN	**DESIGNER** PAUL HASLIP	**DESIGN FIRM** REACTOR ART & DESIGN	**DESIGNER** JOHN SHENG
CLIENT SELECT PAPERS	**DESIGN FIRM** HYNES, HASLIP & PARTNERS	**CLIENT** ONTARIO FILM DEVELOPMENT CORPORATION	**DESIGN FIRM** TAYLOR & BROWNING DESIGN ASSOCIATES
	CLIENT THE GLOBE & MAIL		**CLIENT** CADILLAC FAIRVIEW SHOPPING CENTRES

M A R G A R E T   B O U R K E - W H I T E

P H O T O G R A P H S

1

SILVER AWARD

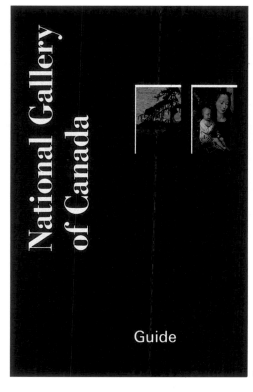

National Gallery of Canada

Guide

2

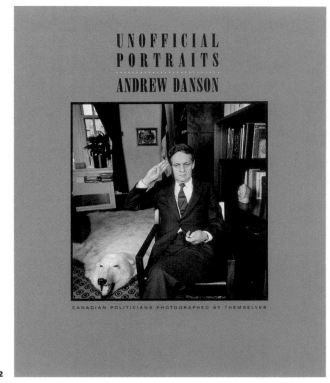

UNOFFICIAL PORTRAITS
ANDREW DANSON

CANADIAN POLITICIANS PHOTOGRAPHED BY THEMSELVES

3

1

TITLE
MARGARET BOURKE WHITE

ART DIRECTOR
CARMEN DUNJKO

DESIGNER
JILL CHEN

DESIGN FIRM
CARMEN DUNJKO ASSOCIATES

CLIENT
JANE CORKIN GALLERY

2

TITLE
NATIONAL GALLERY OF CANADA GUIDE

ART DIRECTOR
IAN C. TUDHOPE

WRITER
SUZANNE LACASSE

PHOTOGRAPHER
NATIONAL GALLERY OF CANADA

DESIGNER
BOB BOUTILIER

DESIGN FIRM
TUDHOPE ASSOCIATES INC.

CLIENT
NATIONAL GALLERY OF CANADA

3

TITLE
UNOFFICIAL PORTRAITS

ART DIRECTOR
PAUL HODGSON

WRITERS
ROBERT FULFORD/MAIA-MARI SUTNIK

PHOTOGRAPHER
ANDREW DANSON

DESIGNER
PAUL HODGSON

DESIGN FIRM
THE SPENCER FRANCEY GROUP

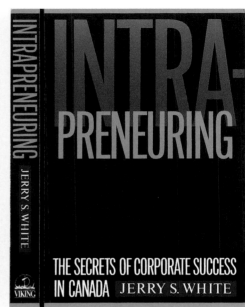

SILVER AWARD

1

TITLE
INTERIOR DESIGN CHOICE #4

ART DIRECTOR
PAUL BROWNING

ILLUSTRATOR
JEAN TUTTLE

DESIGNER
PAUL CAMPBELL

DESIGN FIRM
TAYLOR & BROWNING DESIGN ASSOCIATES

CLIENT
INDECS PUBLISHING

2

TITLE
INTRA-PRENURING

ART DIRECTOR
ARTHUR NIEMI

DESIGNER
ARTHUR NIEMI

DESIGN FIRM
ATLANTA ART & DESIGN

CLIENT
PENGUIN BOOKS

PACKAGE DESIGN

192

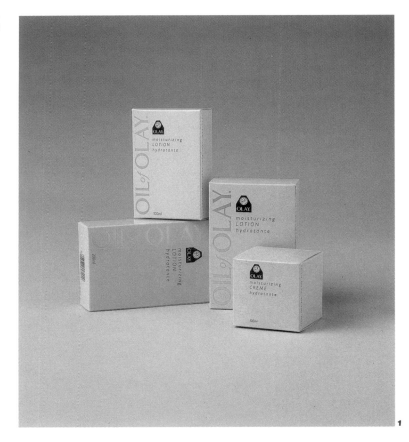

SILVER AWARD

1
TITLE
OIL OF OLAY

ART DIRECTOR
PAUL BROWTON

DESIGNER
PAUL BROWTON

DESIGN FIRM
MICHAEL PETERS GROUP

CLIENT
PROCTER & GAMBLE

2
TITLE
GRENVILLE-MAGICIAN

ART DIRECTOR
HEATHER COOPER

ILLUSTRATOR
HEATHER COOPER

DESIGNER
HEATHER COOPER

DESIGN FIRM
HEATHER COOPER COMMUNICATION BY DESIGN

CLIENT
GRENVILLE PRINTING AND MANAGEMENT LTD.

3
TITLE
SLEEMAN PACKAGING

ART DIRECTORS
PAUL BROWNING/JOANNE VERONNEAU

DESIGNER
JOANNE VERONNEAU

DESIGN FIRM
TAYLOR & BROWNING DESIGN ASSOCIATES

CLIENT
THE SLEEMAN BREWING & MALTING CO.

4
TITLE
ORGANIX

ART DIRECTOR
RON VANDENBERG

DESIGNER
ALISON SLOGA

DESIGN FIRM
BOULEVARD

CLIENT
ORGANIX

PACKAGE DESIGN

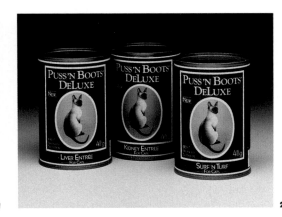

SILVER AWARD

1

2

SIGNAGE, ARCHITECTURAL GRAPHICS OR MURALS

3

1	2	3
TITLE COGNOS PACKAGING	**TITLE** PUSS 'N BOOTS DELUXE	**TITLE** TIME SAVOURS
ART DIRECTORS PAUL BROWNING/JOHN PYLYPCZAK	**ART DIRECTOR** GEOFF SMITH	**ART DIRECTORS** GARY BEELIK/KAREN SATOK
DESIGNERS JOHN PYLYPCZAK/BEN KUNZ	**ILLUSTRATOR** DOUG MARTIN	**DESIGNERS** GARY BEELIK/KAREN SATOK
DESIGN FIRM TAYLOR & BROWNING DESIGN ASSOCIATES	**DESIGNER** GEOFF SMITH	**CLIENT** TIME SAVOURS FOOD ENTERPRISES
CLIENT COGNOS INCORPORATED	**DESIGN FIRM** SMITH & COMPANY	
	CLIENT THE QUAKER OATS COMPANY OF CANADA LIMITED	

SELF PROMOTION

194

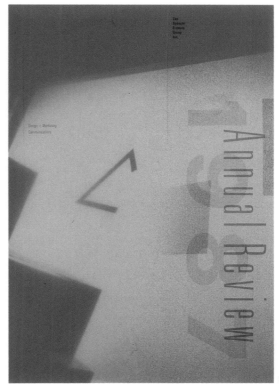

SILVER AWARD

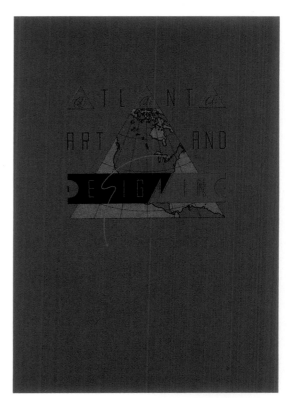

1

TITLE
AGI 88

ART DIRECTOR
THEO DIMSON

ILLUSTRATORS
THEO DIMSON/KEN JACKSON

DESIGNER
THEO DIMSON

DESIGN FIRM
THEO DIMSON DESIGN INC.

CLIENT
THEO DIMSON DESIGN INC.

2

TITLE
1987 ANNUAL REVIEW

ART DIRECTORS
PAUL HODGSON/BARBARA WOOLLEY

WRITER
DESMOND SMITH

PHOTOGRAPHERS
RON BAXTER SMITH/STEVEN EVANS

DESIGNERS
PAUL HODGSON/BARBARA WOOLLEY

DESIGN FIRM
THE SPENCER FRANCEY GROUP

CLIENT
THE SPENCER FRANCEY GROUP

3

TITLE
ART E FAX

ART DIRECTOR
LOUIS FISHAUF

DESIGNER
LOUIS FISHAUF

DESIGN FIRM
REACTOR ART & DESIGN

CLIENT
REACTOR ART & DESIGN

4

TITLE
PRESENTATION FOLDER FOR ATLANTA ART & DESIGN

ART DIRECTOR
ARTHUR NIEMI

ILLUSTRATORS
ARTHUR NIEMI/MARK KOUDYS

DESIGNER
ARTHUR NIEMI

DESIGN FIRM
ATLANTA ART & DESIGN

CLIENT
ATLANTA ART & DESIGN

SELF PROMOTION

1

TITLE
TAYLOR & BROWNING HEAT WAVE

ART DIRECTORS
SCOTT TAYLOR/PAUL BROWNING

WRITER
HELEN BATTERSBY

ILLUSTRATOR
PETER BAKER

DESIGNER
PETER BAKER

DESIGN FIRM
TAYLOR & BROWNING DESIGN ASSOCIATES

CLIENT
TAYLOR & BROWNING DESIGN ASSOCIATES

2

TITLE
TAYLOR & BROWNING CHRISTMAS WINE BOX

ART DIRECTORS
SCOTT TAYLOR/PAUL BROWNING

DESIGNERS
PETER BAKER/JOHN SHENG

DESIGN FIRM
TAYLOR & BROWNING DESIGN ASSOCIATES

CLIENT
TAYLOR & BROWNING DESIGN ASSOCIATES

3

TITLE
1st ANNUAL HAUGHTON BRAZEAU AIR SHOW
& FAMILY PICNIC

ART DIRECTORS
PHILIP BRAZEAU/CATHERINE HAUGHTON

WRITER
CECIL MORRIS

ILLUSTRATOR
PAULA MUNCK/REACTOR

DESIGNER
DERWYN GOODALL

DESIGN FIRM
HAUGHTON BRAZEAU

CLIENT
HAUGHTON BRAZEAU

4

TITLE
JEAN TUTTLE

ILLUSTRATOR
JEAN TUTTLE

DESIGNER
SHARI SPIER

DESIGN FIRM
REACTOR ART & DESIGN

CLIENT
REACTOR ART & DESIGN

CLOSE COVER · REFERMEZ S.V.P.

· DIRECTIONS 88 ·

GRAPHIC DESIGN ILLUSTRATION

197

SILVER AWARD

GOLD AWARD

1

TITLE
IMPRESSIONS

ART DIRECTOR
CARMEN DUNJKO

PHOTOGRAPHER
DEBORAH SAMUEL

DESIGNERS
CARMEN DUNJKO/JENNIFER COGHILL

DESIGN FIRM
CARMEN DUNJKO ASSOCIATES

WRITERS
ELLIOTT COLLINS/RITA YUNGER LINDER

CLIENT
GRENVILLE PRINTING & MANAGEMENT LTD.

2

TITLE
RENE ZAMIC

ILLUSTRATOR
RENE ZAMIC

DESIGNER
SHARI SPIER

DESIGN FIRM
REACTOR ART & DESIGN

CLIENT
REACTOR ART & DESIGN

3

TITLE
THE MAGIC OF ILLUSTRATION

ART DIRECTOR
LOUIS FISHAUF

ILLUSTRATOR
JEFF JACKSON

DESIGNER
LOUIS FISHAUF

DESIGN FIRM
REACTOR ART & DESIGN

CLIENT
BILL HUDSON & ASSOCIATES

1

2

3

SILVER AWARD

1	2	3
TITLE SHAKESPEARE PORTRAIT	**TITLE** STYLE	**TITLE** DIRECTIONS '88
ART DIRECTOR HEATHER COOPER	**ART DIRECTOR** HEATHER COOPER	**ART DIRECTOR** LOUIS FISHAUF
ILLUSTRATOR HEATHER COOPER	**ILLUSTRATOR** HEATHER COOPER	**ILLUSTRATOR** HENRIK DRESCHER & FRIENDS
DESIGNER HEATHER COOPER	**DESIGNER** HEATHER COOPER	**DESIGNER** LOUIS FISHAUF
DESIGN FIRM HEATHER COOPER COMMUNICATION BY DESIGN	**DESIGN FIRM** HEATHER COOPER COMMUNICATION BY DESIGN	**DESIGN FIRM** REACTOR ART & DESIGN
CLIENT STRATFORD FESTIVAL BOOKSHOP	**CLIENT** STYLE MAGAZINE	**CLIENT** ART DIRECTORS CLUB OF TORONTO
		TYPE CANADIAN COMPOSITION

ANNUAL REPORT FISCAL 1988

Tridont Health Care Inc.

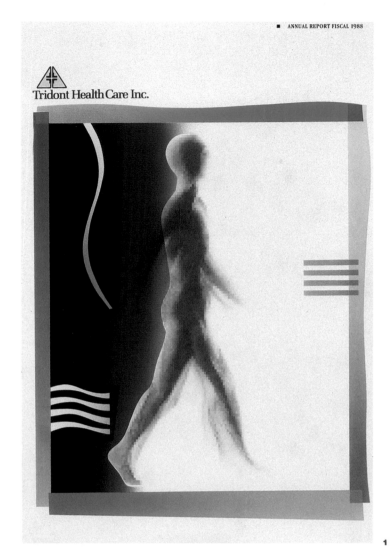

1

THE MUSIC BUILDING
RESTORATION

2

3

1

TITLE
TRIDONT HEALTH CARE

ART DIRECTOR
MARK PINVIDIC

ILLUSTRATOR
KEVIN N. GHIGLIONE

CLIENT
TRIDONT HEALTH CARE

2

TITLE
MUSIC BUILDING RESTORATION

ART DIRECTOR
PAUL GILBERT

ILLUSTRATOR
JEFF JACKSON

DESIGN FIRM
REMARKABLE COMMUNICATIONS

3

TITLE
INTERNATIONAL AMATEUR ATHLETIC FEDERATION, 1988

ART DIRECTOR
BILL SMITH

ILLUSTRATOR
JEFF JACKSON

DESIGNER
BILL SMITH

DESIGN FIRM
BILL SMITH DESIGN

CLIENT
INTERNATIONAL AMATEUR ATHLETIC FEDERATION

GRAPHIC DESIGN ILLUSTRATION

1

1

TITLE
CHEVROLET CAR CATALOGUES

ART DIRECTOR
DIANNE CROTEAU

ILLUSTRATOR
JAMES MARSH

DESIGNER
PHILLIP YAN

DESIGN FIRM
STUDIO INNOVA

AGENCY
MacLAREN ADVERTISING

CLIENT
GM CANADA

SILVER AWARD

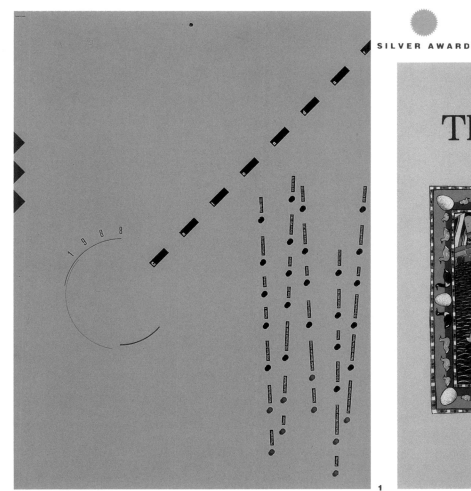

The Wildlife ABC
A Nature Alphabet

JAN THORNHILL

1

2

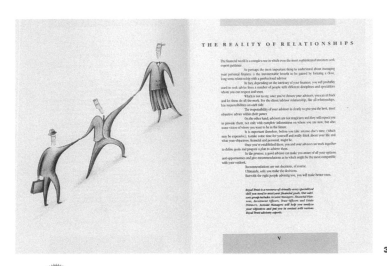

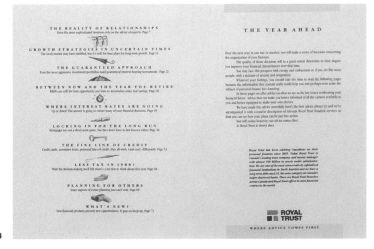

3

GOLD AWARD

1

TITLE
1987-1988 CALENDAR

ART DIRECTOR
MALCOLM WADDELL

PHOTOGRAPHER
MICHAEL NICHOLS

DESIGNERS
ROSLYN ESKIND/GLENDA RISSMAN
MERCEDES ROTHWELL/CHRISTOPHER CAMPBELL
PETER SCOTT/MALCOLM WADDELL

DESIGN FIRM
ESKIND WADDELL

CLIENTS
MICHAEL NICHOLS/ESKIND WADDELL
MacKINNON-MONCUR LTD./GRAPHIC SPECIALTIES LTD.
BARBER-ELLIS FINE PAPERS

2

TITLE
THE WILDLIFE A B C

ART DIRECTOR
WYCLIFFE SMITH

ILLUSTRATOR
JAN THORNHILL

WRITER
JAN THORNHILL

DESIGNER
WYCLIFFE SMITH

3

TITLE
THE ROYAL TRUST PERSONAL FINANCE ADVISOR

ART DIRECTOR
ROBERT BURNS

ILLUSTRATOR
FRANK VIVA

WRITER
JOHN STEWART

DESIGNERS
GREGORY HALAS/PAMELA STRADWICK

DESIGN FIRM
BURNS AND COMPANY

CLIENT
ROYAL TRUSTCO LTD.

1

TITLE
1st ANNUAL HAUGHTON BRAZEAU AIR SHOW
& FAMILY PICNIC

ART DIRECTORS
PHILIP BRAZEAU/CATHERINE HAUGHTON

ILLUSTRATOR
PAULA MUNCK

WRITER
CECIL MORRIS

DESIGNER
DERWYN GOODALL

DESIGN FIRM
HAUGHTON BRAZEAU

CLIENT
HAUGHTON BRAZEAU

2

TITLE
THE MAGICIAN

ART DIRECTOR
HEATHER COOPER

ILLUSTRATOR
HEATHER COOPER

DESIGNER
HEATHER COOPER

DESIGN FIRM
HEATHER COOPER COMMUNICATION BY DESIGN

CLIENT
GRENVILLE PRINTING AND MANAGEMENT LTD.

1   **2**   **3**

TITLE   **TITLE**   **TITLE**
SKYBOX 492 POSTER   PARTY   NATIONAL MAGAZINE AWARDS

ART DIRECTOR   **ART DIRECTOR**   **ART DIRECTOR**
ROBERT HYLAND   PAUL HODGSON   JAMES IRELAND

ILLUSTRATOR   **PHOTOGRAPHER**   **ILLUSTRATOR**
ROGER HILL   JIM ALLEN   BARRY BLITT

PHOTOGRAPHY   **DESIGNER**   **DESIGNER**
SEE SPOT RUN   PAUL HODGSON   JAMES IRELAND

WRITER   **DESIGN FIRM**   **CLIENT**
DAYWRITER   THE SPENCER FRANCEY GROUP NATIONAL MAGAZINE AWARDS

DESIGNERS   **CLIENT**
ROBERT HYLAND/ROGER HILL THE SPENCER FRANCEY GROUP

DESIGN FIRM
ROBERT HYLAND DESIGN

CLIENT
THE INTER-CONTINENTAL GROUP

ART DIRECTOR
ROBERT HYLAND

ILLUSTRATOR
ROGER HILL

206

CARNAVAL PERPETUEL

A collection of works by

HEATHER COOPER

1

2

DALLAS SOCIETY OF ILLUSTRATORS PRESENTS

ANITA KUNZ

AT THE INFOMART IN DALLAS. TEXAS

JUNE 28, 1988

3

1	2	3
TITLE CARNAVAL PERPETUEL POSTER	**TITLE** HEARTBEAT OF RIO	**TITLE** AT THE INFOMART IN DALLAS
ART DIRECTOR HEATHER COOPER	**ART DIRECTOR** CARMEN DUNJKO	**ART DIRECTORS** PAT SLOAN/ANITA KUNZ
ILLUSTRATOR HEATHER COOPER	**ILLUSTRATOR** JOE BIAFORE	**ILLUSTRATOR** ANITA KUNZ
DESIGNER HEATHER COOPER	**DESIGNER** JOE BIAFORE	**DESIGNER** PAT SLOAN
DESIGN FIRM HEATHER COOPER COMMUNICATION BY DESIGN	**DESIGN FIRM** CARMEN DUNJKO ASSOCIATES	**CLIENT** DALLAS SOCIETY OF ILLUSTRATORS
CLIENT CARNAVAL PERPETUEL	**CLIENT** BRAZILIAN BALL COMMITTEE	

1

TITLE
EXTRAORDINARY PRINTING

ART DIRECTOR
CARMEN DUNJKO

PHOTOGRAPHERS
SERGE BARBEAU/DEBORAH SAMUEL
GEORGE WHITESIDE

DESIGNER
CARMEN DUNJKO

DESIGN FIRM
CARMEN DUNJKO ASSOCIATES

CLIENT
GRENVILLE PRINTING & MANAGEMENT LTD.

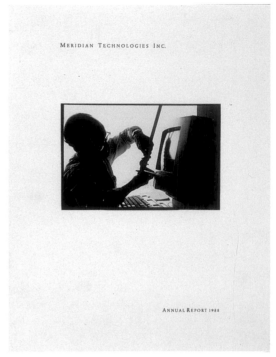

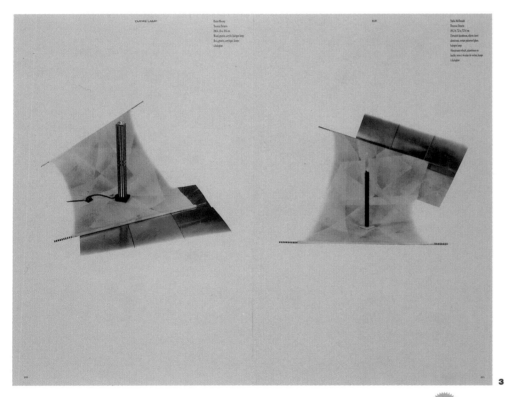

GOLD AWARD

1	**2**	**3**	**4**
TITLE	**TITLE**	**TITLE**	**TITLE**
UNOFFICIAL PORTRAITS	MERIDIAN TECHNOLOGIES	VIRTU 3	FASHION PLATE
ART DIRECTORS	**ART DIRECTOR**	**ART DIRECTOR**	**ART DIRECTOR**
R. FULFORD/M.SUTNICK	LAWRENCE FINN	DEL TERRELONGE	CHRISTINE DOWNS
PHOTOGRAPHER	**PHOTOGRAPHER**	**PHOTOGRAPHER**	**PHOTOGRAPHER**
ANDREW DANSON	SHIN SUGINO	RON BAXTER SMITH	JIM ALLEN
DESIGN FIRM	**DESIGNER**	**DESIGNER**	**DESIGNER**
SPENCER FRANCEY GROUP	LAWRENCE FINN	DEL TERRELONGE	CHRISTINE DOWNS
CLIENT	**DESIGN FIRM**	**DESIGN FIRM**	**DESIGN FIRM**
DOUBLEDAY CANADA	LAWRENCE FINN & ASSOCIATES LTD.	TERRELONGE DESIGN INC.	DOWNS & CO.
	CLIENT	**CLIENT**	**CLIENT**
	MERIDIAN TECHNOLOGIES INC.	FORUM & FUNCTION DIRECTIONS IN CANADIAN DESIGN	SIMPSONS

366-14

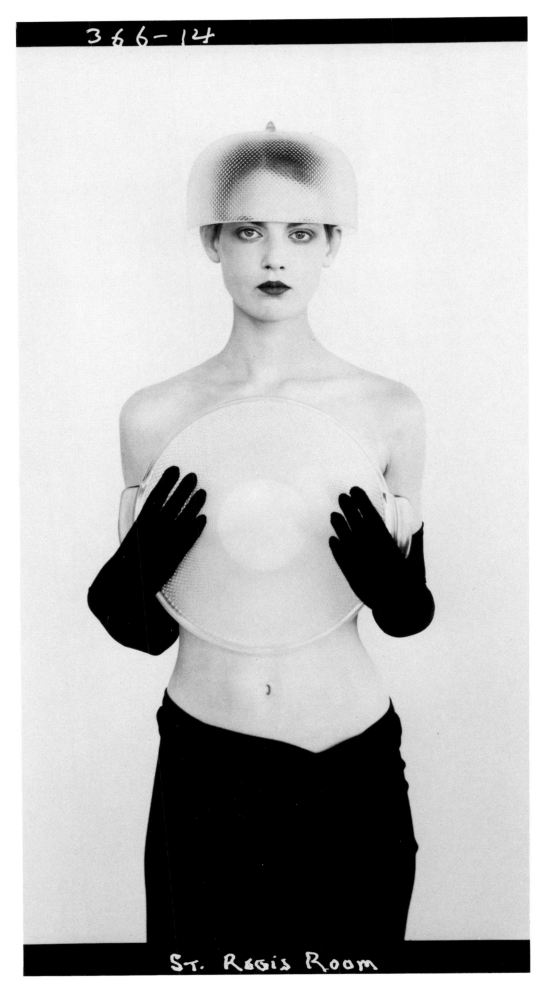

St. Regis Room

ART DIRECTOR
CHRISTINE DOWNS

PHOTOGRAPHER
JIM ALLEN

ART DIRECTOR
CARMEN DUNJKO

PHOTOGRAPHER
DEBORAH SAMUEL

GRAPHIC DESIGN PHOTOGRAPHY

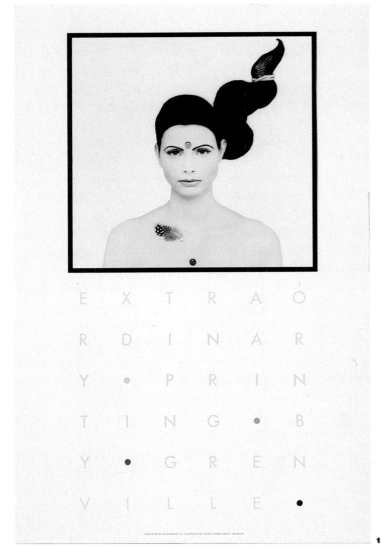

1

TITLE
EXTRAORDINARY PRINTING

ART DIRECTOR
CARMEN DUNJKO

PHOTOGRAPHER
SERGE BARBEAU

DESIGNER
CARMEN DUNJKO

DESIGN FIRM
CARMEN DUNJKO ASSOCIATES

CLIENT
GRENVILLE PRINTING & MANAGEMENT LTD.

2

TITLE
VIRTU 3

ART DIRECTOR
DEL TERRELONGE

PHOTOGRAPHER
RON BAXTER SMITH

DESIGNER
DEL TERRELONGE

DESIGN FIRM
TERRELONGE DESIGN INC.

CLIENT
FORUM AND FUNCTION
DIRECTIONS IN CANADIAN DESIGN

3

TITLE
IMPRESSIONS

ART DIRECTOR
CARMEN DUNJKO

ILLUSTRATORS
JAMIE BENNETT/ANITA KUNZ/JERZY KOLACZ
WENDY WORTSMAN

WRITERS
ELLIOTT COLLINS/RITA YUNGER LINDER

DESIGNERS
CARMEN DUNJKO/JENNIFER COGHILL

DESIGN FIRM
CARMEN DUNJKO ASSOCIATES

CLIENT
GRENVILLE PRINTING & MANAGEMENT LTD.

4

TITLE
FINANCIAL TRUSTCO ANNUAL REPORT

ART DIRECTOR
JULIA HARRIS

PHOTOGRAPHER
RON BAXTER SMITH

DESIGNER
JULIA HARRIS

DESIGN FIRM
JULIA HARRIS DESIGN INC.

CLIENT
FINANCIAL TRUSTCO

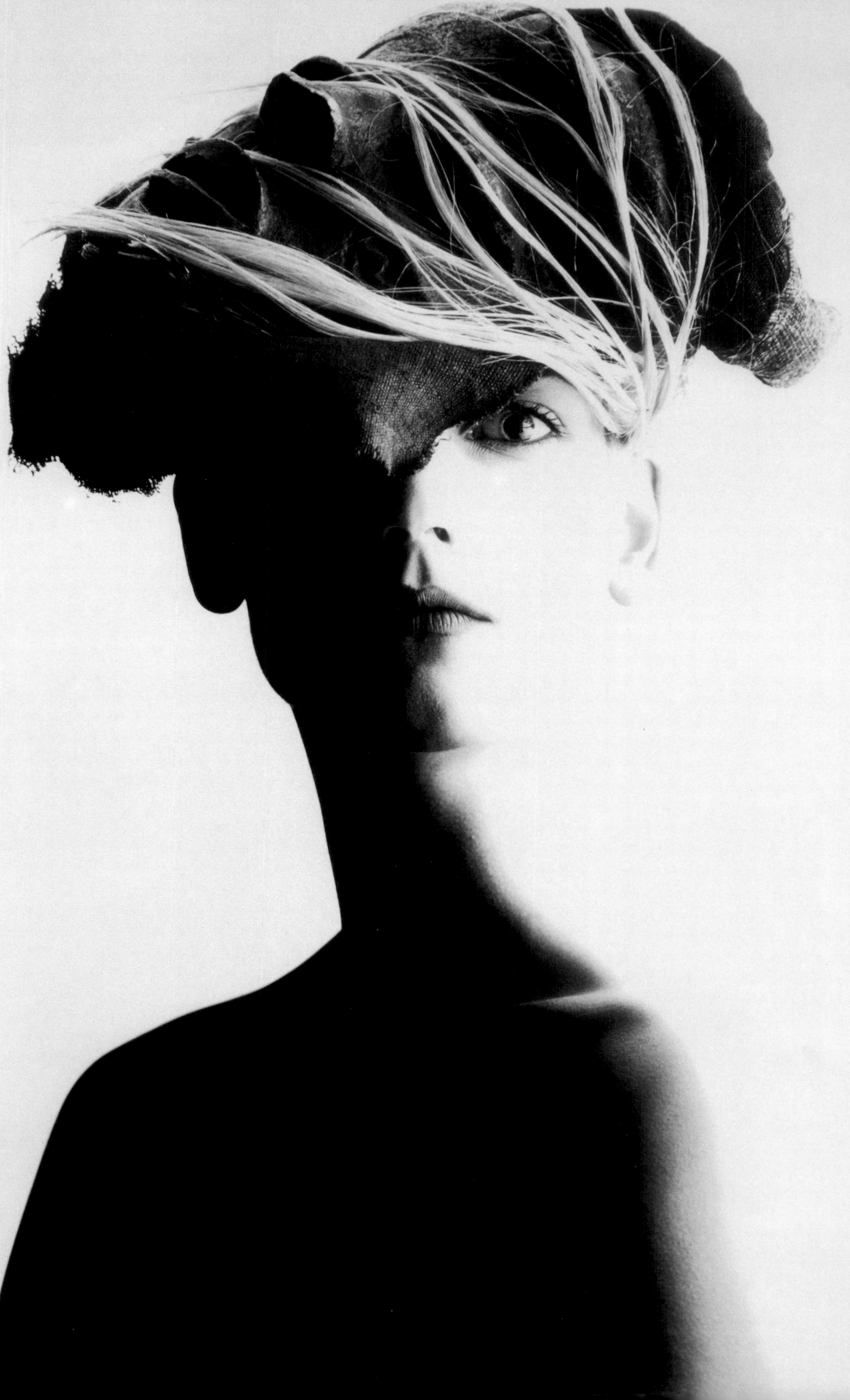

1	2	3
TITLE CAMPEAU CORPORATION 1987 ANNUAL REPORT	**TITLE** EXTRAORDINARY PRINTING	**TITLE** REINHART McMILLAN HAIR BROCHURE
ART DIRECTOR PAUL CAMPBELL	**ART DIRECTOR** CARMEN DUNJKO	**ART DIRECTOR** CARMEN DUNJKO
PHOTOGRAPHER RON BAXTER SMITH	**PHOTOGRAPHER** SERGE BARBEAU	**PHOTOGRAPHER** DEBORAH SAMUEL
DESIGN FIRM TAYLOR & BROWNING DESIGN ASSOCIATES	**DESIGNER** CARMEN DUNJKO	**DESIGNER** CARMEN DUNJKO
CLIENT CAMPEAU CORPORATION	**DESIGN FIRM** CARMEN DUNJKO ASSOCIATES	**DESIGN FIRM** CARMEN DUNJKO ASSOCIATES
	CLIENT GRENVILLE PRINTING	**CLIENT** REINHART McMILLAN HAIR INC.

214

22nd Annual Brazilian Carnival Ball, Saturday, February 6, 1988   **1**

2

3

GOLD AWARD

1

TITLE
HEARTBEAT OF RIO

ART DIRECTOR
CARMEN DUNJKO

ILLUSTRATOR
JOE BIAFORE

DESIGNER
JOE BIAFORE

DESIGN FIRM
CARMEN DUNJKO ASSOCIATES

CLIENT
BRAZILIAN BALL COMMITTEE

2

TITLE
ART FOR THE MASSES

ART DIRECTOR
LOUIS FISHAUF

DESIGNER
LOUIS FISHAUF

DESIGN FIRM
REACTOR ART & DESIGN

CLIENT
REACTOR ARTWEAR

3

TITLE
CFNY VIDEO RD. SHOW

ART DIRECTOR
DAVID SHELLY

DESIGNER
DAVID SHELLY

DESIGN FIRM
GRAPHISPHERE INC.

CLIENT
CFNY FM 102.1

GRAPHIC DESIGN POSTER, SINGLE

SILVER AWARD

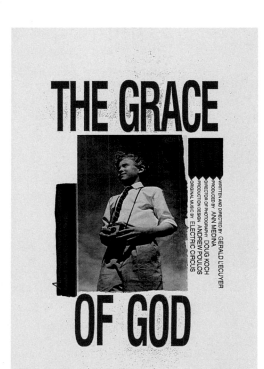

1	2	3
TITLE	**TITLE**	**TITLE**
IIDEX	THE GRACE OF GOD	TAFELMUSIK POSTER
ART DIRECTORS	**ART DIRECTOR**	**ART DIRECTORS**
SCOTT TAYLOR/PAUL BROWNING	KEVIN N. GHIGLIONE	LISA MILLER/PAUL BROWNING
ILLUSTRATOR	**PHOTOGRAPHER**	**ILLUSTRATOR**
WILLIAM LAM	KEVIN N. GHIGLIONE	DAVID CHESTNUTT
DESIGNER	**ILLUSTRATOR**	**DESIGNER**
WILLIAM LAM	KEVIN N. GHIGLIONE	LISA MILLER
DESIGN FIRM	**DESIGNER**	**DESIGN FIRM**
TAYLOR & BROWNING DESIGN ASSOCIATES	KEVIN N. GHIGLIONE	TAYLOR & BROWNING
CLIENT	**CLIENT**	**CLIENT**
ARIDO-ASSOCIATION OF REGISTERED	GERALD L'ECUYER/ANN MEDINA	TAFELMUSIK
INTERIOR DESIGNERS OF ONTARIO		

216

1

TITLE
NATIONAL CITIZENSHIP WEEK

ART DIRECTORS
JEANNETTE HANNA/BRIAN TSANG

ILLUSTRATOR
JEFF JACKSON

DESIGNER
BRIAN TSANG

DESIGN FIRM
THE SPENCER FRANCEY GROUP

CLIENT
SECRETARY OF STATE

2

TITLE
BAR GUIDE

ART DIRECTORS
MANUEL RODENKIRCHEN/PAUL HURREN

PHOTOGRAPHER
MARK MAINGUY

DESIGN FIRM
T.O. MAGAZINE

CLIENT
SOHO PUBLISHING

3

TITLE
RESTAURANT GUIDE

ART DIRECTOR
MANUEL RODENKIRCHEN

PHOTOGRAPHER
ELLEN TOFFLEMIRE

DESIGNER
PAUL HURREN

DESIGN FIRM
T.O. MAGAZINE

CLIENT
SOHO PUBLISHING

1

TITLE
VICKI KEITH SWIMS

ART DIRECTOR
CARMEN DUNJKO

ILLUSTRATOR
JOE BIAFORE

DESIGNER
JOE BIAFORE

DESIGN FIRM
CARMEN DUNJKO ASSOCIATES

CLIENT
VARIETY VILLAGE

2

TITLE
BATA SUMMER MADNESS

ART DIRECTOR
DITI KATONA

ILLUSTRATOR
JAMIE BENNETT

DESIGNER
DITI KATONA

DESIGN FIRM
REACTOR ART & DESIGN

CLIENT
BATA INDUSTRIES LTD.

3

TITLE
BATA WINTER

ART DIRECTOR
LOUIS FISHAUF

ILLUSTRATOR
JEAN TUTTLE

DESIGN FIRM
REACTOR ART & DESIGN

CLIENT
BATA INDUSTRIES LTD.

GRAPHIC DESIGN POSTER, SINGLE

218

1

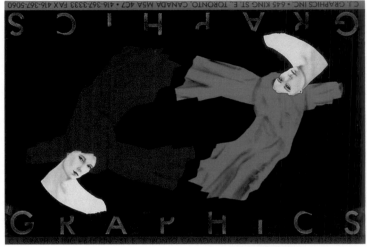

2

3

1

TITLE
CANADIAN OPERA COMPANY POSTER 1987/88 SEASON

ART DIRECTOR
SCOTT TAYLOR

ILLUSTRATOR
SIMON NG

DESIGNER
JOHN PYLYPCZAK

DESIGN FIRM
TAYLOR & BROWNING DESIGN ASSOCIATES

CLIENT
CANADIAN OPERA COMPANY

2

TITLE
C.J. GRAPHICS INC. PROMOTIONAL POSTER

ILLUSTRATOR
GREG HALL

DESIGN FIRM
PHOTO DESIGN

CLIENT
C.J. GRAPHICS INC.

3

TITLE
BATA CHRISTMAS

ART DIRECTOR
LOUIS FISHAUF

ILLUSTRATOR
BLAIR DRAWSON

DESIGN FIRM
REACTOR ART & DESIGN

CLIENT
BATA INDUSTRIES LTD.

MISCELLANEOUS

1

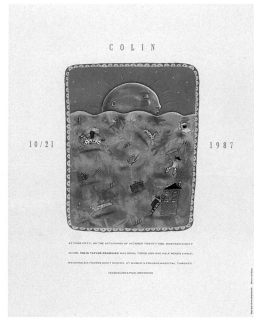

2

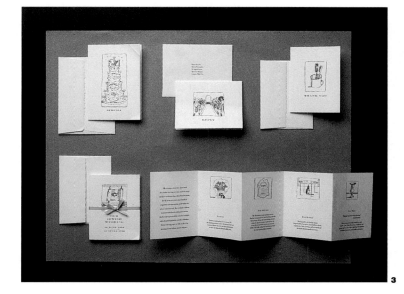

3

4

1	2	3	4
TITLE CRYPTO EGYPTON	**TITLE** COLIN BROWNING BIRTH ANNOUNCEMENT	**TITLE** WEDDING INVITATION	**TITLE** QUADRANGLE NEWSLETTER
ART DIRECTOR LOUIS FISHAUF	**ART DIRECTOR** PAUL BROWNING	**ART DIRECTORS** TERESA FERNANDES/BARRY BLITT	**ART DIRECTOR** BEV W. TUDHOPE
ILLUSTRATOR MAURICE VELLEKOOP	**WRITER** PAUL BROWNING	**WRITERS** TERESA FERNANDES/BARRY BLITT	**DESIGNER** BOB BOUTILIER
DESIGN FIRM REACTOR ART & DESIGN	**ILLUSTRATOR** JAMIE BENNETT	**ILLUSTRATOR** BARRY BLITT	**DESIGN FIRM** TUDHOPE ASSOCIATES INC.
CLIENT REACTOR ARTWEAR	**DESIGNER** PETER BAKER	**DESIGNER** TERESA FERNANDES	**CLIENT** QUADRANGLE ARCHITECTS
	DESIGN FIRM TAYLOR & BROWNING DESIGN ASSOCIATES	**TYPE** BARBARA WOOLLEY	
	CLIENT JACQUELINE BROWNING	**PRINTER** LUNAR CAUSTIC PRESS	

MISCELLANEOUS

220

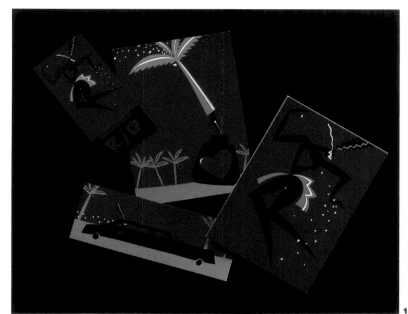

GOLD AWARD

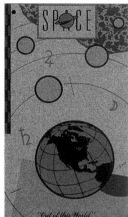

SILVER AWARD

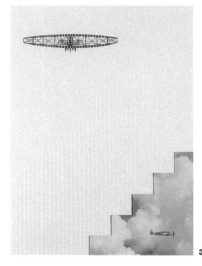

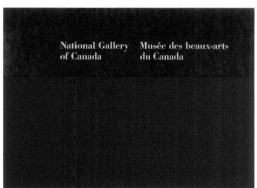

1

TITLE
HEARTBEAT OF RIÓ

ART DIRECTOR
CARMEN DUNJKO

ILLUSTRATOR
JOE BIAFORE

DESIGNER
JOE BIAFORE

DESIGN FIRM
CARMEN DUNJKO ASSOCIATES

CLIENT
BRAZILIAN BALL COMMITTEE

4

TITLE
NATIONAL GALLERY OF CANADA
INFORMATION AND FLOOR PLAN

ART DIRECTOR
IAN C. TUDHOPE

DESIGNER
BOB BOUTILIER

DESIGN FIRM
TUDHOPE ASSOCIATES INC.

CLIENT
NATIONAL GALLERY OF CANADA

2

TITLE
SPACE

ART DIRECTOR
BOB HAMBLY

ILLUSTRATOR
BOB HAMBLY

DESIGNER
BOB HAMBLY

CLIENT
KOSTAR I.T.C. LTD.

5

TITLE
BASF COMMUNICATIONS PACKAGE

ART DIRECTOR
BEV W. TUDHOPE

DESIGNERS
JEAN PIERRE VEILLEUX/YIN HOSKINS/DONNA GEDEON

DESIGN FIRM
TUDHOPE ASSOCIATES INC.

CLIENT
BASF FIBRES INC.

3

TITLE
AVIATION FOLDER & INVITATION

ART DIRECTOR
NEVILLE SMITH

WRITER
WENDY McPEAKE

DESIGNERS
NEVILLE SMITH/AVIVA FURMAN

DESIGN FIRM
SMITH AND FURMAN DESIGN

CLIENT
NATIONAL AVIATION MUSEUM

6

TITLE
CHAIR SHOW/XMAS SHOW

ART DIRECTOR
LOUIS FISHAUF

DESIGNER
LOUIS FISHAUF

DESIGN FIRM
REACTOR ART & DESIGN

CLIENT
THE REACTOR GALLERY

MISCELLANEOUS

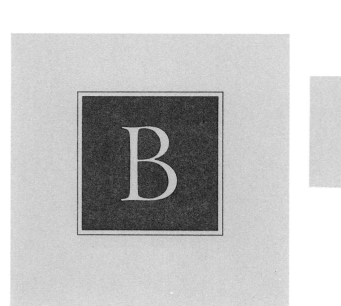

1

2

3

1	**2**	**3**
TITLE BLUE WIND	**TITLE** PLASTIC FANTASTIC LOVER	**TITLE** FACES BY GANDALF
DESIGNER DITI KATONA	**DESIGNER** PAUL SYCH	**ART DIRECTOR** DAVID SHELLY
DESIGN FIRM REACTOR ART & DESIGN	**DESIGN FIRM** REACTOR ART & DESIGN	**WRITER** DAVID SHELLY
CLIENT THE REACTOR GALLERY	**CLIENT** THE REACTOR GALLERY	**DESIGNERS** DAVID SHELLY/LAURA FRANCEY
		DESIGN FIRM GRAPHISPHERE INC.
		CLIENT GANDALF TYPOGRAPHERS INC.

1

TITLE
SKYBOX 492 POSTER

ART DIRECTOR
ROBERT HYLAND

WRITER
DAYWRITER

PHOTOGRAPHY
SEE SPOT RUN

ILLUSTRATOR
ROGER HILL

DESIGNERS
ROBERT HYLAND/ROGER HILL

DESIGN FIRM
ROBERT HYLAND DESIGN

CLIENT
THE INTER-CONTINENTAL GROUP

2

TITLE
1st ANNUAL HAUGHTON BRAZEAU AIR SHOW
& FAMILY PICNIC

ART DIRECTORS
PHILIP BRAZEAU/CATHERINE HAUGHTON

WRITER
CECIL MORRIS

ILLUSTRATOR
PAULA MUNCK

DESIGNER
DERWYN GOODALL

DESIGN FIRM
HAUGHTON BRAZEAU

CLIENT
HAUGHTON BRAZEAU

3

TITLE
NATIONAL MAGAZINE AWARDS

ART DIRECTOR
JAMES IRELAND

ILLUSTRATOR
BARRY BLITT

DESIGNER
JAMES IRELAND

CLIENT
NATIONAL MAGAZINE AWARDS

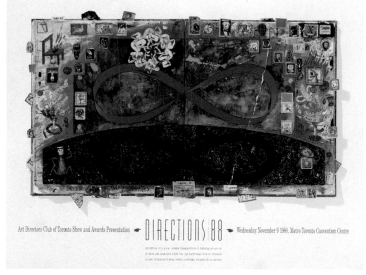

1

TITLE
VIRTU 3

ART DIRECTOR
DEL TERRELONGE

WRITERS
ALLAN KLUSACEK/ESTHER SHIPMAN

PHOTOGRAPHER
RON BAXTER SMITH

DESIGNER
DEL TERRELONGE

DESIGN FIRM
TERRELONGE DESIGN INC.

CLIENT
FORUM AND FUNCTION
DIRECTIONS IN CANADIAN DESIGN

2

TITLE
AUCTION '88

ART DIRECTOR
CARMEN DUNJKO

ILLUSTRATOR
JILL CHEN

DESIGNER
JILL CHEN

DESIGN FIRM
CARMEN DUNJKO ASSOCIATES

CLIENT
ART DIRECTORS CLUB OF TORONTO

3

TITLE
DIRECTIONS '88

ART DIRECTOR
LOUIS FISHAUF

PHOTOGRAPHER
SEE SPOT RUN

ILLUSTRATOR
HENRIK DRESCHER & FRIENDS

DESIGNER
LOUIS FISHAUF

DESIGN FIRM
REACTOR ART & DESIGN

CLIENT
ART DIRECTORS CLUB OF TORONTO

TYPE
CANADIAN COMPOSITION

FILM
LITHO PLUS

PRINTING
GRENVILLE PRINTING & MANAGEMENT LTD.

DIRECTIONS 88

INDEX